STAGE MUM

Lisa Gee is the author of *Friends: Why Men and Women Are From the Same Planet* (Bloomsbury, 2004) and the editor of *Bricks Without Mortar: the Selected Poems of Hartley Coleridge* (Picador, 2000). She has edited the Orange Broadband Prize for Fiction website for ten years and lives in northwest London, with one performing child and her husband, a children's party entertainer.

Lisa Gee

STAGE MUM

Hutchinson

LONDON

Published by Hutchinson 2008

2 4 6 8 10 9 7 5 3 1

Copyright © Lisa Gee 2008

Lisa Gee has asserted her right under the Copyright, Designs
and Patents Act 1988 to be identified as the author of this work

First published in Great Britain in 2008 by
Hutchinson
Random House, 20 Vauxhall Bridge Road,
London SW1V 2SA
www.rbooks.co.uk

Addresses for companies within The Random House Group Limited can be
found at: www.randomhouse.co.uk/offices.htm

The Random House Group Limited Reg. No. 954009

A CIP catalogue record for this book is available from the British Library

ISBN 9780091921392

The Random House Group Limited supports The Forest Stewardship
Council (FSC), the leading international forest certification organisation. All
our titles that are printed on Greenpeace approved FSC certified paper carry
the FSC logo. Our paper procurement policy can be found at
www.rbooks.co.uk/environment

Mixed Sources
Product group from well-managed
forests and other controlled sources
www.fsc.org Cert no. TT-COC-2139
FSC © 1996 Forest Stewardship Council

Typeset by SX Composing DTP, Rayleigh, Essex
Printed and bound in Great Britain by Clays Ltd, St Ives PLC

For Dora: just keep being your (wonderful) self.
For Laurie, thank you for being you.
For the 2006 first run SoM kids and their parents.
For Dad, without whom …

In fond memory of Rebecca Hawes 03/09/1987–19/10/2007

CONTENTS

ACKNOWLEDGEMENTS

Big thanks to …

… Louise Greenberg – much more than just an agent – and her writers' group; Caroline Gascoigne, Tess Callaway, Emma Mitchell, Rebecca Morrison and everyone at Hutchinson; all the SoM kids and their parents, especially Lynn, Helen, Jane, Wendy, Jackie, Nicky and Graham who allowed me to include information about them and their children and who read and commented on early drafts (as did Dora, Jo Hawes and Russ and his family).

…Nancy Carlsson-Paige, June Havoc and Tana Sibilio, Catherine Hindson, Liz Jensen and Raphaël Coleman, Sam Keston, Paul Kirkman, Tracy Land and David Ian, Mark Lester, Paul Morley, Paul Petersen, Russ and Linda Russell, Boyd Tonkin, Mark Williams-Thomas, Sylvia Young and Maggie Melville-Bray who gave their time to be interviewed.

…Claire Russell who allowed her story to be told.

… everyone who discussed this book with me, offered comments, ideas and criticisms.

And, of course, to Dora, Laurie, Dad, Lilli, Auntie Ruth, Nikki and Richard (and also Millie and Freddie) who helped in so many ways.

The author would like to thank the following for the permission to use copyright material. Cover copy from *The Great American Mousical* by Julie Andrews Edwards and Emma Walton Hamilton (Puffin Books 2006). Text copyright © Julie Andrews Edwards and Emma Walton Hamilton. Illustrations copyright © Tony Walton. Reproduced by permission of Penguin Books Ltd.; Extracts from 'Celebrity is the Death of Childhood' copyright © Andrew O'Hagan. Reproduced by permission of Telegraph Media Group Limited; Extracts from *The Story of the Trapp Family Singers* by Maria Augusta Von Trapp (Fontana, 1968). Text copyright © Maria Augusta Trapp. Copyright © renewed 1980 by Trapp Family Lodge, Inc. Now published by HarperCollins Publishers (US); Extracts from *Early Havoc* by June Havoc (Hutchinson & Co. Publishers Ltd, 1960). Text copyright © June Havoc. Reproduced by kind permission of the author; Extracts from *Former Child Stars: The Story of America's Least Wanted* by Joal Ryan (ECW Press, 2000). Text copyright © Joal Ryan. Reproduced by kind permission of the author; Extract from the A Minor Consideration website www.minorcon.org © Paul Petersen A Minor Consideration; Extracts from *Child Star: An Autobiography* by Shirley Temple Black (Headline Book Publishing plc, 1989). Text copyright © Shirley Temple Black; Jo Hawes' emails © Jo Hawes reproduced by kind permission of the author; Extracts from 'To Be Or Not To Be?' by Emily Keston © Emily Keston reproduced by kind permission of the author.

LET'S START AT THE VERY
BEGINNING

'Do you think Dora might be interested?' My father was calling from Vienna where he spends several months each year, visiting friends, absorbing culture and going for long walks in the woods. He'd been watching the news (in English) on Sky TV, when an item came on about the open kids' auditions for Andrew Lloyd Webber's forthcoming West End production of *The Sound of Music*. We – Dora, me, my fiancé Laurie and his mother Lilli – were sitting round the dining table in Lilli's flat a few minutes' walk from the Bournemouth seafront on a freezing April Fool's Day. We were debating, heatedly, the relative merits of mushroom vol-au-vents and smoked salmon bagels as wedding fare and wondering whether to brave the wintry weather to build a token sandcastle.

'She'd have to sing "Somewhere Over the Rainbow",' my father continued, before telling me where and when she'd have to sing it. He sounded a bit excited by the idea, which means he was actually quite excited. The only time I remember him sounding really excited was when my parents' house was struck by lightning. Even then his excitement was tinged with regret at having been elsewhere at the time. He had missed the huge bang as the roof exploded, terrifying my mother, who was hiding in a windowless bathroom, clutching the cat.

The auditions were due to take place at the London Palladium in a few days' time. It was the Easter holidays and there was nothing else in the diary. 'Would you like to go?' I asked Dora. Silly question. Dora, aged six and a bit, already had an impressive track record of volunteering enthusiastically. Naturally she wanted to go.

It would probably have been more sensible to think about whether *I* wanted to go before raising the possibility with her. But I didn't. I was, however, very good about nixing any unrealistic expectations she might have. 'There's no way you'll get a part,' I told her. 'We'll have to queue for hours, you'll get to sing for one minute and then they'll say "thank you" and "goodbye".'

She still wanted to go, and as we didn't have any better offers for that day, I Googled the song lyrics, printed them out for her, downloaded the Judy Garland version from iTunes and copied it seven times on to a CD. I sang it to Dora. She put her hands over her ears and cried. I stopped singing and let her practise along with Judy. I told her again and again that there was no way she'd get a part. Was she really, *really* sure she wanted to go? Yes. Did she understand what I was saying? Yes. But she wanted to have a go and thought it might be fun. I thought it probably wouldn't be fun. I thought it would be a lot of very boring standing about, followed by her singing two lines while I got to do more boring standing about. Then I would have to comfort a humiliated, fed-up and frustrated child who'd been treated appallingly and dismissed carelessly by a panel of thoughtless Simon Cowell types. But, like many people, I was curious about what it would be like. How would Dora get on? What kinds of children (and parents) would turn out? What would the directors be looking for? Would we get to meet anyone interesting? My curiosity triumphed over my concerns. There is, after all, such a thing as being overprotective, and a day standing in line outside the London Palladium didn't seem *that* risky.

'The other parents will be awful,' advised my sister Nikki, who, having done some performing herself as a child, had taken her very pretty daughter to a couple of modeling castings and hadn't enjoyed the experience. 'They'll all be from *Essex*.' I wasn't convinced that coming from Essex was, of itself, reprehensible, but without entirely buying into her stereotyping (she does, after all, live in *West Hendon*), I thought I understood what she was getting at.

A couple of days before the audition, I went online to see if I could find out any more about what would be happening. What time would we have to be there to make sure Dora wouldn't miss out? How many children would turn up? Would they have to sing in a particular key? What should she wear? After some serious surfing, I came across the online ad on the Really Useful Group's website. At the bottom was an email address for someone called Jo Hawes, the Children's Administrator – whatever that meant. So, just after 11 p.m., having nothing better to do, I emailed her:

Hi there
Am planning on bringing my 6-year-old daughter along on
Thursday – it will be a first audition for both of us.
Please would you let me know
a) will the children sing accompanied or unaccompanied – does
it matter what key she sings in?
and – you may not be able to advise on this!!!
b) the time you expect people to start queuing on Thursday
morning
Thanks very much

Probably won't reply, I thought, but worth a go.
Fifteen minutes later she replied.

She will be accompanied and the key may vary. She should just
know the tune.
All I can tell you is that every single child will be seen but not
necessarily on Thursday. It will depend where you are in the
queue but on an open audition it is impossible to say how long

the queue will be or what time it will start building up. Experience
tells me they will start queuing at 6 or before and I am expecting
1000+ children.
Further info attached.

No way was I going to get up *that* early.

Thanks so much for getting back to me so rapidly and for the
extra information!
A bit cheeky to ask this, but if we're not going to be
superhumanly keen and start queuing at daybreak, is 9 a.m. the
cutoff point, or might it be more sensible to turn up a little later,
knowing that she might not be seen for a day or so?

It was, Jo replied immediately, entirely up to me.

On Thursday, 6 April 2006 we left home at a very civilised
8.30 a.m., arriving in front of the London Palladium about an hour
later. The multipley-braided, be-ribboned and even, in places,
dirndled queue snaked around the theatre and off into the distance.
Girls outnumbered boys massively, and the majority looked between
nine and thirteen years old: there weren't so many, it seemed, of
Dora's size and age. A couple of crews were filming groups of over-
excited children, who were thrilled that they might be on telly. A few
adults – those who had phoned in sick to bring their kids along – were
hiding under their coats, worried that they might be on telly.
Meanwhile, a smiley man with grey hair was joking with the children
and brandishing a measuring stick to check that they didn't exceed
the five-foot height limit. It took us at least five minutes to reach the
end of the queue.

A thousand hopefuls were waiting (although the media reported
that there were three thousand), the keenest, I later discovered,
having shown up before five that morning. There was, obviously, no
chance that Dora would be seen that day, and about twenty minutes

after we arrived, I was handed a form to complete with name, address, height and weight details, and told that I would be contacted with the venue, date and time of her audition. Despite her insistence at having her growth regularly marked in biro on the kitchen doorpost, I didn't have a clue how tall or heavy she was. Unless I'm baking a cake – a rare occurrence – I don't do measuring. This has led to some entertaining (for me) situations involving doorways, sofas, badly scratched paintwork and cross men. Feeling slightly smug at having avoided the mind-numbingly dull queuing bit, I tracked down the nice man with the stick to determine Dora's height and took a random guess at her weight.

Five days later when we hadn't heard anything, I emailed Jo just to make sure the form hadn't gone AWOL. There was, she replied, a letter in the post, and auditions would be the following Wednesday. That would be the first day of the summer term. Dora attends one of the local state schools, headed by the formidable but twinkly Mrs Kendall. It's a great school, happily diverse, within which the children are encouraged – pushed even – to work hard and to have high aspirations. The uniform is purple, popular with the girls (and may partly explain why, in Dora's class, they outnumber the boys two to one). Mrs Kendall strongly disapproves of children missing school for any reason not involving a communicable disease, so I had to summon all my courage to phone the office and seek permission for Dora to skive off for her audition. Permission was granted much more readily than I expected. Surprisingly, Mrs Kendall actually seemed excited at the prospect.

We arrived at the Urdang Academy in Covent Garden half an hour before our appointed time, climbed several flights of stairs and, after a quick loo visit, edged our way into a hot, stuffy studio-type room with scuffed wooden floors. It was buzzing with excited children and anxious parents and the few token chairs were all occupied. Because I wasn't sure what she'd be asked to do (also I have zero dress sense and my hairdressing talents don't stretch to straight central partings), Dora was wearing trainers, tracky pants and t-shirt, a broad grin and lopsided bunchies. I'd avoided twee, partly for reasons of taste, but mostly because it tends to involve pleats and plaits: both are beyond me. I gave Dora's name to a woman leaning over a trestle table, managing a clipboard, a marker pen and a long strip of white stickers. She was obviously in charge, so I also handed over the small passport-sized photo we'd been instructed to provide (child's name on the reverse), which featured Dora in her school uniform, another broad grin and more lopsided bunchies. 'Aaaw,' said the woman, looking at the photo and running her finger down the list on her clipboard. Halfway down page three of many, she put a tick by Dora's name, wrote 'Dora Gee' on a sticker which she gave me to stick on Dora's chest, shuffled through a pile of yellow paper to find the form I'd filled out at the Palladium, and fixed the photo to it. The auditions were running late, but after a lifetime of hanging around in doctors' waiting rooms (mostly, but not entirely, due to low-level hypochondria), I'd expected this and brought along colouring book, pencils and something to read.

The woman shushed everyone and called out a long list of names. About twenty assorted children bounced into a raggedy line, and were led out of the room. A couple of minutes later the previous group surged back in, three or four triumphantly waving letters, most shrugging and a couple in tears because they hadn't got through. It was, I thought, a bit brutal to tell them then and there. But maybe better to know straight away: no restless waiting, you could start picking up the pieces immediately. 'You won't mind if you don't get through, will you?' I asked Dora, anxious that she might be returned to me sobbing her heart out, permanently scarred by the rejection. 'No,' she said. 'It's my first audition. I know I won't get a part. I just want to try.'

Perhaps drumming into her that she'd be highly unlikely to succeed at her *first* audition was a mistake. *First* implied that there might be other opportunities to try out for other shows. That having taken her to one audition, muggins here would schlep her along to another, then another and another, cheerfully abandoning work, wedding planning and, eventually, own life in the cause of supporting the aspiring starlet and tending to its every need.

Had taking Dora to her 'first' audition inadvertently committed us to a life of kiddie showbiz? Would it turn me into a pushy mum, desperate for the reflected glory blazing off my spoiled child and pathologically and mistakenly convinced that she was better at everything than anyone else? Could today be the first small step on a downward spiral that would see me lying, cheating and demanding special treatment for her, telling directors how to do their job, and competing with other stage mothers, putting them and their children down whilst promoting my own flesh and blood. Would I – like Rose Hovick, immortalised in the musical *Gypsy*, who slathered her child-star daughter June in make-up and pushed her out on to the stage even when she had chicken pox, mumps and measles (although, to be fair, she did let her stay in bed with German measles) – fetch up putting my own, vicarious, ambition over Dora's welfare? Would I turn into . . . (dun dun dun) – STAGE MOTHER?????

As the group who'd just finished their audition left with their parents, we managed to snag a couple of vacated seats. I handed Dora her colouring book and pencils. But she soon found something more interesting to do. We'd been joined by a pretty little girl with long, straight, well-behaved dark hair, deep, sassy blue eyes and a cute grin. Inordinately self-possessed, she was accompanied by both parents and dressed as impeccably as her perfectly turned-out mother. Sitting down, she took her white Nintendo DS Lite out of her impossibly fluffy bag. Dora went shyly over to say hello and to watch her playing, and the girl made space for Dora to join her, while her parents and I made stilted, polite conversation. They had come up from Southend, and it was Adrianna's first proper audition too, but she was already the star of her dance and drama schools, and had performed in local productions of *South Pacific* and *The King and I*.

Although much smaller and slighter than Dora, she was a year older. Dora, I figured, stood no chance against this competition. She's about average height for her age, and I remembered from my sister's childhood acting days that small kids are usually preferred because it's easier to work with an older child who can pass for younger than a younger one who isn't yet mature enough to take direction.

The girls' names were called, and they disappeared out of the room in a cloud of children. Adrianna's parents and I looked at each other nervously and made more polite, stilted conversation, without actually listening to anything the other said. A few minutes after the girls had been shepherded off, we parents ran out of conversation. I opened my book, read the same paragraph several times and worried about Dora being upset if – as was more than likely – she didn't get through. I wondered whether she might actually have a chance. I smiled at Adrianna's mum and read the same paragraph again. I worried about whether Dora was enjoying herself. What were they all doing in there? Singing? Solo? Together? Sometimes, apparently, auditions can be good, clean, melodic fun. Participating children have been known to form lasting friendships. They go in, sing, do some fun drama games and burst out bubbly and excited, while their parents chat warily and size up the opposition. But often kids are told whether they've got through not at the end of their slot, like today, or a few days or even weeks later, but part way through their audition. On those occasions, it's usual for more than one or two to come out crying.

I was, it turned out, a lot more anxious than I had anticipated being. And, despite my expectations to the contrary, I really *really* wanted Dora to come out with an even broader grin than she went in with... and a letter. An unfamiliar urge was bubbling up in my stomach, provoking vague nausea enhanced by a wishy-washy sense of right-on liberal shame. I was silently willing Dora to open her throat and wow 'em. I don't consider myself either highly competitive or a particularly ambitious-for-my-child mother (well, not very). But every now and then – and this was one of those occasions – a petite and slightly passive-aggressive dragon uneggs itself inside me, mewling quietly for victory. Naturally, I try to conceal it under an 'I-couldn't-be-more-delighted-for-your-success' kind of smile, but I strongly suspect that it's still visible, pulsing away underneath. If Dora did get any further, could I rein in this obnoxious part of me?

It's not even as if I ever wanted to go on the stage myself. As a geeky pre-teen I'd been forced into attending a local drama training institution for after-school lessons. The Studio School was run by Miss Jones – a distinctly colour-boosted redhead with terrifying diction and no-nonsense eyeliner – and Miss Hudson, a gentler, quieter soul and a hazier, greyer presence in my memory. It was in my own best interests: I was so mumbly as to be borderline inaudible, and my parents decided that elocution and acting lessons would cure me. I hated it. It was, I felt, hard enough figuring out how to be myself, without having to pretend to be other people, however fictional, and even if for only a couple of hours a week. Nikki, younger than me by three years, much more outgoing, cheeky and tiny for her age, loved performing and had real talent. She was spotted by an agent during one of the Studio School's annual shows and earned a lot of money (for a nine-year-old) bouncing across a Birds Eye advert, dressed as a giant fish finger.

My father was also a good actor. In his teens he won a place at RADA's preparatory academy. He turned it down, choosing to study civil engineering instead: it was, apparently, just as much fun, and meant his National Service was deferred (though he was disappointed when it was, ultimately, cancelled as he'd been looking forward to travelling abroad and playing lots of table tennis). And Dad could still exercise his dramatic flair by miming, dressed in a conservative suit and a less conservative curly brown wig, to Shirley Bassey doing 'Hey Big Spender' at company Christmas parties.

And although Dora had no previous acting experience, my father's suggestion that she might like to try out for *The Sound of Music* wasn't completely random. After their (very happy) time in daycare, Dora and her two best friends were each about to start a different school. To ease the pain of separation and ensure that they could still get to hang out regularly, we parents got together and enrolled them into the littlies ballet class at Adele's Dance School. I was ambivalent. I knew Dora would have fun dancing with her friends and hoped (rather optimistically) the discipline might calm her down a tad. But it was already perfectly clear that with her three-year-old proto-warrior physique and habit of barrelling into people head-first for ferocious, spine-shattering cuddles, she was never going to mature into the kind of quietly bendy, baby-pink stick insect that gives good ballet, and I felt that it was important to protect her from thinking that she should. There's more than enough pressure on young girls to starve themselves unnaturally thin, without over-exposing them to the extremes of that particular part of the dance world. But given that she and her friends were only three, and this was local, inexpensive, conveniently timed ballet-for-fun, where the teacher welcomed children of all shapes, sizes and abilities, I decided that my worries were, if not excessive, at least previous. If, at some point, doing ballet did start having a negative impact on Dora's sense of self, I'd just have to divert her into tap or Kathak instead.

One Tuesday afternoon, a year after the three of them had skipped into their first lesson, wearing their favourite 100% polyester fairy dress-up costumes, I arrived late, someone else having delivered Dora for me. Unlike many dance schools, at Adele's, parents and carers are encouraged to stay and watch. This is sometimes cute, sometimes hilarious and sometimes tortuously boring – especially as you get told off for chatting. To my dismay, I discovered everyone except my daughter standing in line, swaying along to the opening strains of 'Do-Re-Mi'. Dora was fidgeting off to one side, watching. Adele's Dance School is determinedly and cheerfully inclusive. What terrible sin, I wondered, could Dora possibly have committed to get herself excluded from the line-up? It didn't look like anyone was bleeding . . .

She hadn't, it transpired, done anything wrong. The class was starting to rehearse its contribution to the school's annual show. Earlier in the lesson, her hand had shot up and she'd volunteered – possibly without knowing what one was – to sing a solo. She was merely waiting on her cue. Striding out purposefully in front of the other little girls, she took her place and sang loudly, clearly, confidently and with evident gusto. Afterwards, Adele's pianist Carl – who, in addition to accompanying little girls' dance lessons, has also posed as Liberace for the entertainment of guests at Matt Lucas's wedding party – took me aside. 'Where did she get that voice?' he asked. 'She's like Shirley Bassey.'

Er . . . From her grandpa?

A few of the kids trickled back in. It looked like there was a higher concentration of letters in this group. Adrianna was waving one. 'That's brilliant. Well done!' I said, with as much enthusiasm as I could muster – which was, fortunately, quite a lot – while her parents cuddled and praised her. I looked anxiously towards the door. Dora was nowhere to be seen. Then, suddenly, there she was, leaping into my lap and shoving a piece of paper into my face. 'I've got a recall,' she announced proudly.

I gave her a big hug and told her she'd done fantastically, especially as this was her first time, and that it was completely brilliant to have got a recall, and asked lots of questions. Did they sing together or by themselves? Did they have to do anything else? Was it scary or fun? And I reminded her that she had only got through the first stage and that it didn't mean that she'd get a part, which she still definitely wouldn't.

It was almost a month and only one anxious email (I exercised impressive restraint) from me to Jo Hawes before details of the next audition plopped into our messy hallway. The two-page letter from Jo explained that there would, most likely, be several more rounds of auditions, which would be quite spread out, 'with final casting not taking place until well into August'. She explained that they were looking for three Friedrichs, Louisas, Kurts, Brigittas and Martas, four or five Gretls 'since she is such a young child', and no Liesls: the role of the oldest von Trapp child would be played by a grown-up, sourced elsewhere. We were also urged to 'make sure you understand the commitment involved with a show like this', and to check with the children's schools that they'd be happy for them to take part. 'Rehearsals,' she continued, 'will be arduous and require time away from school although the statutory 15 hours' schooling a week will be applied. Either this will take place at your own school or we will hire a tutor.' Also, 'Please note that no holidays will be permitted during the contract which will be from the start of rehearsals until March/April 07.' The schedule would not be changed to accommodate anyone's special occasions 'or to allow time off for any reason during rehearsal and performances apart from illness – we require 100% commitment'.

I avoided taking much notice of any of this: mostly because Laurie likes holidays, and I was nervous of raising the possibility of a six-month ban on them in the run-up to our wedding. Especially as, unlike me, he thought Dora had a good chance of winning a part. There were already more than enough, mostly catering-related (if we were refusing vol-au-vents, then *surely* we had to have mini-latkes) disputes to manage. Family members on both sides were muttering that we simply weren't competent to organise the event ourselves: they seemed particularly worried about insufficiently padded seating, plates with the wrong patterns on, and no bridge rolls.

Also I was slightly hazy about exactly what – should it come to pass – '100% commitment' might involve. Would I need to look after Dora while she was rehearsing and performing? If so, would I be paid? How much? Did 'no holidays' mean we were confined to London for six months, or did it just mean no long trips to exotic locations? Anyway, I didn't waste too much time thinking about it too deeply. She'd only got through one audition. All that meant was that she could sing in tune and was under five foot tall. There were still hundreds of children in the running. Watching *The Sound of Music* on video for approximately the millionth time (we did actually wear it out), I did, however, notice that she looked like Kym Karath, who played Gretl, nearly drowned during the boating scene and about whom Christopher Plummer reputedly exclaimed, 'I'm not carrying that bloody fat little kid up that mountain' (after which they stuffed a skinny local into Kym's costume and filmed the scene with her instead).

More of my attention was absorbed by the three pages of sheet music attached to the back of Jo's letter. Dora needed to learn all three parts of an a cappella harmony extract from the title song, plus fifteen bars of 'The Lonely Goatherd'. I couldn't help her with that, nor could Laurie: we didn't have a piano and I hadn't tried to read music for over twenty-five years. Not since I'd failed my Grade 5 trumpet exam for the second time.

A little over a month before our wedding, there was still a lot to organise. I wasn't terribly bothered about things like clothes and flowers. Actually, I was so not bothered by flowers that it hadn't occurred to me that we might need or want some. Clothes were slightly more of a concern. The feeling of sartorial inadequacy that thrums constantly at the edge of my consciousness was gradually gaining volume and would, I knew, at some point – probably when it was too late to do anything about it – erupt into full-blown neurosis. But I was way behind Lilli, who was threatening to spontaneously combust over Laurie's reluctance to invest in a new outfit. She had a point: his attachment to the three pairs of well-worn Clark's lace-ups that comprised his entire shoe collection did seem slightly unnatural, and his trouser-knees were universally shiny. 'I'm an ascetic,' he lamented. 'Or I used to be. All I ever needed was one pair of yoga pants and a prayer mat.' Which was true. Before becoming a children's entertainer (how we met), my husband-to-be used to travel the world practising and teaching Sufi meditation, dance and Middle Eastern drumming.

I was more concerned that we hadn't yet sent out the invitations, or even decided exactly who we were going to invite. What was the point of ordering 250 smoked salmon bagels if there was no one to eat them? After a bit of toing and froing between Laurie and me, my dad and Lilli – Dora had already invited about ten of her closest friends (including a couple of boys) to be bridesmaids – we settled on a guest list long enough to include everyone who had to be invited and most of the people we wanted to be there. We just about managed to keep it short enough to ensure that none of the older generation would be trampled in the post-ceremony scramble for a cup of tea (and, obviously, a bagel).

On that guest list was the solution to our audition music problem: Ruth Franks, jazz-singer-turned-children's-music-teacher – a lifelong family friend of Laurie's.

Two weeks before her recall – four before our wedding – we dropped Dora off at Ruth's flat with sheet music, my minidisc recorder complete with blank disc and some garbled instructions on how to use it and what to use it for. Handily, Ruth lives just round the corner from the rabbi who was going to officiate at our wedding. We took the opportunity to visit his house with a packet of kosher biscuits, so we could chat about the service and discuss those delicate matters that needed raising and, more critically, avoiding in his speech.

An hour and a half later, marginally wiser and only slightly confused (did we get the things that needed raising and avoiding the right way round?), we were back at Ruth's. Dora had had a fantastic time, and Ruth had recorded the melodies she needed to learn. 'How did she do?' I asked.

'She's pitch-perfect,' said Ruth. 'She might be exactly what they're looking for.'

'But she's got no experience, and with all those stage school kids out there . . .'

'They're probably not looking for stage school kids.'

I thought she was wrong. I was certain they'd be after stage school moppets, old pros by the age of seven, who could cry convincingly on cue like Shirley Temple, sing like Cyndi Lauper, dance like very small versions of Ginger Rogers and all of whom would have been genetically modified using DNA carefully extracted from Jenny Agutter.

I copied each of Dora's four tunes three times on to a cassette tape, and left her to practise, only interfering occasionally. Or, to be more accurate, only when I couldn't help myself, which was quite often. When I wasn't annoying her, she worked hard to learn the songs, and by a couple of days before the audition had mastered all but the bottom part of 'The Sound of Music'. I figured this didn't matter too much – surely that was what the boys would be for? She'd probably be singing the top or middle parts. But I made her do a bit of extra work on it anyway, despite Laurie's very sensible advice that she'd be better off concentrating on the parts she knew well. On the up side, she took to belting out 'The Lonely Goatherd' like she was born to yodel. Unfortunately, so did I, and I wasn't. Worse than that, the song wormed itself into my brain. I spent the best part of a year humming it to myself, and occasionally bursting into off-key song, sometimes in deeply inappropriate situations.

We were due at the Really Useful Group's head office in Covent Garden at 3.30 p.m. on Tuesday, 30 May, half-term, so no need to ask Mrs Kendall for time off. As usual we arrived ludicrously early. As usual, Dora was hungry and demanded food, so first of all, we popped round the corner to a café, where I bought her an apple and a bottle of water, promising something unhealthy after the audition. As we were now slightly less ludicrously early, we wandered back to Really Useful's HQ. A few kids and parents were leaving. 'How did it go?' I asked one father. He shrugged, smiling, and told me that this time they weren't letting the children know immediately whether they would be recalled. Round the side of the building, a mother was critiquing her son's rendition of the top part of 'The Sound of Music'. I thought it sounded better than Dora's rendition of the bottom part. But then he was much older.

I pressed the buzzer, and the door released. To our left was a curved dark wood reception desk, behind which sat a smiley young woman. Rather unnecessarily, given that I was attached to a small, grinning girl, I explained what we were there for. She directed us into the boardroom, which, with its thick carpet, comfy sofas, huge oval dining table and big plasma telly, looked like it wanted to be a lounge when it grew up. There was a grand piano (covered) in the corner and a sideboard with half-empty bottles of water, cartons of orange juice, jugs of tea and coffee and nothing clean left to pour them into. And lots and lots and lots of people. One family of older girls and boys were huddled in a corner practising perfect three-part-harmony singing. Others were bunched together trying to peek through the closed white Venetian blinds into what was obviously the audition room. Groups of children were chatting excitedly amongst themselves. As new people arrived, there were the occasional shrieks of recognition, followed by excited hugs, as children met up with old friends. The adults also seemed to know each other. I didn't recognise anyone. It crossed my mind that this was what our wedding might feel like.

Dora tugged at my sleeve. 'I need the toilet,' she whispered. So did I. But we found a woman with a clipboard first, so Dora could be ticked off the list and stickered. She was wearing tracksuit pants and bunchies again, as these had done the trick last time, and I was very proud that her hairdo was marginally more even. Although I hadn't exactly achieved the Roman road of all partings, I'd managed to get one or two sections of it quite straight.

There was a short queue for the loo, followed by a long wait for the audition. We'd managed to grab one of the chairs around the big table. Dora sat on my lap and I read to her, whilst trying to listen to the singing that wafted out of the audition room whenever the chatter in the waiting area died down slightly.

Eventually her name was called, and after a few minutes of trying to concentrate on reading a novel, and smiling friendlily at some other parents, I joined the huddle at the Venetian blind. It was almost closed, but if you squinted at the right angle, you could just catch the odd slice of feet, ankles and table legs. If you focused hard, it was possible to hear muffled instructions being issued, although impossible to work out what was being said. These would be followed by short snatches of singing (audible and uplifting), more muffled talking and then laughter. Once or twice I thought I spotted Dora's Scooby-Doo trainers. But strain as I might, I couldn't identify her voice. This made me feel slightly inadequate: surely as a concerned parent, I ought to be able to distinguish my own daughter's singing, even when it was parsed through a double-glazed window and a mostly closed blind.

I wandered back to the table. Someone else had taken my seat, so I picked up my book, found a spare bit of floor to sit on and leaned against the wall. Judging from the laughter – it sounded genuine – the children seemed to be having lots of fun. I wasn't, but for some reason I was less nervy this time. I knew we wouldn't find out whether she'd got through that day, so there'd be no immediate consequences to cope with. And we weren't far enough into the process for a part to feel like it might be a nail-bitingly real possibility. I felt that having got through the first round, Dora had, in some small way, proved herself. Neither of us would be remotely disappointed if this was as far as it went. We would, on the other hand, be quite excited if she got further, even though I was starting to realise exactly how ferrying my little darling to auditions might gobble up large chunks of time and money.

Two things made it feel doable. Having only one child meant I wouldn't have to factor in any additional school pick-ups, swimming lessons, packed lunches and screaming tantrums. And I work freelance. All I really need to get on with whatever I'm working on is my laptop, a book or two and a small square of reasonably clean floor. Table and chair optional, wireless internet access desirable. But I could, in theory at least, beetle away at whatever I was being paid to do and still become a stage mother. Not that I expected to become one. But I could. If I had to.

About twenty-five minutes after she'd gone in, Dora resurfaced.

'How was it?' I asked.

'Great,' she said. 'I'm hungry.'

'Was it fun?'

'Yes. Can I have a packet of crisps *and* a muffin *and* a drink?'

'What did you do?'

'Singing. Can we get some food now?'

'Did you have to sing all the different parts? Did you have to sing by yourself? Were the other children nice? Were the grown-ups nice?'

'*Please* can I have some crisps and a muffin and a drink?'

Further grilling (over a muffin and a bottle of that disgusting with-a-hint-of-fruit-and-a-ton-of-aspartame water that Dora loves and that I feel guilty about allowing her to drink sometimes – I drew the line at crisps as well) revealed that everyone, children and adults, was nice, but she didn't know anybody's name, except that there were two people in there called Jo, one of whom had long curly hair and played the piano, that they'd all had to sing parts of 'The Lonely Goatherd' solo, although they'd yodelled in chorus, and that the youngest children had been asked which parts of the harmony in 'The Sound of Music' they wanted to sing.

'You've done very well to get this far,' I said

'I know,' she said. 'I'm still hungry. *Please* can I have a packet of crisps?'

There was no news for another week. Fortunately, we were all very busy. Dora had plenty of play-dates to keep her occupied over half-term and Laurie and I were hectic with work and wedding planning. As we were having a Jewish do (hence the rabbi and the bagels), I needed a veil – so that Laurie could do the traditional thing and, before the main ceremony, peek underneath it to check that he was getting hitched to the right woman. Or, at least, the one he expected to be marrying. Because of all the friends Dora had invited to be bridesmaids, it had to be a long one. Thank heavens for eBay. Then Dora and I popped down to Bournemouth for a couple of days to visit Lilli. She helped sew tiny gold beads on to my BEAUTIFUL VEIL PERFECT FOR YOUR WEDDING NEW COST £150! (£24.99 + postage) so it went with the dress I'd decided to wear: a tight-fitting, knee-length gold brocade vintage number that my maternal grandmother wore to my parents' wedding.

On our return to London, we heard.

This is to let you know that *Dora* will be recalled for THE SOUND OF MUSIC but I have no other details such as dates at the moment. All such details will come by email or by post when I know.

Best wishes,

Jo

Oh Gawd. What if the next round clashed with our honeymoon? Couldn't cut that short just to take Dora to an audition. Not without an entry in the *Guinness Book of Records* for the shortest ever marriage, anyway. Still, it would be a pity for her to miss it, especially as she wasn't coming with us. My dad would just have to take her: it was all his fault, after all. But what if the details were sent by post and the letter arrived while we were away and we didn't get it in time? Or we got it in time for her to be there, but not in time for her to learn whatever it was she needed to learn beforehand?

After several minutes of frantic agonising over what might possibly happen when, and what all the implications might be, it occurred to me that what I was actually feeling anxious about was getting married and that this recall business was fairly simple to manage. So I emailed Jo to check when it might possibly happen and she confirmed that the next round wouldn't be during our honeymoon, but there was a chance that Dora would be needed the day we were due to arrive back. I gave her my mobile number just in case. Sorted.

In the event, we managed to get through both wedding and honeymoon without any *Sound of Music*-related interruptions, although the beautiful veil perfect for my wedding slipped sideways as, accompanied by a herd of small, over-excited children and my father and sister, I did my supposed-to-be-dignified processional walk from the front door, round the side of my father's house, to the chuppah – the canopy under which the wedding ceremony takes place. As the repeated attempts to secure the veil delayed my appearance by several minutes (the walk should have taken thirty seconds – we're not talking a hike round Hampton Court here), the rabbi leant forward to Laurie and whispered, 'Are you sure she's coming?' I spent the entire ceremony looking like I'd lost a fight with a net curtain and the rabbi concluded his description of Laurie with the words 'and so we can only hope, Lisa, that you are a practical person'. Oh dear.

Two days after Laurie and I returned from our romantic trip to Tuscany, most of which we spent in a basic wooden cabin on an idyllic seaside campsite, where I thrashed him at table football and we tried, but failed, to ride a tandem, Jo sent the following email

Dear Dora
We are delighted to be able to offer you a further recall.
DATE: Monday, 26 June
VENUE: Pineapple Langley Street Covent Garden
TIME: 2.05 p.m.
Please bring – the music that you have already learnt.
A piece of prose or a poem not longer than one min to be
recited by heart.
A school letter indicating support for participation in the show,
not just the audition. I already have this from some children.

Since our return, Dora had been skipping round chanting parts of one of Michael Rosen's poems, 'Don't', which, she told me, formed the basis of a playground game. As it involved being instructed not to pour gravy on a baby, put ants in pants or throw fruit at the computer, I quietly hoped that she and her friends weren't acting out the rhyme too literally, using props or torturing any small insects. The children had discovered the poem in one of the books in the classroom, so, with the teacher's permission, we borrowed it, and that afternoon I timed Dora reading it.

It was the ideal length and, whilst not very *Sound-of-Music*-ish, suited Dora's bouncy personality perfectly, which saved me the trouble of sourcing something that was both appropriate (where to start?) and that she wouldn't turn her freckly little nose up at. Besides which, she had virtually memorised it already. As there were only five days until the next audition, why give us both extra work? I typed it up on my computer and printed it out for Dora to learn completely by heart, which, as she nearly knew it anyway, didn't take long. Then Laurie, who's done a bit of acting and drama teaching in his time, helped her add more expression at one or two points, and tone it down at a few others. I found myself thinking that 'Don't' might be a bit different from the other children's offerings in a way that could possibly give Dora the edge. The little internal dragon was unfurling its wings, mewling softly, blowing smoke rings and preparing itself for a fight. A nice, constrained middle-class kind of fight, naturally: one that would take place almost entirely inside me. The creature was, I realised, my inner stage mother. There are whole schools of therapy based on the idea that it's important to embrace and express one's inner child. Should I do that with my inner stage mother, or would the right thing be to ignore and suppress her? If that was the right thing to do, could I do it?

I encouraged Dora to recite her poem a couple of times on the way in to Covent Garden, but pretty soon she'd had enough and told me to stop and I did what I was told. There were a lot of stairs at

Pineapple, and a café, so while we were waiting (early again) I bought Dora an apple and a bottle of unflavoured water. I'd made sure to feed her before we left home on something with no milk or cheese or yoghurt in it, as I'd overheard someone at the last audition saying that they should avoid eating dairy before singing, because it could make them all mucusy. As instructed, we'd brought the music she'd learned, a copy of the poem and a letter of agreement from the school. 'Hmmm,' Mrs Kendall had frowned. 'She'll be in Year Two. Missing school in her SATs year. I'm not sure I approve.' But after I'd explained that there were loads more rounds of auditions to go and hundreds of children still in the running, she'd signed a letter to say that the school was happy for Dora to be in the show. 'You never know. She's got this far. She might just be in with a chance.' She smiled.

I did manage not to stick my fingers in my ears and shout 'LA LA LA LA LA LA', but only just. 'She might be in with a chance' was the position I was trying to avoid coming round to. Not because I didn't want Dora to get a part, but rather because I didn't want to think about the possibility that it might happen. Although I might not be the most practical person in the world, I am emphatically – and by choice – not a fantasist. Having been obsessed with *Champion the Wonder Horse*, *Dr Who* and *The New Avengers* during my impressionable early years, by the age of eight I'd moved on from pretending to be a pony to daydreaming up an entire alternative existence in which I led a team of international troubleshooting detectives called the Black Cats. We wore black catsuits (well, this was the 1970s), flew speedily to trouble spots using personal helicopter-like transportation devices that strapped around our waists, and communicated via state-of-the-art walkie-talkie systems (mobile phones weren't invented). In my daydreams I was lithe and athletic. This was in stark contrast to my usual painful clumsiness, which was so extreme that my mother sometimes wondered if I might have sustained minor brain damage affecting my motor skills when deprived of oxygen during the birth process. Eventually, finding the transition from dream life to real life too painful to negotiate on a regular basis, I chose to anchor myself in what passes for reality. It took more than a decade to reach that point and I could just as easily have gone the other way.

Before I let Dora eat her apple or drink her water, I made sure we found the lady with the clipboard, made small talk, got Dora's sticker and handed over the school letter. I tried to read what was on the clipboard to see if I could work out how many children they were seeing, and which parts they might be being considered for, but I couldn't, although a G in front of Dora's name could, I thought, stand for Gretl. Judging from the length of the list (many sheets of paper) and how crammed the café area was (there was only enough space at any of the picnic-style tables-and-benches to accommodate one buttock), there were still hundreds in the running.

Fifteen minutes before her audition was due to start, Dora had eaten her apple and drunk about half her water. I suggested she save the rest for when she went in, and took her to the loo. She protested that she didn't need to go, but I insisted. 'You don't want to have to run out of your audition.' She pulled a face but complied. While I waited for her I asked another mum, who was brushing her daughter's silky blonde hair, how old her child was. 'She's seven,' she replied proudly, 'but she sings like a ten-year-old.'

'That's nice,' I said, feeling I ought to reciprocate in kind. But what should I tell her in return? 'My daughter's six but she sings like Shirley Bassey'? 'My daughter is quite good at ballet'? 'My daughter watches TV like a pro'? In the end I blurted out, 'My daughter's face is quite big, so she shows up well on stage.' Which, along with her big voice, was something I'd noticed during school assemblies. The other mother looked slightly shocked.

When I look at Dora I am, sometimes, silenced by her breath-takingly big-eyed, radiantly cheeky beauty. Of course I am. I'm her mother. I also think she's very funny, even witty; clever; sometimes wise beyond her years, and talented in ways that often take me by surprise and leave me slightly in awe (though obviously I'd never let her know about the awe bit). But although I think she's fantastic, I know, as her mother, it's my job to think that. And it feels wrong to big her up to complete strangers. It's almost like walking around wearing a t-shirt with 'I'm brilliant, I am' written on it in huge letters, then winking and pointing at it every time you catch someone's eye. It's not that I think we should all go around being demurely modest in a head-bowed, ribbons-and-bonnets don't-show-your-ankles Victorian kind of way. I just wouldn't expect anyone to believe me if I told them how brilliant my child was. For starters, I'm not convinced that any of us can achieve the detachment and perspective necessary to judge our children (or our parents, spouses or siblings for that matter) accurately. Nor do I think, in most circumstances, that we should even try. Which doesn't mean that we should be blind to their faults or their talents, just that we should be aware of our proper and necessary bias.

A few minutes later Dora's name was called. I stuffed the sheet music and poem into her hands. She gave the music back, saying she didn't need it, but took the poem. 'Good luck!' I called as she headed off. 'Have fun.' 'I will,' she shouted, skipping off without a backward glance as she was led off down a corridor, along with about fifteen other children.

I don't remember talking to anyone while I was waiting for her to come out again. I think I just stared at people, and eavesdropped. 'I hardly got to say any of my poem,' one girl from the previous group complained to her father. 'One of the girls completely forgot the thing she'd learned,' a boy told his mum quietly. 'She cried.' I tried not to think about whether Dora would remember her poem. I suspected she'd probably be quite good at reciting it – but what did I know? There was no predicting what might happen if conditions weren't right. At the end of the ballet school show a year and a half ago – the one at which Dora had sung 'Do-Re-Mi' – there had been a slight incident. Carl-the-pianist had been so impressed by her singing that he'd suggested to Adele-the-teacher that Dora join with a couple of older girls to sing another solo – a short part of ABBA's 'Thank You For the Music' – in the finale. All had gone swimmingly in rehearsal, but on the first of the two nights, disaster struck. A big girl accidentally sat so that her voluminous tutu settled itself over the microphone that Dora had been instructed to sing into. Unprepared for this eventuality, Dora didn't know what to do, and consequently did nothing, except look distressed and uncomfortable. She felt awful, and so did I. The following night – the last – the problem was, happily, solved: one of the bigger girl singers held a microphone under Dora's nose and started the singing with her.

Dora bounced out of her audition bubblier than a can of shaken lemonade, which was quite scary, but more informative than usual. This time she couldn't stop talking about what had happened, and needed no prompting whatsoever. She'd got all the way to the last stanza of her poem before they stopped her reciting, and had remembered to cross her eyes and stick out her tongue on the 'Don't pull faces' line. 'We played games,' she told me excitedly. 'We had to line up with the tallest at one end and the shortest at the other. We got that right. I was at one end,' she added. 'Then we had to line up again in order of who lives nearest and who lives most far away.' She paused. 'We had to work it all out by ourselves. I was on the end again. We got that wrong.'

'Did any of the grown-ups say anything to you?' I asked.

'Yes. We all had to go up one at a time at the end and they said I was the loudest and clearest.'

'In a good way?'

I deserved Dora's response: rolled eyes, raised eyebrows and a dismissive shrug. In fact, I deserved something louder and clearer. She hadn't been told off for mucking about in class, shrieking at the library, or having a tantrum in the quiet coach of a train into which I had accidentally booked us. Of course being loud and clear in an audition was a good thing. It might mean, I thought, that she'd get another recall. This, on the one hand, would be another good thing. On the other, from what Jo had written in an earlier letter, it was likely that the auditions would continue through the summer. And would it be fair on Laurie if the process interfered with our holiday plans? I could, I reckoned, possibly argue that as we'd already been on our honeymoon, it didn't matter quite so much, but I wasn't entirely sure whether that would be the right thing to do. What should my priorities be?

There was also, on the new husband front, a decision to make about names. I had been married before – I was nineteen when we got hitched, we stayed together for ten years, split amicably and are still good friends – and had reverted to my maiden name after the divorce. I had also changed Dora's surname to match mine when her father and I split up (am I difficult to live with?), and I wasn't sure if it would be sensible to change either, or both our names again. Should we ditch our surname and take his? Should we go double-barrelled? Or should we save the hassle and expense of changing all the documentation and just stay as we were?

A big envelope arrived four days later. It was Dora's school sports day, and she was not happy.

'I won't win *anything*,' she sobbed. 'I don't want to go.'

'It doesn't matter about winning. It's about joining in and having fun.'

'It's *not* fun if you never win.' Then she brightened up. 'Perhaps I'll come second in the potato-and-spoon race.'

'I can't run fast,' I told her. 'And it doesn't matter. You're good at lots of other things. You can't be good at everything.'

'Why not?' I chose to ignore her, because I couldn't think of a good, satisfying answer whilst simultaneously making sure she had everything she needed and getting us both out the door in a generally calm, positive way. It was time to walk to school, join up with the rest of her class, then turn around and walk straight back the way we came, past our house and on to the City Academy, where we would experience the joy of sports day.

It was the usual chaos. Dora didn't place in the potato-and-spoon race, but achieved a creditable third in throwing what appeared to be a miniature primary-coloured intercontinental ballistic missile.

Eventually it was time for the mothers' race. I walked up to the line, along with about twenty other mums. We took our places. The gun went off. We ran. I went as fast as I could, legs pounding away beneath me, arms pumping, heart racing. I didn't come last, but that was only because another mum fell flat on her face. I passed her, and the friend who'd finished and then come back to make sure she was still breathing, seconds after everyone else had hit the finish line. It was the fastest hundred metres I'd done in twenty-five years. Possibly ever.

'You looked really funny,' said Dora, with a six-year-old's grasp of both tact and the taking-part spirit I'd been attempting to role-model. 'Everyone in my class was laughing at you.'

I felt okay until the walk home, during which my right leg started to hurt. By the time we made it home, I could no longer stand on it.

I phoned NHS Direct and was put through to a male and perky Australian nurse who compared my injury to Michael Owen's (he thought I'd damaged my cruciate ligament) and instructed me to go straight to A & E. I didn't buy the comparison and, hence, the diagnosis. And as I didn't fancy spending three hours waiting in the local hospital, only to be rewarded with a don't-waste-our-time-again scowl and a free tubigrip, I tracked down the number of the local minor injuries unit. A rather weary nurse asked me if I'd taken ibuprofen. I hadn't. 'Don't come in,' she said. 'We'll only send you away with a couple of ibuprofen to see if it gets better.' Not even a tubigrip. I took two tablets, settled down on the bed to read Dora's recall letter and started wondering if the cycling holiday we'd been contemplating was such a good idea.

The letter contained details of the next audition together with two and a half pages of genuine *Sound of Music* script, the scene where the children introduce themselves to Maria. Dora had to learn all their lines (including the boys') by the next audition on 6 July. I helped, by being Maria, correcting Dora when she went wrong, and making her repeat and repeat until she got it right. Out of sheer curiosity, I timed how long it took her to memorise everything she needed to learn. It took two sessions on successive days, a total of one and a half hours, at the end of which I hadn't managed to learn the few lines Maria speaks – a fraction of what Dora had absorbed – and still, much to her frustration at how hopeless I was, needed the script.

The letter said there would be more auditions on Friday 7th, too. Did that mean, I asked Jo by email, that everyone would be seen on the Friday too, or just those who shone on Thursday? Everyone, came the answer.

Two more half-days off school and still no complaints from Mrs Kendall. 'Do you think she's going to get a part?' she asked, grinning, her perfectly applied plum lipstick stretching from one ear to the other.

'Well,' I admitted grudgingly. 'It's not impossible. This'll be the fourth round.'

'How exciting! Wouldn't it be wonderful? I wouldn't be at all surprised!' she enthused, looking astutely confident in both Dora's abilities and her suitability and without mentioning any adverse side-effects on her education or her Key Stage 1 SATs score, which was simultaneously reassuring and alarming. In fact, Adele, Dora's ballet teacher, had told me that she wouldn't be surprised, either. Nor would Carl-the-pianist. Or Dora's father Steve, who works as a theatre techie (sound and light) whenever he's bored being a computer techie. The only person, it seemed, who would be surprised if Dora ended up strutting her stuff on the London Palladium stage at the age of six was me. But just in case, I ordered a replacement for our worn-out *Sound of Music* video from Amazon. A new DVD. The singalong edition.

And I dared to email Jo again: 'Are you still seeing hundreds?' to which Jo's immediate one-word response was 'No!'

At this point, my inner stage mother woke up and smelled the greasepaint. She took over the keyboard

Aaahh . . . Do you know how many more stages there are likely to be? And (I've never done this sort of thing before), can I ask, on the basis of what you've seen of her so far, what Dora's chances might be?
Thanks!

There are likely to be two more auditions at least, I think. I have no idea what her chances are – a lot of people have a say in it. Also if they don't find what they want we will start again. So it is best to just take it as it comes.

Well, that told me. I clamped down on the stage mother part of me and tried to douse the fizzling excitement I wasn't admitting to in public – or even in private – and started planning an October half-term trip to visit Laurie's sister and niece in New York. That way, whatever happened, we'd have something to look forward to. And I could pretend that I hadn't started counting chickens. Which, three months and three recalls along, I now had. I would, I realised, be disappointed if she didn't get at least to the last round, and kept reminding myself – and my inner stage mother, who had already started planning her opening night party outfit – that Dora had done very well to get this far.

'You've done very well to get this far,' I told her, several times, as she recited her lines (I still couldn't do Maria without a script, or with conviction. I'm not nun material).

'I know,' she said. 'But I might get a part, mightn't I?'

'It's not impossible,' I replied, 'but let's not think too much about it.'

'But I might, mightn't I?'

'Yes,' I finally admitted to both of us. 'You might.'

'I wonder if I'll be Gretl or Marta,' she mused.

'Time for supper,' I said, changing the subject.

'But I don't like fish.'

'Tough.'

'Do I have to eat all of it? Do you think I might get a part?'

'Eat your fish.'

'Do I have to?'

I raised my eyebrows and did my best stern face, which, after six and a half years of practice, was quite good, even if it rarely achieved the desired effect.

'Not fair.'

The day before the next audition, we received a hurried email from Jo Hawes. The venue had been double-booked, so they'd shifted us all from one church hall (Catholic) in west London to another (Baptist) a couple of minutes away. Dora was due at two, and because I had trouble finding a parking place and change for the meter ('All right. You can have a packet of crisps. But only Ready Salted Lite ones. And save the face-pulling for the audition, okay?'), we were only twenty minutes early, which is almost the same as being on time. It was easy to find the church. It was the squat modern building set back from the road opposite Ravenscourt Park station and largely obscured by a swarm of mostly chattering children of distinctly Aryan appearance, around which the occasional anxious parent orbited erratic as a malfunctioning satellite.

There were two ways to get to the front door: up a flight of concrete steps, zigzagging round or stepping over the kids sitting talking, rehearsing their lines or daydreaming. Or by negotiating a ramp, which several auditionees' younger brothers were neeeeyoowwing down, arms outstretched in fighter plane mode. Dora hurtled up the ramp while I picked my way up the stairs, peering down on partings so straight and plaits so perfect that creating them must have involved slide rules, spirit levels and abstruse algebraic calculations. We made our way inside and signed Dora in. This time, the woman with the clipboard and stickers was Jo Hawes herself, commandingly tall and straight – imagine Boudicca in a business suit – with a direct, unblinking blue-eyed gaze and precise Home Counties diction. Not someone you'd want to get into a fight with, unless you happened to have a sports day ICBM or two up your sleeve.

She was very smiley and welcoming and explained that there'd be a bit of a wait as they were running slightly behind. The group before Dora's hadn't gone in yet, which was why there were children bursting out all over the place: once the next lot were called we would, she thought, be able to sit down comfortably. We wandered outside again. A few of the kids were rehearsing lines with the assistance – or, in the odd case, extreme encouragement – of a parent. I asked Dora if she wanted to practise. She wrinkled up her nose and shook her head: she thought she knew it and didn't, anyway, want to rehearse in front of everyone. I tried not to look up towards the front of the building where a mother was comforting a sobbing girl who had, I found out later, run out of her audition distressed because she kept getting everything wrong. I glanced down at Dora: 'You've done very well . . .'

'I know,' she interrupted.

'When it's your turn, just enjoy yourself and try your best,' I said, sticking to the healthy manipulate-your-child-into-doing-her-best-without-putting-pressure-on-her-to-achieve parenting script that every middle-class parent believes to be far more effective (and far less work) at generating achievement than traditional-style, overt pushing.

What I really wanted to say was: *It doesn't matter if you get it wrong, but it would be brilliant if you did get it right and are you sure you don't want to run through the lines just one more time to be a hundred per cent*

*sure that you know it really well and please concentrate and whatever
happens don't run out of there in floods of tears because I'm starting to
think you might be in with a chance and if you do that you'll blow it just
when it's starting to get interesting and I'd really like you to get a part so
please don't blow it. Oh yes, and also I don't want you to be upset.
Obviously.*

My inner stage mother mostly agreed with me, but didn't think I
should have bothered to include the bit about not wanting her to be
upset.

A surge of children and parents left the building, which seemed,
suddenly, to have inhaled most of the people who had been waiting
outside. Dora and I went back in and Jo directed us past the
reception desk and into a waiting area, where a handful of mums and
comparatively quiet kids were fidgeting gently. Dora was instantly
drawn to a slightly older girl, blonde, slender and lively, who was
playing games on her mum's iBook.

Bethany was eight and had been pulled out of the queue at the
Palladium by Jo Hawes to try for the role of young Cosette in *Les
Misérables*. She'd won the part, and was enjoying her first West End
job. Her mother, Rachel, a slim, sensible redhead, now comfortably
ensconced in a second career running a very techie website business
and writing articles and books explaining how to use complex
software applications, used to be a dancer, and had been reluctant to
let her daughter follow in her pointy-toed footsteps. But Bethany had
nagged and nagged and, eventually, Rachel had given in, going so far
as to enrol her in stage school.

We nattered while the girls played. I was delighted to meet a fellow
laptop-toting freelancer, an open, personable individual who, having
lived it herself, had a down-to-earth, sceptical attitude towards
showbiz. We swapped the bowdlerised highlights of our life stories,
and went into more depth once the girls had been called through to
their audition.

This one lasted much longer than the previous rounds: they were in for over an hour. And in Dora's absence, I learned a lot. I found out about how doctors test for narcolepsy (electrodes, bed, stopwatch: how quickly does the patient fall asleep?), about the best diet for people with arthritic conditions (lots of fruit and veg; no dairy). And about how much fun these auditions were, and how well the children's feelings were being taken into account, compared to others these mums had taken their kids to.

'Did you see that mother outside shouting at her son because he couldn't remember all his lines?' asked one of the mums. 'Awful. The lengths some people will go to.'

I confessed to missing this brazen display of pushiness and rewound my involvement in Dora's progress so far to check whether I'd committed a similar crime. Recalling that I might have been a little overcritical when she was learning 'Somewhere Over the Rainbow': 'you don't have to do it, but if you're going to, you do have to do it properly', I immediately suppressed the memory.

'Does that kind of thing happen much?' I asked, switching my features into what I hoped was an expression of innocent shock.

'If you think that's bad, you should try the festival scene,' chipped in an earth-mother type, a comforting presence who had told us that she hadn't originally wanted children, but had one, then didn't want to stop, and ended up with five. All of whom were into singing, dancing and acting in a big, schedule-boggling way, and busy progressing through ballet, tap, modern and music theatre exams. I didn't even know there were music theatre exams to do. 'My eldest has had to stop for a while,' Comforting Earth Mother explained. 'It's better not to do the higher grades with more grown-up songs until they're older. Some of the songs just aren't appropriate.'

Earth Mother wouldn't be the last person to tell me how pushy the mums could be at the drama and dance festivals. For the uninitiated, these are highly competitive weekend celebrations of the performing arts, featuring singing, dancing, acting and instrument-playing accompanied by devastated sobbing, violent tantrums and hysterical parental disagreements with judges who have inexplicably failed to recognise their child's genius. 'I gave up in the end,' one former festival judge told me. 'It got too much. I needed a bodyguard.'

I dimly remembered taking part in one such festival during my reluctant speech-and-drama-lesson years. We performed an extract from Brecht's *Mother Courage and her Children*. I was badly miscast in the wrong half of the title role, by a new young teacher who mistook my lack of aptitude for and interest in acting for intelligent and spirited rebellion. It might have worked okay if I could have been *and her Children*, but at twelve, being neither remotely maternal nor very brave, I was a poor choice for *Mother Courage*. We came bottom of our section. I wasn't the least bit upset by what the judge wrote about my contribution to the performance. I agreed with him.

As if to counterbalance all the waiting-room chat about how appallingly pushy so many (other) mothers could be, I was also initiated into the world of www.notapushymum.com. 'I'm Catwoman,' said one of the other mums. 'That's nice,' I said.

'There's loads of information and gossip on the site,' said Catwoman. 'Especially gossip. It's addictive. Very.'

I was twitching to get home and check it out. It sounded exactly like my sort of website, one where I could waste hours and hours finding out about things that I didn't really need to know about in minute detail, whilst fooling myself that I was engaged in serious and productive research. It was, as Catwoman said, highly addictive. Over the successive months, I lost hours – probably days in total – immersed in the discussions and jokes. I followed individual stories with interest and occasional prurience, enjoyed the community feeling – supportive rather than competitive – and, just occasionally, contributed myself, under the moniker 'inconspicuous'. On notapushymum.com, people post details of upcoming auditions, and parents who've taken their children – and sometimes the older kids themselves – share information about castings they've attended. It is, as Rachel had told me, great when you've been for an audition and heard nothing, because you can find out if everyone else is in the same boat, or if people have already been told about recalls. Or if only the 'nos' have heard.

Meanwhile, back at the Baptist church, the kids emerged from their audition. 'We learned a dance,' Dora told me. 'A man called Frank taught us. It went like this.' She started to demonstrate, then stopped. 'No,' she said, 'not like that' and started again, got confused, waved her arms around a bit and '. . . well anyway. I can't remember it.'

'And did you do the lines?'

'Yes.'

'Did you have to do one of the boys' parts?'

'No.'

'Which parts did you do?'

'Only Gretl. It's not fair. I hardly got to say anything, just to do this.' She stamped her foot. 'And I wanted to be a boy. Did you get me anything to eat? I need to practise the dance at home. Can I go and play at Beth's house?'

'No. Not today. She lives too far away.'

'Can she come to mine? Oh please. Please please *please*?'

'Not today, sweetie.'

'But *why*?'

'Because you have another audition tomorrow, and you need an early night.'

'No I don't. I'm not tired. Can I go to her house tomorrow?'

'Say bye, now, you'll see her at the audition tomorrow.'

I used one hand to wave goodbye to the other mums, the other to guide Dora, still demanding a play-date with Bethany – which she would continue to do for the entire journey home, with the odd break for a quick and tuneful yodel – firmly out of the room and back to the car.

The following day's audition was back at Really Useful's offices, after lunch. Rachel was there with Bethany, as were one or two others I recognised and several I didn't: they'd mixed the groups up from the previous day and also some of the other mums had been nattering outside. The office was much less crowded than last time we were there, and there were enough cups and glasses to go round. While we mums sat up at the table, drinking the complimentary drinks and talking, the kids bounced round the room, chatting, laughing and practising the dance, getting it wrong and saying 'no, not like that, like *this*', and laughing more.

'Look,' one of the mums pointed out. 'Even though they're all competing with each other, and they know they are, they're still helping each other out.' And they were. There was no sizing up of the competition, no putting anyone else down, or withholding of information that might help another child, just open friendliness. And if I've managed to make that sound a bit vomit-inducingly Pollyannaish, it wasn't. It was heartwarming.

And perhaps the parents were taking their cue from the children, because if any among us were wondering whether there was any way we could sabotage someone else's chances, in order to give our own offspring a better chance, we'd concealed it extremely well. All was sweetness, light, empathy and laughter. I began to wonder if maybe Dora and I had stumbled into a parallel universe that neither of us might ever want to return from. Perhaps that's the start of the slippery slope to stage motherhood. At first, you try just one audition. Just one – it won't do any harm. Then your child gets a recall and another until, eventually, he or she lands a part. It's all so much fun, you want to do it again. And again and again. Pretty soon, you're hooked. And that's when it starts going bad – or, more accurately, when *you* start going bad. You need your next fix. So you do everything, no matter how mean, nasty and underhand, you can to make sure you get it. Before you know it, you're dressing your acutely embarrassed son in lederhosen and yelling at him to smile whilst simultaneously demonstrating a faux-Germanic leg-and-bottom-slapping dance and keeping his place only 123rd in the audition queue (you made him stand there alone while you counted. Twice. From his spot to the front and then back again, to make sure that no one had pushed in in your absence). Or you threaten your little darling that unless she sneaks to the front and pretends she's someone else's daughter – someone so keen that they got out of bed obscenely early so *their* little darlings could legitimately be amongst the first seen – you'll NEVER TAKE HER TO ANOTHER AUDITION AGAIN. *UNDERSTAND???!!!???* Or, on a freezing cold winter's day, you make your pubescent daughter bind her chest, remove her shoes and socks and stand in the gutter, hoping that the nice man with the measuring stick won't notice that she's too tall and too physically developed to audition for the role you've set your heart on her playing, and when he does notice, you scream, 'SHE HAS TO BE SEEN. SHE'S PERFECT FOR THE PART! I SHOULD KNOW, I'M HER MOTHER!'

The children were called in. A few of the parents popped out for coffee, the rest of us sat round the table or sprawled on the sofas. We talked about our children: which, if any, shows they'd been in before – this ranged from none to every major West End musical with kids in it as well as the odd high profile film – and which *Sound of Music* roles we thought they might be being considered for. The occasional sounds of angelic singing wafted through into the waiting area and temporarily silenced us.

During these interludes, I wondered how the people responsible for selecting eighteen or twenty children – people who were, if Dora's information was correct, mostly called Jo – from the sixty or so they'd whittled it down to could possibly do it. How could they decide which talented moppets were the right talented moppets? In the early stages it must've been comparatively easy – if they couldn't sing and didn't look feasibly Austrian, they were out – but surely all those who'd got this far must be capable of doing the things they had to do to play the parts.

Although, to be fair, they hadn't yet been tested on their ability to stay awake and continue functioning in front of a few thousand paying theatre-goers way past bedtime. I had concerns about this, but decided not to mention them to anyone connected with the production.

The children were returned to us on reasonably good and only slightly hyperactive form, and we were told they'd let us know soon about the next round. Predictably, the first sentence out of Dora's mouth was 'Can I go to Bethany's house?'

Predictably, the first word out of mine was 'No.'

But we did go for coffee and cake together at a local café.

'Did you get to be a boy today?'

'Nah. Just Gretl again.'

'I had to be Brigitta today,' said Bethany, who'd been Marta the day before.

Having failed in her attempt to secure an invitation to play at Beth's house, Dora upped the ante and asked Rachel if she could move in with them. Rachel took the request in her stride. She didn't look remotely panicked or even slightly fazed. 'Not today,' she replied. 'Dora,' she wrote, in an email to me the next day, 'reminds me of how Bethany was at the same age. Beth has started to get more "grown up" and serious these days, but every now and again it all breaks loose like she can't help herself.'

It was the first time anyone had ever said to me that Dora reminded them of their child. It's not that my daughter is an uncontrollable wild thing. She's just exuberant, strong-minded, vocal, extrovert and determined. In most circumstances, this is a good thing.

Jo Hawes called that evening to say they wanted to see Dora again. The audition was the following Tuesday, would take about two hours and would again be at the Really Useful offices. She needed to remember the dance Frank had taught them, her lines and the music.

They were, Jo said, hoping to cast that day.

'Sorry,' I told Mrs Kendall on Monday morning. 'She has to take tomorrow afternoon off. She's been recalled again.'

'She's going to get a part, isn't she?'

'Um . . . well, er, I suppose . . .'

'She is.'

'Well, yes. She might well. We'll probably know after tomorrow.'

'How exciting!'

The audition was at 2 p.m. on Tuesday, 11 July. We arrived at Really Useful's offices with the customary apple, bottle of water and time to spare. Rachel had emailed to say that that Bethany hadn't been recalled, which Dora and I were both a tad sad about, although, naturally, not quite as sad as Bethany had been. But, Rachel said, her disappointment had been short-lived: she'd been upset when first told, but by the next morning she'd bounced back and started to feel excited about the tap exam she was due to take the following week. 'It's always much more traumatic for the parents,' Rachel told me. 'The kids are straight on to the next thing, and we're left reeling.' You'd need, I thought, to be pretty tough to survive doing this on a regular basis. The more auditions, the more knockbacks. This could, I supposed, be character-forming: good preparation for the difficult realities of adult life. Or it could be confidence-destroying – and anyway, how early *should* kids start preparing for adult life? Should you protect them – as far as is parentally possible – from exposure to life's cruelties, or should you allow them to experience, or at least know about, what can happen out there so they're forewarned and forearmed?

'I want to be prepared for adult life,' said Dora, when I read her that last paragraph, a year and a half later. 'Definitely. Can I start walking to school by myself? Now? When I'm in Year Four?'

You would, I thought, as I recharged my Oyster card, also need plenty of time and cash. I hadn't expected expenses to be reimbursed for early rounds of auditions – but then neither had I anticipated recharging my Oyster card quite so often. To be fair, I hadn't given that side of it much consideration as I hadn't thought beyond the first audition.

We were amongst the first to arrive, and found a seat at the boardroom dining table from which I would be able to get a good look at everyone else coming in. As others arrived, I counted round and noticed that there were only six or seven potential Gretls. I figured Dora stood a fair chance, as they were looking for four or five of them. On the other hand, they were all slight, big-eyed, gazelle-like creatures, who looked delicate as glass next to my meteorite of a daughter.

Adrianna – who we'd met at the first audition – was there with her parents, Darren and Shana. Dora attached herself to a slightly taller and, it turned out, quite a lot older girl called Yasmin and her mum, Wendy, an attractively trendy, laconically funny and down-to-earth woman, who worked at her daughter's school as a teaching assistant. Dora left me, climbed on to Wendy's lap and wrapped her arms around her neck. Nuzzling into her cheek, she skipped the whole 'can I come to Yasmin's house to play?' stage and cut straight to the chase, asking hopefully if she could move in with them.

There were also a set of twins, a minuscule but feisty and disturbingly strong five-year-old, who bounced around picking up children three times her size, a pair of Viking-blonde sisters – one Gretl-sized (competition!), one much bigger – whose mum, Jackie, I had a quick chat with, lots of older girls and nine or ten older boys, some of whom came in, slightly late, in a giggling horde of shiny, smart, well-behaved children, all dressed in the uniform of the Sylvia Young Theatre School. These were the last twenty-six children culled from the original thousand auditionees who'd queued outside the Palladium three months earlier. I apologised to Wendy for Dora's forwardness. She laughed. In my (now extensive) experience, people don't seem to mind too much when someone else's child asks to come and live with them: I suppose it counts as a compliment.

Although, of course, I don't know what they say behind my back after we've left, about how terrible Dora's home life must be for her to want to move in with complete strangers. Anyway, I expect it would only get really scary if she turned up on their doorstep at dusk, unannounced and unaccompanied, pulling her small purple wheelie suitcase with a smiling picture of Cinderella on it with one hand, and clutching her formerly white cuddly unicorn by the leg in the other.

I looked around the room. *She's in with a good chance*, I found myself thinking. *Oh no she isn't*, I argued back at myself. *They'll take the skinny little ones. The Gretls will need to be picked up and carried.* Dora is not, and has never been, fat, but she looks well constructed and feels even more solid than she looks. Once she hit five I could only carry her for very short distances, and only if she was riding piggy back. *But, on the other hand, I'm not very strong. And they probably aren't testing the kids for portability . . .*

I waved and shouted 'good luck!' as she joined the line of children being shepherded off, then started forcing myself to focus on how well she'd done to get this far, and tried to look forward to my first ever visit to New York.

The atmosphere in the waiting area was noticeably more tense than it had been the previous week, or, in fact, during any of the earlier auditions. A couple of anxious fathers were pacing up and down, looking as if they were expecting their partners to give birth any minute. A quick glance around the room revealed that most of us mums seemed to have got our faces stuck. We formed a panorama of frozen little smiles hanging under unblinking terrified eyes: like a herd of meerkat trying to think up a polite way of introducing ourselves to an oncoming juggernaut. Our few attempts at conversation dwindled rapidly into silence, and only one or two brave or, possibly, seen-it-all-before types managed to concentrate on the newspapers they'd brought with them.

A lot more noise emanated from the audition room this time, and none of it was angelic singing. One of the other mums told us that there was a window from the corridor outside the loo, through which, if you stood on tiptoe (small kids = short parents), you could see what was going on. It wasn't exactly appropriate audition etiquette, but it was irresistibly tempting. I took a trip to the toilet. On my way out again – just as I was wondering whether I could summon the chutzpah to peer through the window (which, it turned out, had been papered over) – the door (also papered over) to the audition room swung open, and a young woman with a long, straight, white-blonde ponytail and a gentle smile ushered three small chattering girls out towards me. Through the doorway, I caught a glimpse of groups of kids sprawled on the floor, reading magazines, playing card games and talking while they waited.

The door swung shut and, one by one, the girls went to the toilet. 'How's it going?' I asked the young blonde woman who, I now knew, was 'chaperoning'. 'Oh, fine,' she said, giving absolutely nothing away. Damn. Should have asked a better question.

I went back to my seat at the table in the waiting area. The same mum who'd told us about the potential viewing window said that she thought Andrew Lloyd Webber *himself* was in there with the kids. 'Really?' I asked. 'Did you see him?'

'I think so,' she said

I fleetingly contemplated another trip to the loo so I could try to see if she was right, but decided against it, partly because I had an unaccustomed attack of inhibition, but mostly because I wasn't that interested in catching a split-second view of Andrew Lloyd Webber *himself*. Discounting those teenage years during which – demonstrating either admirably catholic taste, or the disturbingly random impact of raging hormones – I was simultaneously besotted with David Bowie, Bob Geldof and David Coverdale (for the uninitiated, the very macho and hairy lead singer of Whitesnake and, before that, Deep Purple), I have never been either particularly starstruck, or any good at recognising celebrities. A few years ago, in the space of two weeks, I failed to recognise Bianca Jagger, Eddie Izzard and Jonathan

Dimbleby at close quarters. Mr Dimbleby answered very politely when I asked him, over the plate of crisps I was offering, who he was and what he did for a living.

It was a long two hours. There was no singing, and no knowing what was going on in there.

Eventually the kids were let out. One older boy told his mother that he was pretty sure he hadn't got a part as they'd shuffled the kids into families and he and a few others had been left sitting to the side.

Dora came out smiley, but not as bouncy as on previous occasions.

'It was a bit boring,' she said. 'We had to sit down doing nothing for lots of the time. And one of the girls was very rude.'

'Rude?' I asked, as we headed out the door.

'Yes,'

'What did she do that was rude?'

'She said she has an oval face. But she hasn't. Her face is round, so I said "Your face is round", but she said "No it isn't, it's oval. My mum said." '

'So she said her face was oval when you think it's round?'

'Yes. But she was wrong. And she was very rude.'

My attempt to explain the nature and purpose of tact – and of the difference between opinion and fact – simply did not compute. At that age, Dora hadn't yet grasped the idea of either difference of opinion or white lies. There was simply the truth, which was good, and lies, which were bad. And very rude. 'I'm hungry,' she said, changing the subject.

'Were you with her for a lot of the audition?' I asked over fried egg, beans and chips – her treat of an early tea at the closest thing we could find to a greasy spoon in Covent Garden.

'Yes,' said Dora, baked bean sauce dripping from her chin.

'What did you have to do this time? I didn't hear any singing.'

'I had to be Marta,' she told me.

'Not Gretl?' I asked.

'For some of the time at the beginning. I've had enough. Can I have an ice cream?'

'Just eat a bit more of the egg white. And then you had to be Marta?'

'Can I stop after one more mouthful? I had to say "I'm going to be seven on Tuesday and I want a pink parasol."'

'That's nice,' I said, my heart sinking. 'So you got to say more lines. Did you get to be anyone else? Friedrich or Kurt?'

'No, but they said maybe I could be Liesl next time. Can I have an ice cream?'

'Yes,' I said, thinking, after Bethany's experience, that this must be the end of the road. 'Were you with the same group of children for most of the time, or did you change round?'

'Most of the time but changed a bit. Can I have a chocolate ice cream?'

'How many children were with you?'

'Dunno. Can I have my ice cream now?'

'In a minute. Was there anyone there called Andrew?' I asked.

'Andrew?' she mused. 'Hmmm. Yes.'

'What was he like?'

'Nice. Can I have my ice cream *now*?'

'Of course. You deserve a treat for getting to the final round. You've worked very hard learning singing and lines and dancing and done brilliantly well. Especially as it's your first time. You won't mind if you don't get a part, will you?' I asked, feeling that I might mind more than Dora.

'No. I've done very well to get the last audition.' My brainwashing had, evidently, proved successful. 'But I might get a part, mightn't I? I'd like to be in it.'

'Yes, you might. But if you don't, we'll go to New York and see Auntie Louise and Talya and have a fantastic time! Do you want to ring Daddy and tell him what it was like while you're waiting for your ice cream?' When, the previous September, Laurie and I had told

Dora that we'd decided to get married, she had announced that, straight after the wedding, she'd start calling Laurie 'Daddy'. And she did.

I dialled his mobile and they chatted. Whilst half listening to Dora's side of the conversation (just in case Laurie managed to extract more information from her than I had done), I mulled over how I'd take it if she fell at this, the final hurdle. Would I be able to conceal my disappointment from her? Would I actually be that disappointed? It would probably feel like we'd started off along the Yellow Brick Road, only to be dropped straight back into black and white Kansas before we'd had any proper adventures or even met a Munchkin. There would be compensations, though, even if these were just the comfort and familiarity of home and routine (well, as much routine as two freelancers and a child with an active social life can cobble together).

Dora scraped the last drip of melted chocolate ice cream – 'Don't squish it all up like that.' 'I *have* to. I'm making ice cream soup' – out of the little stainless steel bowl, and wiped her mouth with the back of her hand, at which point I noticed exactly how long and dirty her fingernails were. Then we made our way, hand in hand, humming 'The Lonely Goatherd' back to Covent Garden station, and travelled home. We counted the stops and talked about all the things we would do if she didn't get a part, and all the things she wouldn't be able to do if she did. We arrived at our house, fought our way past the piles of shoes, bikes, scooters and things that we'd sorted out to take to charity shops several months ago but hadn't got round to taking, and flopped on to the sofa.

Laurie quizzed Dora further while I ran her a bath.

At about 7.30, I called her up so I could bathe her and, most importantly, cut her fingernails. I snuggled her into bed, read her a story and said good night. As I was on my way back downstairs, the phone rang and Laurie answered it.

I ran downstairs and hovered, while Jo Hawes told Laurie that

Dora was being offered a part. They wanted her to play Marta, the second youngest von Trapp child. She'd done it! My little girl, at the ridiculous age of six, with precisely no acting experience, no more dance training than a million other small, pink-obsessed poppets and one singing lesson under her belt had sung, acted and danced her way happily and unconcernedly through five rounds of auditions and landed a role in a West End musical. It was one of those rare moments when you suddenly zoom out and get a completely different perspective on your child and catch a glimpse of what other people see. Like when you read her school report to discover that she's been consistently thoughtful about volunteering to help tidy up after every lesson and wonder whether this could possibly the same child who, when asked very nicely to put her own plate and cutlery in the sink, or to tidy away one, *just one*, naked Barbie, consistently doesn't (Dora would like you to know that, now she is older, she does clear up her Barbies and dinner things).

We jumped up and down, hugged each other, woke Dora up to tell her and jumped up and down some more. Then we shrieked the news over-excitedly down the phone at our nearest and dearest. They all said 'I told you so!' Especially my father, who, sounding as if his excitement had almost reached house-struck-by-lightning pitch, reminded me of what his Austrian friend Elfi had joked a year and a half earlier when they'd gone to see the first major staging of the musical in Vienna at the Volksoper Theater (where the director, Renaud Doucet, replaced the phrase 'schnitzel with noodles' in 'My Favourite Things' with 'goulash mit nockerl' as no self-respecting Austrian would ever eat schnitzel with noodles): 'You must take Dora to see this when they do it in London. What am I saying? When they do this in London, Dora will be in it.'

★

It wasn't until the following morning that reality set in. 'What do you mean, no holidays for six months?' Laurie demanded. '*No* holidays?'

'Well, *Dora* can't go away . . .' I countered lamely, as he was well aware that, having recently left her in the care of my sister for a week while we went on honeymoon, we had a lot of return-favour babysitting to do before we could legitimately claim another Dora-free trip. Also, I wasn't sure I'd particularly want to go away while Dora was in the middle of rehearsing or performing this show. It would be a very demanding time and I couldn't possibly know in advance how she'd cope with all the pressure. After all, although I understood what a six-month commitment meant, I wasn't remotely sure that, at her age, she did or could. I could quite easily envisage a situation in which, two weeks into rehearsals or, having clocked up three or four performances, she'd turn round to me and say, 'That was fun. I've had enough. Can I stop now, have a packet of crisps and a chocolate ice cream and watch TV?' Not to mention the fact that – although I was now sufficiently inducted into the world of performing children to know that a chaperone wasn't a maiden aunt charged with accompanying two young people of good breeding and opposite sex on a walk round the garden of Northanger Abbey – I didn't yet know whether I'd have to be one while Dora was rehearsing and performing. *Should I take up knitting?* I wondered, imagining myself sitting on a hard wooden chair in the backstage dark, one of a long row of grinning, wide-eyed mothers, ears straining to catch our children's voices over the clicking of our knitting needles, while unevenly striped wonky woollen scarves grew down over our knees.

'I'm not sure if I want to do any more films,' says thirteen-year-old Raphaël Coleman, whose acting talent was noticed by a family friend who works as a casting director. Raphaël is the veteran of two movies: *Nanny McPhee*, in which he appeared at the tender age of nine, and, more recently, a low-budget remake of seventies horror flick *It's Alive*, which features a baby that morphs into a monster. The latter job involved spending two freezing winter months filming in Bulgaria, where his mother, novelist Liz Jensen, who was chaperoning him, caught pneumonia. He enjoys the work – 'It's a great job and you learn a lot' – and being on set. 'He loved playing around with all the special effects,' Liz told me. 'Because it was a horror movie there was lots of blood, and one of the special effects guys gave him an ear to take home.' But there are down sides. The hours can be horrendously long: whole days waiting around, after which filming can go on until one o'clock in the morning – although the chaperone can and should call a halt if it's too much for the child. And by law, the children also have to keep up with their schooling. 'Sometimes I find it too difficult,' Raph admits. 'But you've agreed to what you've signed up for. If you've signed up for it, you should want to do it.'

On the one hand, an important life lesson learned early. On the other, that's okay once you're a teenager, and have some experience under your belt. But when you're younger and you've never done it before, you may think you want to do it, but how do you know until you've tried?

Meanwhile, as it was still termtime, Dora was at school, practising joined-up writing, learning her two and three times tables and refining her skipping technique. In her spare time, she enjoyed her dance classes and play-dates with her friends and cousins, and started learning to swim and to ride her bike without stabilisers. Her school report was calmly complimentary. A couple of days before the holidays started, I met with the teacher she'd have the following year: Mrs Arin; very dedicated, very bright and switched-on, who leads the school choir, thinks singing is important and believes that learning should be fun. We discussed how Dora would keep up with her work whilst rehearsing and performing, and Mrs Arin handed me a thick wodge of maths worksheets for Dora to complete over the summer.

The confirmation letter from Jo Hawes arrived on the last day of term, welcoming us to *The Sound of Music* and enclosing the licence forms I needed to complete so that Dora could legally work on the show – all children working in the entertainment industry must be licensed by their local authority: there are strict legal controls on the amount of time they can spend on stage or set

The first UK regulations limiting the employment of performing children were introduced in the Prevention of Cruelty to, and Protection of, Children Act 1889. Chapter 44 – which, incidentally, defined a child as a boy under fourteen and a girl under sixteen – prohibited adults getting children to perform on the streets for money (this counted as begging), performing anywhere not licensed for public entertainments between 10 p.m. and 5 a.m. and prohibited all children under ten 'singing, playing, or performing for profit' anywhere. Contravention could be punished by 'a fine not exceeding twenty-five pounds, or alternatively, or in default of payment of the said fine, or in addition thereto, to imprisonment, with or without hard labour, for any term not exceeding three months'.

If, however, it was 'shown to the satisfaction of a petty sessional court, or in Scotland the school board, that proper provision has been made to secure the health and kind treatment of any children proposed to be employed thereat', local authorities could license any fit child over seven to perform professionally. These regulations were refined in the Children & Young Persons Act 1933 and then again in Children (Performance) Regulations 1968.

Also in the letter was a list of documents and details that we were required to provide, and five pages of information 'regarding your child's appearance in THE SOUND OF MUSIC'. Because Dora's name had been changed, as well as her birth certificate I'd need to provide a photocopy of her passport. While I was working out what was required, it occurred to me that this would be a bad time to change our last names again. Not only would there be all the faff with the documentation, but Laurie's surname is Temple. You can't change a little girl's surname to Temple when she's just about to go on the stage. That looks like hubris. Anyway, I like 'Gee'. It was my grandfather's stage name: he changed the family's (from Goldstein) to match it after another violinist also named Harold Gee got in

contact from Yorkshire and complained that Grandpa had stolen his
name.

'You might,' Jo wrote, 'need to sit down with a drink or a cup of
tea' to wade through the information.' I settled for a glass of orange
juice, worrying about how I was going to write a 'short biography' for
a child too young to have one, where I'd stashed her birth certificate
and whether our doctor would still write a letter saying Dora was fit
to perform even though she had an enormous verruca on her left foot.

The five-page information pack included details of which teams
the children would be in – with a couple of gaps as they were still one
Louisa and one Brigitta short – with the caveat that this was likely to
change. It confirmed that rehearsals were due to start on 25
September, and stressed very strongly that 'Children will be expected
to attend school whenever they are not in rehearsal and it is vital that
they do because failure to do so could result in the licence being
revoked . . . If they are not well enough to attend school they are not
well enough to do the show!' There would be no time off for any
reason except illness, and if our child was ill, we had to let Jo know
as early as possible in the day, so she could get someone else's to
cover. If you were the someone else whose child she was asking to
cover, you would be expected to jump to it: 'I appreciate that it may
be inconvenient but it is part of the job.' As she didn't have an agent,
Dora's 'salary' would be paid straight to her – time to open her first
bank account – but travel expenses would come to me. I wondered
idly if they'd cover the costs of a taxi home from the theatre, as the
prospect of getting Dora home by tube at 11 p.m. at night was not
one I wanted to entertain, any more than I wanted to pay congestion
and parking charges to drive her in.

I read on. Parents, I discovered, were required to provide a packed
lunch or tea for rehearsals that we would not be permitted to watch.
We also had to check regularly for head lice – a problem that Dora
had, hitherto, happily been free from, and phone Jo the moment a nit
reared its ugly egg. We would also be barred from backstage (no need

to take up knitting): the children would be chaperoned by 'professional, licensed chaperones'. We were also sternly warned against discussing our child's performance with them. 'Occasionally,' Jo explained, 'a child will deliver a completely different performance once their mother has watched – believe me, it happens!'

A few days later I heard – from another source – a story about a little girl who'd been in *Annie*. She played her part brilliantly throughout the rehearsal and preview periods. Then, on opening night, the poor little orphan arrived at the stage door dolled up like a pop star, and once the curtain was raised proceeded to do her best to upstage the rest of the cast. When asked why she'd deviated from the director's instructions, she said, 'My mummy told me to do it like that.' Apparently, it didn't do her 'career' any good.

Aside from all that, it was made very clear that the children had to behave themselves in a disciplined and grown-up way, keeping unnaturally – but necessarily – quiet while waiting to go on stage, and being extremely sensible at other times.

I wasn't too worried about sensibleness as far as Dora was concerned. Remarkably, given both genes and environment, she has always been pretty sensible. I've never, for instance, had to extract a Hama bead from her left nostril, a pencil from her ear or any of her fingers from an electric socket. Nor have I regularly needed to shout at her to *STOP* at the kerb, look, listen, think and *WAIT FOR ME!*

I was most worried about controlling my own curiosity. How would I cope with being excluded from rehearsals, barred from backstage? I need to know what's going on, who said what to whom, why and when they said it. And my experiences of trying to get Dora to tell me what had happened during the auditions had proved to me that no matter how much chocolate ice cream you wave under its nose, you can't bribe that kind of information out of a six-year-old. Not only was the information she provided in most cases as sparse as the hair on her grandfather's head, it was also, I found out later, inaccurate.

At the back of the pack – after *The Sound of Music* Anti-Bullying Policy, four to-the-point bullet points detailing how any unkindnesses would be dealt with swiftly – a team list was attached. There were three teams – red, blue and green. Dora's name was in the red team. The green team had two gaps, still needing a Louisa and a Brigitta.

I rang Jo Hawes that evening to ask a couple of questions about the licence forms and ended up having a long conversation about what to expect now my child would be working in the West End. During this conversation I discovered that one of the grown-ups called Jo involved in the auditions – the one with long curly hair – was, in fact, Ros Jones, the children's musical director, and that Andrew Lloyd Webber had never been there.

Jo also told me that children in musicals have a fantastic time, but the parents don't. We would have to drop our children off in good performing order and pick them up at unsocial times. There would be nowhere comfortable for us to wait – 'I've had breast-feeding mums who've had to spend all evening sitting in the car with their babies, because there's nowhere for them to go.' Our kids would get tired and fractious and, because they had to be on their best behaviour around the theatre, would save all their tantrums for us. There was, in short, nothing in it for us. It would, Jo said cheerfully, be 'hell' for the parents. That was encouraging. As was the way she laughed at me like I'd said something hilarious when I suggested that being in *The Sound of Music* might be a one-off experience for Dora. Apparently, once they've done one show, children never want to stop. 'Most of them end up at Sylvia Young's,' she explained briskly, as if it was an obvious case of predestination. 'If not at the school itself, then at least with the agency.' I thought back to the party of smiley uniformed children who'd arrived en masse at the final audition, chattering amongst themselves and looking, in my opinion, unnaturally keen and clean. In my head, I briefly superimposed Dora's face on top of one of their bodies. It fitted, but my stomach rebelled. I had a visceral aversion to the idea of any stage school: the appalling children I was convinced would fetch up there, not to mention the uneven education I was sure they'd receive, one which, focusing on performance skills – singing, dancing and acting – at the expense of the academic subjects they'd need for real, adult life, would deprive them of a productive Plan B should – as was likely – their ambitions for a career in showbiz come to nowt.

Then it was the summer holidays. Towards the end of July, the three of us spent a few days down in Bournemouth with Laurie's mum, Lilli, admiring the beautiful job she'd done of displaying our wedding photos and watching the first *How Do You Solve a Problem Like Maria?* – the BBC reality TV show through which Maria von Trapp was to be cast. This was, as far as we were concerned, *serious* reality TV. The outcome of the vote would affect our lives – well, Dora's life, anyway. What if the public chose a Maria who loathed children? Someone who could act well enough to come across all maternal on the telly and onstage, but morphed into the Wicked Witch of the West the moment the lights went down? Or who was just grandly self-obsessed, humourless and slightly scary? Or who was so keen to demonstrate how much she *adored* children that she was loveyishly all over them in a yucky cheeks-covered-in-lipstick-kisses kind of way?

We fell for Connie Fisher's vivacity, determination and perfect-for-the-part voice from the first time we saw her twirling, eyebrows raised, in her tacky orange pseudo-dirndl (which was in programme four – we missed two and three). But we were also, Laurie in particular, quite taken with Siobhan, the tall and stunningly beautiful Maria with the heart-stopping voice who eventually came third. There were also a lot of wider-family debates about the merits of Abi – known as Tomboy Maria. Should we support our own and vote for her because she was also Jewish? Personally, I was against voting along sectarian lines.

Dora loved watching. 'I want to vote for *her*,' she shrieked, every time any one of the girls sang a song, irrespective of whether they were even in tune. And I let her – at least once. That way, whoever ended up getting the gig, Dora could sidle up to her shyly at rehearsal and whisper innocently and truthfully, 'I voted for you,' which could only be a good thing.

On our return to London, after a long chat with a very helpful woman at the World of Camping, we bought an enormous two-bedroom tent – and by enormous, I mean the mansion of all tents, the sort of thing designed for an entire troop of Girl Guides to earn their camping, firelighting and first aid badges in – and sundry other bits of equipment. With some trepidation, we headed off towards Totnes for a ten-day alternative camping experience at the Sharpham Barton Family Camp.

On 9 August an email arrived from Jo Hawes asking a couple of the kids – Michael (Kurt) and Yasmin (Marta) – if they could pop in to the Really Useful offices on the following Monday as they were auditioning for the last Louisa and Brigitta and wanted to make sure that they got ones that were the right height. The email also contained some information about rehearsals. They would be happening at the Jerwood Space starting, as expected, on 25 September. 'All children will be called all day that day 10–6. After that the plan is that the children will be called in the afternoons and all day Saturday. Every child will have a complete day off every week apart from Sunday which will be a day off for everybody. Every child will be called every Saturday.' Jo promised 'more precise details soon', and also asked us all for our holiday dates, so they could work out if a couple of 'music calls' could be fitted in before rehearsals started.

I Googled the Jerwood Space. It looked very posh: all artworks, stripped wood and sparkling glass. Luckily for us, it was close to Southwark station, on the Jubilee line, which meant we could park near Dora's school, walk from there to Neasden station and get a direct train. It also, I noticed on the 'About Us' section of its website, had a café. Great. I could sit there with my computer and get on with my work.

On the 14th, another email from Jo. This one informed us that they were now fully cast. An updated team list was attached, with two new names: Georgia Russell (Louisa) and Grace Vance (Brigitta) added to the green team.

Meanwhile, in the two-month hiatus between the casting of the von Trapp children and the start of rehearsals, my curiosity about *The Sound of Music* morphed into a full-scale research project. I surfed the web for any information I could find about the film, the stage show and the original true story of the von Trapps. I ordered *The Trapp Family Singers* – Maria von Trapp's autobiography – from www.abebooks.co.uk. A very cheap and musty thirty-eight-year-old Fontana paperback arrived a few days later. It said 'The Sound of Music' in big pink, lime green, turquoise and orange gothic lettering above the author's name, which was much smaller and in a very plain black upper case type. Then – much larger – 'Julie Andrews', followed, in fluffy pink italics, by 'stars in the 20th Century Fox Film based on the touching romantic story of THE TRAPP FAMILY SINGERS'. The confection was completed by an extravagantly lime-green-bordered circular still from the film showing Julie as Maria, standing in front of a lake looking winsomely lovely and appropriately chaste in pale aqua chiffon and a straw hat.

I opened the book and browsed the foreword. Maria writes that her book is 'introduced as a canticle of love and gratitude to the Heavenly Father in His Divine Providence'. Blimey, I thought. This all sounds a bit pious. Then I engaged my brain. The real-life Maria was training to be a nun. Of course she'd be pious. What did I expect?

Certainly not what I went on to read, which was a story that was, if anything, more astonishing than the familiar movie version. Maria describes herself as the 'black sheep' of the abbey where she was a novice nun, always getting told off for whistling, sliding down banisters and indulging in an early Mitteleuropean form of parkour, jumping over chimney pots on the flat roof of the abbey's school wing. She had just finished training as a teacher when she was packed off to Captain von Trapp's place, not as governess to his entire brood, but as tutor to one of his children also named Maria, who was poorly following bouts of scarlet fever and influenza.

Von Trapp was shortly expected to announce his engagement to a Princess Yvonne: the pair had been discussing marriage for three years. Fantastic! thought Maria – just like in the movie – the children will have a new mother. But the princess shocked Maria by blithely telling her that the children would all be sent off to boarding school as she was marrying Georg, not them. Then she explained that Georg was falling in love with Maria because she was kind to his children – but these feelings were of no consequence. Maria, feeling thoroughly compromised, tried to leave, but Princess Yvonne got a priest to persuade her that it was God's will that she should stay at least until she was due to return to the abbey. The princess left, and in the following weeks Maria did her best both to distance herself from the captain and persuade him to get himself properly engaged as soon as possible. Then he left, putting a completely unqualified Maria in charge of his household, as his housekeeper had broken her leg while on a visit to her sister and was unable to return.

Every day Maria dutifully sent brief letters to the captain telling him that children, house and farm were fine. Eventually, as the time for her return to the convent approached, she added a PS asking when he would get engaged. He sent her a joking reply to which she fired off an angry response by registered return. Von Trapp was about to propose to the princess when the letter arrived. Reading it, he realised that he could not marry Princess Yvonne as he was in love with Maria, so he broke off their relationship and returned home to Salzburg, where he hid in his study, ostensibly writing his memoirs.

A few days before Maria was due to leave, she noticed, from the top of the ladder she was balancing on whilst spring-cleaning a huge crystal chandelier, the three youngest von Trapp children disappearing into their father's study. They burst out again shortly afterwards, and yelled at her, 'Father says he doesn't know whether you like him at all!' Maria – concentrating on the chandelier, because this was the first time she'd ever washed one – replied that of course she liked him. The kids dashed back to their father with the news.

Later that evening, Maria was arranging some flowers when the captain came over to her and said 'That was really very nice of you.' Maria, who couldn't work out what he was talking about, was astonished to discover that she had, inadvertently, accepted a proposal of marriage. She said she couldn't get married as she was going to be a nun and it wasn't possible to do both. Then, as Georg was upset, she suggested that she ask the mistress of novitiates what she should do and promptly escaped back to the convent.

Her stay there lasted only a few hours. The mistress of novices consulted the mother superior. The mother superior summoned the whole community for a meeting and a prayer, and they decided that it was the will of God that Maria should marry the captain. Maria doesn't indicate whether God might have wanted her to do that partly to relieve the convent of a nun who spent her time jumping over chimney pots, sliding down banisters and whistling inappropriately. All she tells us is that, once she realised that she had no alternative but to serve her Maker 'whole-heartedly and cheerfully' as commanded by the mother superior, she dawdled reluctantly and miserably back to the captain's house, where she found him waiting for her. At which point she burst into floods of tears and explained, 'Th-they s-s-said I have to m-m-m-marry you.'

The wedding took place on 26 November 1927. There followed healthy camping holidays, normal family life, two more children (both girls, so the boys were now outnumbered seven to two), loss of the family fortune and the start of their singing career before some eleven years later, a few months after the Anschluss, the family – including a pregnant Maria – had to flee Austria. It was becoming impossible to resist the Nazis, and once von Trapp had refused a commission in the Ostmark navy; Rupert, the eldest son – a newly qualified doctor – had said *nein danke* to the offer of a senior medical job at a Viennese hospital (there were lots of vacancies because the Jewish doctors had been sent to concentration camps); and the family had turned down an invitation to sing for Hitler at his birthday celebrations, it wasn't safe to stay.

Stateless, penniless and homeless, they fetched up in the US, where, relying on the kindness of strangers, they learned English, sang their way round the country, and Maria gave birth to her third child – a boy this time – who brought the total to ten. Then their visitors' visas ran out and they had to leave for Europe. On their return, seven months later, so delighted was Maria to be back in the US that instead of saying what she was supposed to say when the immigration officer asked her how long she intended to stay in the country – the correct answer was six months, as she and her family were again on visitors' visas – she 'blurted out, "Oh, I am so glad to be here – I never want to leave again!"'

As a result, the entire family – except for Rupert, who, as a doctor, had been granted an immigration visa – were shipped off to jail on Ellis Island.

Several years and much-water-under-the-bridge later, the family bought a rundown farm in Vermont and settled there. Today, the Trapp Family Lodge – now a ninety-three room, 2,700-acre resort, where holidaymakers can enjoy healthy outdoor activities and musical recreations, spend an afternoon with a pastry chef and even buy a luxurious villa – is still family-run.

Browsing the Trapp Family Lodge website, a thought sprang into my head. It was mid-August, and we had a couple of weeks to kill before Dora was due back at school. We couldn't afford to visit the

Lodge, but if the flights were cheap enough, and I could find somewhere inexpensive to stay, I could take Dora for a short trip to Salzburg, where the movie was filmed and where the von Trapps really lived before they fled and their home was requisitioned by Himmler. It could be a mother–daughter bonding weekend (Laurie didn't want to come) and we could do all those tacky *Sound of Music* sightseeing things that I'd turn my semi-cultured and generally intellectually snobbish nose up at under other circumstances. But this time, I could justify and enjoy doing them because they would count as research and not mere time-wasting. I could help Dora learn about some of the true story behind the musical she was soon to start rehearsing, thus ensuring that it would be an Educational Experience as well as lots of fun.

Our first official *Sound of Music* event took place on 24 August. It was a costume fitting. I took Dora to the Cambridge Theatre in Covent Garden, where a young woman called Katie shepherded us up several flights of stairs to a small office. In the office was a smiley and efficient-looking woman called Lynette, who had a tape measure draped round her neck, curly greying hair and the kind of direct gaze that has you sized up the moment it settles on you and made me wonder whether she would actually need to use the tape measure. She whipped it off and applied it to every inch of Dora while asking me about shoe sizes. 'She has very wide feet,' I told her, having just, in an unaccustomed feat of pre-planning, taken Dora out to buy her school shoes for the following term – size 12½ H.

'How many different costumes will they have?' I asked.

'Six,' Lynette replied.

'That'll keep you busy,' I said, trying to imagine exactly how much work would be involved in sorting out at least fifty-four outfits and then adjusting them as the children changed shape and size over the next few months.

'And we have to do the adults too.'

Dora's contract arrived the day before we were due to head off to Salzburg. It was all very straightforward: she would be paid £17.50 per rehearsal – up to a maximum of £100 per week – and £35 per performance. I was shocked. Thirty years previously, my sister Nikki had earned £40 a day being a fish finger. I knew – from friends in the business – that theatre pay was ludicrously low, but I had imagined that with a show this high-profile, the kids would be paid at least £50. As Dora didn't have an agent, I thought I'd better ring Jo to check whether the amount was at all negotiable. 'No,' she informed me firmly. 'It would be a nightmare situation with this many children to have some earning more than others.' Still, although it seemed like peanuts to me, to a child too young to be getting regular pocket money, it felt like all her birthdays had come at once.

'How much money will I get?' Dora asked me. 'Will it be enough to buy a bike with gears?'

I assured her that it would.

'And Heelys?'

'Hmm. Maybe.'

More disappointing was the news on travel expenses. Those of us living in London would receive ten quid a week. I did my sums. This could, I worked out, almost cover the costs while Dora was performing, so long as I hung around while she was on stage and dragged her back on the tube late at night, which was clearly not practical given that she was six, there was a long, poorly lit walk at the other end and it would be winter. And then there was getting her to the rehearsals five days a week for six weeks. Ten pounds would only cover a third of our actual costs during that period. And – living nearer the centre of London than most of the other kids – we were comparatively well off. Unnecessarily stingy, I thought, given the amount of money the company stood to make on this production. Thank goodness Ken Livingstone had introduced free travel for under elevens and both Dora's dance teachers (she was doing Grade 1 ballet and fun, express-yourself-with-friends general dance) had agreed that I only had to pay for the classes she could attend while she was doing the show.

It was also made abundantly clear that the company reserved 'the right to terminate the contract' with two weeks' notice if the children behaved badly or unprofessionally or grew too much, if their voices broke or for any other reason. 'It means,' another parent later explained to me drily, 'that they can do what they like and we have no rights at all.' The producers had us firmly not by the short and curlies, but by the place we keep our love for our children and our desire to see them happy. After they'd worked so hard for so long, done so well and were so excited, who among us was going to pull our kids from the show just because we'd end up a few hundred quid out of pocket? Especially as the money would be siphoned slowly and almost unnoticeably out of our bank accounts over a six-month period. And we were, I found out, being better treated than parents with kids in other shows: many companies don't give parents any contribution whatsoever towards travel expenses. After all, they reason, they don't cover the adult performers' costs. Adult performers, however, aren't required by law to be dropped off and picked up by a total idiot who not only isn't being paid at all for ensuring that actors essential to the show's success arrive at the stage door on time, well fed and in a fit state to play their part, but is actually forking out for the privilege.

Still, I'd save some money on Dora's after-school activities and I'd hold off signing her up for more swimming tuition and piano lessons. Anyway, there was no point in letting this rampant exploitation of my parental goodwill and excitement ruin that excitement. Especially when Dora and I were about to head off to Salzburg for a three-day multi-sensory *Sound of Music* experience.

Our flight was due to leave from Stansted at 18.30 on Wednesday 31 August. Laurie dropped us at the airport, now wishing that he was coming with us. Several days earlier, I'd visited TK Maxx with a tape measure and invested £11 in an oblong grey rucksack that just fitted the new, terrorist-induced hand baggage size restrictions and bought Dora a Scooby-Doo backpack as her purple pull-along case was slightly too big.

Although our flight was delayed, and the overpriced cheese toasties the airline served tasted like they'd been made from cereal packets and flour-and-water glue by enthusiastic five-year-olds, the journey was uneventful. We arrived at our hotel – the Kolpinghaus Salzburg – just before midnight.

We woke early the next morning. It was grey and drizzly, but we stuck to our plan and caught a bus to visit the surprise fountains and then the zoo at Hellbrunn, which was enormous, if damp, fun. I was particularly taken with the hydro-powered automata – small moving tableaux of workshops with mechanical potters potting, forests with woodcutters chopping wood, and one enormous, bustling cityscape – as well as the golden crown that danced on a jet of water and the deer's head with spouting nose and antlers. Dora's favourite bit was feeding the alpaca and getting gently butted by a very small but very determined goat in the petting zoo. I think she spotted a kindred spirit.

The sky brightened and we returned to the hotel tired, happy, but also hungry. We ate a hearty dinner and retired to bed. Dora decided she couldn't possibly sleep on the other side of the room as it was too far away from me and she was lonely. She climbed into my single bed and snuggled me so ferociously that I was crushed cartoon-flat against the wall.

Next morning, I experienced a sudden-onset stomach bug, which ruined my breakfast but, thanks to some rapid evasive action on my part, no one else's. We were due for the highlight of our trip that morning – The Original *Sound of Music* Tour – but once I'd made it to our bedroom, it was clear that the only trip I would be taking was a rapid stagger between bed and en suite followed by a slow crawl back again. Fortunately, the Kolpinghaus staff helped. They whisked Dora on to the final day of their summer childcare programme, draped her in a gigantic bright orange t-shirt and introduced her to the joys of graffiti art – toxic fumes and all. At lunchtime, by which point I could stand, I tiptoed fragilely downstairs to discover her, with the assistance of two much bigger boys, putting the final touches to a large sheet of jagged-edged metal, spray-painted the same bright orange as Dora's t-shirt, with my name zigzagged across it and surrounded by rather wobbly hearts.

'We're allowed to take it home,' she told me, proudly and only slightly addled from the fumes. I thanked the boys for helping her and said that, regretfully, we couldn't, as it wouldn't fit on the aeroplane.

Meanwhile, the hotel staff had also rebooked our *Sound of Music* tour for that afternoon. Fortunately for my stomach, the front seats of the coach were free. 'Ah, and you must be Gretl,' boomed the large and very blond tour guide, as Dora climbed the coach steps. 'No, Marta, actually,' I intervened, before the stage mother in me took over and explained, entirely unnecessarily, when and where and in which production she was due to be Marta. Essentially, I kvelled. Kvelling, for the uninitiated, is an important part of being Jewish – especially if you happen, like me, to be a Jewish mother. To kvell (Yiddish) is to burst (or beam) with pride and pleasure, usually over your children's (or grandchildren's) achievements. 'My son, the doctor.' That sort of thing. *The Sound of Music* provided me – and the whole of Dora's extended family – with a fantastic kvelling opportunity. By the end of her run, it had gone so far that when Laurie's uncle and aunt went to play bridge with a couple of my father's friends they were all at it.

The Original *Sound of Music* Tour *was* slightly blink-and-you've-missed-it, omigod-is-there-time-to-get-to-the-loo-and-buy-Dora-an-ice-cream-before-the-coach-sets-off? but was lots of fun. We drove past the Mirabell Gardens where the cast were filmed skipping along and singing 'Do-Re-Mi', then hopped off the coach to peek at the back of Leopoldskron Castle, where Julie Andrews and company fell out of their boat and Kym Karath, who played Gretl, nearly drowned. We hopped back on again and were whisked off to Schloss Hellbrunn, where we were shown the summerhouse in which Liesl and Rolf sang and danced 'Sixteen, Going on Seventeen', and which has been closed to visitors ever since an elderly woman tried to recreate the young things' leaps from bench to bench, fell off and broke her leg. Which was one better than Charmian Carr – Liesl in the movie – who, when she fell off, only sprained her ankle and broke a pane of glass (you can, if you watch closely, just spot the make-up-covered bandage on her dancing leg).

Next, we drove past Nonnberg Abbey – the oldest female convent in German-speaking Europe, dating back to 714 – where the real Maria was a candidate for the novitiate and the Julie Andrews version was a novice. Had Maria really run there from the Untersberg, as Julie Andrews appears to do at the beginning of the movie (having been repeatedly knocked over by the downdraught from the helicopter filming the opening shot), it would have taken her much longer than the minute or so the film allows, as she would have sprinted approximately fifteen kilometres. Still, I suppose it was Julie Andrews doing it, so anything's possible . . . Next, a mountain drive up to St Gilgen on Lake Wolfgang for the chance to use a pay toilet and buy a yodelling, lederhosen-clad rag doll (we demurred), whilst looking at some pretty yachts, and then on to Mondsee cathedral, where the wedding scene was filmed.

It was all good, healthy fun: I didn't feel too sick and Dora didn't get too bored. Our tour guide, Peter, joked his way round the sights in a way a few American purists have allegedly, on previous tours, found slightly offensive. In between his jokes – Dora still enjoys mistelling one, which features a family of tourists running out of petrol, an old castle, Dracula and the punchline 'the Hills are alive with the sound of music' – we were all encouraged to sing along to the movie soundtrack. There were lots of British people on board that day, so the singing was muted. We were also introduced to the fizzy delights of the Austrian national soft drink – Almdudler, a kind of not-quite-ginger-beer, the first few glugs of which are fruit-and-herbily thirst-quenching. Overdo it, though, and it feels like the inside of your mouth has been shrink-wrapped.

We finished up back in Salzburg, where the tour guide presented each of us with a tiny and tasteful edelweiss lapel pin. Back to the hotel to change, then into Salzburg again for our evening treat – The Sound of Salzburg. Bound to be toe-curlingly tacky, I thought as I rushed us into town on a bus. After all, the tour had been fun and superbly lowest-common-denominator, so I anticipated more of the same. We got off too soon and spent a hurried half an hour asking the way and dashing off in the wrong direction. Eventually, I found someone who both understood English – my German being restricted to *bitte schön, danke schön, grüss Gott*, several *schokolade-*related items and now Almdudler – and knew where the Sternbräu Dinner Theatre was. I dragged a dressed-up and grumbling Dora through the Mirabell Gardens, promising her that we'd return the next day to see the dwarf statues that Peter the tour guide had told us about, across the bridge over the river and into the old town.

We found the venue and entered. It was an old-fashioned oak-panelled space. A man behind a high reception desk took our money and told us we were too late to book a dinner. This was something of a relief, as I was still feeling slightly fragile, and the prospect of schnitzel (well, chicken escalope, actually) with noodles (even though no self-respecting Austrian would eat it, it's served up for tourists by popular demand) followed by crisp apple strudel with whipped cream was more than I could stomach. A big bowl of chips or two, though, was another matter. 'Back to healthy food as soon as we get home,' I told Dora, trying not to feel guilty about all the junk I'd been feeding her while we were in Salzburg.

Despite my expectations to the contrary, the show was terrific – even better than the chips. The evening started with the showing of a film interview, in English, with the real Maria von Trapp. Then a troupe of performers who could really sing performed a selection of songs from *The Sound of Music* and a few of the folk numbers that the original Trapp Family Singers sang in the concerts they gave, then treated us to a variety of light opera extracts. There was audience participation in which Dora refused to participate, although I allowed myself to be coaxed up on to the stage along with several others, to join the cast in a simple folk dance, which I persisted in getting wrong.

The following morning we ate as much as we could for breakfast, checked out of our room, dragged the suitcase to the hotel office for safe-keeping, donned our backpacks and set off to catch the bus into town. It was a gloriously sunny day, perfect for exploring. We bounced round the Mirabell Gardens, hunting for the dwarf statues and then taking photos of each other with them. We crossed the bridge over the river into the old city. Dora wasn't interested in visiting Mozart's house, so I bought her a present – a very pretty and very cheap china doll dressed in a green checked dirndl, who was loved intensely for the next few days and then tidied into a box, where she's languished ever since, her broken right leg in severe need of glue – and we wandered for a while, in the general direction of the fortress that has loomed over the city for the best part of the past thousand years. En route we listened to a girl playing the harp, laughed at a man dressed as a skeleton with a giant skull, hands and feet, and watched a whole troupe of Chinese dancers rehearsing for a show.

Then we hopped on the funicular railway and explored the fortress, taking in the spectacular views, the torture room and the marionette museum, until Dora got bored and needed lunch. So it was back down the funicular and into a little café, where we ate more chips and drank a final glass of Almdudler. A bit more wandering, and that was it. Time to go home. Laurie met us at Stansted and drove us home while Dora fell asleep.

WHEN THE DOG BITES

Early September, and school was about to start. I bought Dora some supermarket school uniform shirts and skirts to go with her new shoes. Routine set in. It was more than six weeks since we'd heard she'd been cast, and there was still almost a month to go before rehearsals were due to start. It was impossible to sustain our excitement. I'd read everything I could in books and on the internet about *The Sound of Music* and digested the financial implications of my daughter's involvement. So it was time to start worrying about the other potential down sides of propelling a six-year-old on to a West End stage.

Child performers are not famous for going on to live happy, fulfilled adult lives. Addiction, anorexia, misery, tragically early deaths and terrible plastic surgery are their lot. Was that what I was condemning my daughter to by allowing her to go on the stage so young?

Because it hadn't occurred to me when I took her to the first audition that she might actually end up getting a part, I'd only prepared her to handle the disappointment of not being cast, not how to cope if she was picked. In technicolour contrast to the stereo-typical stage mother approach, I was geared up for, and anticipated, failure, not success. I'd considered the consequences of her being eliminated at each round, and decided that she was sufficiently robust and well-cushioned to handle the rejection. There were, I felt, no major risks: we could just say 'oh well' and get on with our lives the same as before. It would, I knew, be no big deal supporting her through that: a hug, a 'you did very well, darling, to get this far on your first go' and a quick diversion into some other fun activity, and that, I was confident, would be that.

Because I was completely unprepared for it, I hadn't thought about how to help her handle success. Or whether I'd been nuts to start the whole process in the first place. Would it be possible for her to do this and come out okay? Might Jo Hawes be wrong: could this be a happy one-off experience? Could it even be good for Dora? And if it wasn't going to be a one-off experience, was showbiz something she could be involved in without it taking over her life and the lives of those of us she lived with? Why do some well-known child performers turn out all right, when others – the ones we hear most about – crash and burn? Why do we expect child performers to end up terribly scarred? Why do we expect their mothers to be horrid? Was I horrid? Was I being a terrible mother to let her get into this sordid, destructive, vicious business? And if Dora did go horribly wrong after spending six months pretending to be Austrian twice a week in front of 2,300 theatre-goers, would it all be my fault?

Like many other ordinary mothers, I've sat aghast in front of television documentaries wondering why on earth any parent would tart up their four- or five-year-old daughter and train her up to pose and pout like an apprentice prostitute on the US pageant circuit. Like many others I was shocked and distressed – though not overly surprised – when one of them, JonBenet Ramsey, was murdered, and her parents treated as prime suspects, while local cops missed signs of a break-in. It is fundamentally wrong to put little girls on display in such a sexually charged way. It's one thing for them to clatter around the house in plastic dress-up high heels, smeared in cheap, lurid-coloured kiddie make-up, making believe that they're grown-ups in the privacy of their or their friends' own homes, quite another to do it on stage, in front of strangers, as part of a competition.

I was also, more recently, discomforted at the sight of Connie Talbot, the six-year-old who made the finals of *Britain's Got Talent*, singing 'Somewhere Over the Rainbow' and then 'Ben' – songs popularised by Judy Garland and Michael Jackson, neither of whom exactly managed to grow up into happy, well-grounded adults. And yet I'd popped my own six-year-old daughter into a big, professional stage production. What was so different about what Connie Talbot was doing? Where should I draw the line? Had I, in my naivety and over-excitement, already overstepped it?

To be honest, I didn't know. I worried. There's a long list of child performers who've gone on to lead short and troubled adult lives. Visit US journalist Joal Ryan's blog Former Child Star Central (www.fcscentral.com) for a less-than-comforting picture of the grown-up experiences of showbiz kids. There's a lot of rehab, attention-seeking kinds of crime, car crashes (generally under the influence), broken relationships and fighting. Judy Garland on slimming pills at twelve. Lena Zavaroni, anorexic from her mid-teens, penniless and dead from the illness before she hit forty. Michael Jackson, troubled in so many ways. Jack Wilde – the Artful Dodger in *Oliver!* – dead of alcohol-related liver disease at fifty. Lindsay Lohan, Britney Spears in and out of rehab. And yet despite all these very public, horribly sad stories, so many of us parents encourage, support or simply allow our children to go out to work in the entertainment business. One glimpse of a spotlight and we make like moths.

In the US in particular, there are books, websites and courses dedicated to informing and assisting parents who wish to turn their little darlings into stars of stage and screen. You must, these exhort, ensure that your offspring become 'triple threats'. That is, they must be able to sing, dance and act, and even when they tick all those boxes, on top of that, they must look cute. Pure natural talent isn't enough. You must pay for them to go to the best singing, dancing and acting teachers. You must pay for portfolios of professional photographs. You must get them the best agent. You must take them to audition after audition after audition. Success comes at a heavy price in terms of investment of money, time, hope and energy. Failure costs just as much – although maybe not in the long term, if the child's wellbeing is considered. Oh – and if your child isn't naturally cute/classically good-looking, you need to get them to cultivate a niche persona. Geek, for example. Or fat kid.

American child TV star Paul Petersen started off as a Mouseketeer, made *Houseboat* with Cary Grant and Sophia Loren and spent his teenage years on *The Donna Reed Show*. He recovered from his alcoholic, drug-addled and generally dangerous-living twenties to write a string of adventure books and found A Minor Consideration, the US organisation dedicated to protecting performing children from the exploitation common in the industry: exploitation in which the children's parents are so often enthusiastically complicit. It was his own experiences in the business – and his recognition that so many other child actors had to cope with the same difficult issues – that led him to set up the organisation in 1990. Since then he has worked with the entertainment unions, the US government and even the United Nations to improve the lot of working children. The issue that starts most of the problems in the US, he told me, is a legal and financial one. 'The law requires that an adult person attend the child's workplace to be within sight and sound of their child at all times. They receive no compensation.'

This adult is usually mum or dad – who else would do it for nothing? They have to be there, looking after their working child, and so can't be somewhere else, earning a living or caring for any other children. They become financially dependent on the working child and 'it's an all-too-familiar story, that these young people come to their eighteenth birthday and discover, to their horror, that they're the only one in the family that's working'.

And then, suddenly, they're not. After *The Donna Reed Show* ended, Paul Petersen's career – like that of many juvenile actors when they reach adulthood, especially if they are identified with one particular role, like Petersen was – stalled. He went off the rails.

Whether the ratio of child performers who grow up wild – or, at a minimum, live out dangerously feral late teens and early twenties – is higher than it is for the general population, I don't know. And I don't think anyone does. Certainly, at eighteen or twenty, having worked in film or TV, they most likely have access to more money to buy more alcohol and narcotics and faster cars than most other kids – excepting, of course, those with very rich parents, who may get into similar trouble when they come into their trust funds. Being that age, having lots of money and no gainful employment is dangerous.

Petersen reckons that 'about half' of his troubles would have happened if he'd never set foot in a TV studio. He'd been a rambunctious child, sacked from his first job as a Mouseketeer for 'behaviour unbecoming', regarded by his teachers as one of the brightest boys in the class, but also amongst the most disruptive. He says he's 'genetically predisposed to being an alcoholic', and 'didn't learn how to say no' until he was well into his forties. 'That's on my back, I get that and I'm responsible.' But 'a significant chunk of the rest, I was either driven to, or encouraged to do by people who were not supportive of my efforts, but were envious and jealous and couldn't wait for me to fail'.

'I was very lucky,' Mark Lester (most famous for playing the title role in the 1968 film version of *Oliver!*) told me, 'to go from one film to the next up until the age of eighteen when the work just didn't come in.' At the same time as the work stopped, he gained access to his earnings and spent the next couple of years spending them on the traditional drink, drugs and fast cars. Then he went into rehab, came out, got into martial arts and then, having developed an interest in sports injuries, trained as an osteopath. He seems a very practical, down-to-earth person, not given to speculation. 'I don't know,' he said when I asked if he thought he'd have gone off the rails whether or not he'd gone into the entertainment business. 'But it's probably in my genetic make-up. Maybe I was given more opportunity to do it, but I probably would have done anyway.'

Danny Bonaduce – famous as Danny Partridge in *The Partridge Family*, and for his subsequent hellraising – is fond of pointing out that when he was in rehab, 'he was the only former child star among forty-eight patients – nine of whom, he added, were dentists'.* So, if you worry about your kids growing up to have drug problems, keep them out of the medical professions: it's not only dentists that get hooked. Lots of doctors do, too. They have access to all sorts of substances that other people don't and, because they are clever and know the telltale signs, tend to be highly skilled at concealing their own addictions. And a paramedic told me recently that loads of ambulance crews rely on diazepam to help them sleep. 'Otherwise,' he said, 'we couldn't cope with the shift patterns.'

Anxious to explore what I might be condemning my child to, I read some former child performers' autobiographies. Shirley Temple had come through it all with flying colours, even though she ended up with very little of the money she earned through her movies. Her autobiography *Child Star* is dedicated 'lovingly' to her mother. Miraculously, despite the fact that her mum was the archetypal, ultra-pushy stage mother, Rose Hovick, June Havoc survived childhood stardom and struggled her way to adult acting and, much later on, writing and directing success. Her story, told in two volumes of memoirs, is an extraordinary one.

At the height of her career in the early 1920s, 'Dainty Baby' June's act earned a staggering $1,500 a week as she headlined around the lucrative vaudeville circuit. But then puberty and moving pictures struck, work became harder to find, and wages dropped. Her mother grew increasingly hysterical. In 1929, June secretly married and tried to run away with Bobby Reed, a dancer in her act. She might have

*As Joal Ryan reports in her book *Former Child Stars: the story of America's least wanted*.

been thirteen – at least, that's how old Rose told her she was on her birthday: 'My baby is thirteen today. I just can't believe it!' June told Bobby she thought she was 'at least sixteen'. But she couldn't be sure. As she explained to him, she had an impressive collection of birth certificates that her mother had had forged so she could work illegally young. 'Two of them make me twenty-one now. The others can't be used. They make me over thirty.'* Mrs Hovick discovered and attempted to foil the newly-weds' escape plans. Following a scene in a police station during which she tried to shoot Bobby – but didn't have a clue how to use her gun and left the safety catch on – the pair got away.

Marriage was June's only way out of the embarrassingly childish act that Mrs Hovick was still touting round the remains of the vaudeville circuit. June had wanted out for a while. A couple of years earlier, she'd realised: 'I was much too big, not only for the act and the clothes, but for my billing: "Dainty Baby June". I was gangly. Nothing about me pleased me. I was still doing the same wretched baby-talk kind of act . . . The same act that was remarkable for a little child . . . [was] completely uninteresting for a gangly teenager . . . Maybe I no longer looked like a ferret, but I hadn't emerged a beauty . . . I knew I was no longer cute.' June was offered the chance of training with Samuel L. 'Roxy' Rothafel, renowned for producing the best stage shows of the time at his New York theatre, the Roxy. 'Give me this little girl for three years,' Roxy said, offering to take care of them whilst June was training – provided they forgot about their act – 'and I'll give you a star.' But Rose Hovick was having none of it. Despite her daughter's desperate entreaties, she bawled Rothafel out: 'Mother's voice was shrill. "She *is* a star! She's head-lined in vaudeville since . . . You want to separate us! That's what you're trying to do – separate me from my baby. How cruel!" '.†

Meanwhile June's older sister Louise *was* emerging a beauty.

Early Havoc, by June Havoc pp. 174–5.
†*Early Havoc*, pp. 129–34.

During June's starring years, Louise – blessed, allegedly, with none of her sister's talent – was forced by their mother to wear boys' clothes. She was kept firmly in her younger sibling's shadow to ensure that all attention focused on June. When June married and left the act, Louise stepped into the spotlight and within a few years had achieved a much higher level of fame than her child star sister. She became the world's best-known burlesque artiste, Gypsy Rose Lee, feted for the sassy humour of her striptease act, and able to get away with revealing comparatively little flesh.

In her memoirs, Gypsy described their archetypal stage mother as 'charming, courageous, resourceful and ambitious. She was also, in a feminine way, ruthless.' Once Gypsy hit the big time, Mrs Hovick didn't bother with June, who by the early 1930s was separated from Bobby and struggling to scrape a living doing the rounds of the gruelling dance marathons. The first volume of June's extraordinary memoirs is very matter-of-fact about her mother's coldness. I wondered how she felt about it, imagining a combination of sadness, disorientation, a sense of abandonment, but also relief and freedom after all the years of intense attention and pushing. Now in her mid-nineties – and just over a decade into her retirement – Miss Havoc explained, via her assistant Tana:

'Yes, of course that's how I felt, but I also experienced bewilderment at the sense of relief and freedom. I did love my mother but found those feelings a little uneasy to have. And by the time that happened, I was more cognisant of my mother's ways than I had been as a child; and while things were hard, I held on to my dream. That occupied me emotionally – that and taking care of my infant daughter.'

Miss Havoc also told me how, despite the kind of upbringing that would drive most people to drink and drugs – or at least extended bouts of unproductive self-pity – she got up, dusted herself down and worked incredibly hard to forge herself a successful adult career

'I gained the uproarious, unconditional acclaim of the audiences I played to – waves and waves of love coming over the footlights. This, along with the approval and guidance of many of the vaudevillians with whom I worked, gave me a strong foundation of self-respect, and knowledge of talent and achievement.'

She went on to explain how most vaudevillians prided themselves on their family values. 'I learned right from wrong by being among them backstage. I hate to see the young actors of today being exploited when so many of them have had little opportunity to plumb the depths of their talent and instead are being turned into "icons", whatever that means.'

There is, in other words, a big difference between being a working child actor and a child star. June Havoc was both, but she was both at a time before the press and public felt entitled to invade a star's personal space, and in a place – vaudeville – where the focus was on teamwork, on the responsibility performers had to each other and to their audience, to keep going even when they felt rotten, to hone their skills and to work hard. As Tana told me, if you were working in vaudeville, you 'went on stage no matter what. I suppose the odd missing limb might excuse you, or a coma, but other than that, you went out there because the rest of the people in the act – perhaps all the acts on the bill – depended on you.'

And then came film, and then television, video, DVD. With the evolution in media came a change in how we, the audience, respond and relate to the performers. With traditional theatre, the differences between us and them and – crucially – between performance and real life are clear. As filming techniques and technology increased in sophistication, as television arrived in our living rooms and started taking over our lives, the relationships between audience and performer changed. The more our lives are ruled by TV, the more proprietorial we feel towards the people on it and the less we are able to distinguish between real life and drama.

In her book *Former Child Stars: the story of America's least wanted*, journalist Joal Ryan posits the theory that 'a TV kid makes a more personal impression than a movie kid'. Her idea is that kids on TV shows are watched over years by children, grow up with us and are seen as peers and attainable, whereas children on films are movie stars and different. I think it's more that anyone who appears on a regular basis in our living rooms along with our families feels familiar. Because we're used to them being in our homes, we feel – on some primordial level – as if they are kin.

Weirdly, it works the other way round, too. A few years ago, a family friend, an actor, was in a TV series called *A Thing Called Love*. I watched avidly. During one episode, his character was rounded on by several of his friends who all shouted at him a lot. I can't remember why. What I can remember are the emotions this scene evoked in me. I got very cross and upset with the people who were being horrid to my friend, and felt very protective towards him – which is embarrassing and, given the fact that he's six foot tall and works out (I'm four foot eleven and don't) and perfectly capable of looking after himself, hilarious. I am – like most people – intellectually sophisticated enough to distinguish between real life and TV drama. On a deeper, emotional level I can't tell the difference.

Some months after Dora finished in *The Sound of Music*, she went to audition for a prestigious TV police drama. We knew only that her role involved cavorting round London Zoo, posthumously, as a figment of her grieving father's distressed imagination. That, I thought, would be enormous fun for her, and given that was all it involved, I reckoned I could cope with the fact that her character was dead. After the casting she told me that she'd had to lie still without breathing for thirty seconds. 'Why?' I asked. 'Dunno,' she replied happily, having thoroughly enjoyed herself. I had a fairly good idea, but consoled myself with the conviction that she wouldn't get the part anyway.

A few days later we heard that she had been cast. The job would start in two days, when she would have to wear a party dress and have her picture taken with penguins. That was very exciting. Then we heard that they needed to know how tall she was so they could buy a body double to use for when they showed her having her operation. And could I please bring in some family photos of her, but, naturally, none with her real family in. Then I discovered that her character was due to die as a result of a (routine) operation that, in real life, the sister of one of her best friends was waiting to have. And that viewers would see her character lying on a mortuary slab, as her grieving father – who spent more time than was strictly healthy visiting his dead daughter there – wouldn't let her be buried.

I pulled her. It was all too much. Although she would undoubtedly have had a fantastic time, and got to work with a highly respected director, top-notch cast and award-winning company, it felt wrong. It would have been a brilliant career opportunity, but might have caused her friend worry and upset, completely unnecessarily. And then there was my reaction to consider. Although I would know, indisputably, that Dora was alive and well, if I watched her performance and saw her lying on that mortuary slab, in the context of a realistic, contemporary drama, I would feel that something terrible had happened to her. Given how strong my emotional reaction was to my friend's character being shouted at, I could imagine exactly how this would affect me. I'm still not sure whether my response was flaky or normal. I am sure, however, that she'll have plenty of other brilliant career opportunities when she's old enough to have a career.

Dora, to her credit, took the disappointment very well. She had been very much looking forward to meeting the penguins, but was pleased that she wouldn't miss seeing the results of the science experiment they'd been conducting at school (leaving an egg in a variety of different liquids – Coke, tea, milk and water – to see which stained the shell the most). 'Oh well,' she said, philosophically, 'I didn't really want to be dead anyway.' She changed her tune a few months later, though, when she watched the brother of one of her *Sound of Music* colleagues playing a boy who died in the BBC drama

Cranford. 'It's not *fair*,' she complained. 'Haydon was allowed to be dead. Why wasn't I?' I opened my mouth to tell her and then closed it again. I didn't think I could explain how a realistic drama has a different impact on the viewer than a period drama does. 'You would be allowed to play a character who dies in period costume, but not in contemporary costume,' simply wouldn't compute in Dora's brain.

One of the things, I realised, about all the child star casualties was that they were child *stars*. And stars of films or TV shows. To keep things in proportion, Dora was not about to become a child star. She was going to be one of a team of children performing in a stage musical, a show that would be seen by thousands, but not by millions. And lots of them would be sitting a long way from the stage, and so, despite her highly visible face and those annoying red opera glasses that you have to pay fifty pee (FIFTY PEE!) to use and then have to give back at the end of the show and don't really work, wouldn't be able to see her that well anyway. Also, from what I'd read, most of the child performers who went on to have major problems were those who earned shedloads of money and were recognised whenever they walked down the street. I soothed myself with the thought that *The Sound of Music* would make Dora neither famous nor rich, nor lead to me becoming financially dependent on her. Appearing in it would probably make her no more likely to spend her late teens and early twenties going wild than she was anyway – than I had been. She had already, two years earlier, expressed a strong interest in motorbikes.

We were sitting in my car, in a traffic jam. A man on a moped wobbled past us, L-plate slightly askew. 'That man is riding his motorbike well,' Dora informed me, impressed in a way that only someone with stabilisers on their pushbike could be. 'When I grow up, I want one.'

'Dora,' I said, taking a deep breath and trying to imbue my voice with gravitas, so that she'd always remember the significant piece of guidance I was about to impart, 'there are only two things that I really, really don't want you to do when you grow up. One is smoke cigarettes. The other is ride motorbikes.' I've seen too many casualties and consider both even more dangerous than going on the stage.

'Mummy,' replied Dora, who at four was already able to muster more gravitas, with less effort, than I ever could, 'I will never smoke a cigarette. But I'll get a motorbike when you're died, because you won't be able to know anything about it.'

Oh well, I thought. She's obviously grasped the concept of death.

With Dora starting back at school, I had some more immediate worries to deal with. She'd been begging to be allowed to switch from packed lunches to school dinners, longing for those delicious meals of pasta, pizza, chips and bread followed by chocolate pudding with chocolate custard sprinkled with brightly E-number-coloured hundreds and thousands that you never find in a health-conscious, middle-class lunch bag, which is, instead, bursting with nectarines (in season), carrots, cherry tomatoes and some very tasty lettuce. As rehearsal and performance schedules were likely to mean that she'd be missing lots of hot meals at home over the winter months, I caved in, on the condition that if she had pudding at school, she could only have a healthy snack when she came home, but if she had fruit for afters, she'd be allowed a couple of biscuits.

Meanwhile, another email had arrived from Jo Hawes.

Hi guys,
We would like to get all of you together on the morning of Monday 18 September in order to decide on teams and for Jeremy [Sams – director] and Arlene [Phillips – choreographer] to see you all together.
Please confirm that you will be able to attend – it does need everybody of course or we cannot achieve what we are setting out to do!!

As Dora settled into the new term and the excitement of being-put-into-teams-day and the start of rehearsals – 25 September – drew nearer, I started thinking about the impact it would all have on her school life. Academically, I suspected she'd be fine. She's not way out ahead of the other kids in her class, but is bright. Unlike me she enjoys, and has a natural flair for, maths. She reads well, writes carefully and neatly (also unlike me), and settles happily and conscientiously to do her homework. So I was fairly confident that she'd be able to make up for any schoolwork she missed while rehearsing or performing. She was, after all, only six, was contracted for only six months, and hence would have plenty of post-*Sound of Music* time to catch up before embarking on her PhD in rocket science.

I was more concerned about her friendships. Her best pals don't go to the same school as she does, and although, from what I could make out from her reports of school life, she nearly always had someone to play with at playtime, she wasn't particularly close to any of her peers. This was partly because she tended to, er, 'direct' them. The previous term, for instance, she'd come home one afternoon and flopped on to the sofa. 'Phew,' she announced, as if she'd just returned from a hard day at the office. 'I needed *a lot* of people today to play Barbie and the Magic of Pegasus.'

'And did you get them?' I asked, one eyebrow raised doubtfully.

'Yes,' she said, adding an 'of course,' to demonstrate her annoyance at my lack of faith in her persuasiveness and directorial talent.

Given this history, I was worried that her frequent absences and the reason for them might further increase the distance between her and her classmates. At the auditions a couple of the other mums had told me how, once they'd started working on the stage, their daughters had been targeted by other girls at school and bullied. One mother – who works at her daughter's school – told me how the ringleader had picked her daughter up and dangled her upside down.

'The teacher said it was happening because she'd got this part, and what did I expect?'

Perhaps it's different for boys. Mark Lester remembers his childhood relationships being normal and uncomplicated. He attended a stage school for a while and then moved on to his local grammar school, where his friends were unfazed by his celebrity status. 'They were okay. You have mates like anybody else. Kids are great levellers, they don't really care if you've got one leg, or one eye. It's only later in life that prejudices come in. Kids just get on, and get on together.'

On 14 September, Dora's licence arrived. She was now authorised 'to take part in performances on the dates specified below . . . subject to the restrictions and conditions laid down in the Children (Performances) Regulations 1968 and to such other conditions as the local authority or the licensing authority may impose under the said Regulations'. Then there were the what, when and where details, followed by the names of the chaperones and then the regulations:

On days where the child is required to take part in both afternoon and evening performances the child must not be present at place of performance no earlier [*sic*] than 1000 hrs and leave the place of performance no later than 2200 or 30 minutes after their required part is completed, [hooray, a comma!] whichever is the earliest; child must vacate location between performances for no less than one and a half hours for purposes of rests and meals; on single performance days child must leave the place of performance no later than 2200 hrs or 30 minutes after their required part is completed, whichever is the earliest. If the child has taken part in the performance on the previous day she may not be present at the location until 16 hours have elapsed; this does mean that she may return to a place where she would normally be the next morning.

She was allowed to be absent from school on the days she was due to perform, but there was no mention of rehearsal dates – and it was during the rehearsals that she'd miss school most frequently. Had there, I wondered, been a mistake? Could this be a problem? Did it mean that Brent Council had authorised her to perform, but not to rehearse? Would it all go horribly, horribly wrong?

I was thrilled to see the performance dates – but slightly confused by their presence. If the kids hadn't yet been sorted into their final families, how could Jo – and Brent Council – possibly know the dates on which they would be performing? Could Jo, as well as being terrifyingly efficient and able to work round the clock on sub-Thatcherite amounts of sleep, also see into the future? I wouldn't have been surprised.

The popularity of the *How Do You Solve a Problem Like Maria?* TV show meant that *Sound of Music* tickets were selling fast. The five pages of information about the show that Jo had sent included the bombshell that we had to book our seats through the box office like everyone else: i.e., no freebies or reductions for stage parents. On top of everything else, it seemed a little unfair. But by then I'd resigned myself to spending the money and was more concerned that, given the show's popularity, tickets might have completely sold out by the time I knew the dates when Dora would actually be performing.

So I emailed Jo Hawes hopefully, asking if there was any chance that the dates on Dora's licence might be accurate and could I, therefore, book tickets? No chance. They would, she responded, almost certainly change. And some councils just didn't include rehearsals in the licence. So that was all right then, Dora could attend the rehearsals. I didn't book tickets, but continued to monitor availability on seetickets.com, the Really Useful Group's ticket sales website. Most of the top-price tickets were already sold out for the first month or so, but at fifty-five quid apiece, I couldn't see myself forking out for many of those anyway. There was plenty of availability in the upper circle, though, so I probably would be able to watch her long distance. Not to worry, I already knew what she looked like . . . I just wanted to make sure I could be there on her first night. Whenever that might be.

SOMETHING GOOD

Dora had settled well into Year 2. She tackled school and homework industriously, enjoyed Mrs Arin's teaching and played with her friends and her cousins, Millie and Freddie, who we visited most Saturday mornings. There were the usual rounds of play-dates and sleepovers. She rode her scooter to school most days (I rode it home) and arabesqued happily around her dance classes. It was a fairly busy routine, but she still managed to fit in plenty of telly-watching. Life would be like this for another week.

Monday, 18 September, I was up bright and early for our trip to the Really Useful Group's offices. It was only when I found myself standing stretching my formerly black, now a sophisticated shade of dark grey, Fenn Wright Manson silk top (bought *circa* 1990) over our ancient wobbly ironing board and pressing the button so an extra spray of steam and limescale burst through the base of the cracked iron that I should have replaced years ago, showering everything with white chalky stuff, that I realised how excited I must be. I only iron on really important occasions: posh parties, job interviews and live music – doing it for the latter being a complete waste of time as it's always really dark anyway. Mostly I wear casually creased trousers and even more noticeably distressed t-shirts (you'd be distressed if you spent most of your time crumpled up in an overstuffed drawer). Dora was sporting her trademark almost-even bunchies – my technique was improving – together with jeans, pink t-shirt and trainers.

After much pleading from Dora, I'd recently started reading *Harry Potter and the Philosopher's Stone* to her at bedtime. We were still near the beginning, but, like millions of others, were both already engrossed in Harry's story. Realising that, on the journey into town, I had a choice between reading aloud from it, potentially irritating the other passengers who didn't care what happened to Harry, Hermione et al., and Dora playing a game where she tries to rearrange my face by pulling and squishing my features in different directions, I plumped for irritating the other passengers. The journey passed without us needing to count the stops, and at the end my nose was still in its usual position. We weren't the first to arrive at the Really Useful offices, but there were only a couple of other people there when we arrived – an older boy sitting quietly with his mum on one of the sofas. They'd come from Birmingham, and Jack, who was going to play Kurt, and had done lots of other theatre work, would be staying with a friend in London for the duration of the show.

It wasn't long before the room filled up, and there were soon nineteen excited, chattering children, and about the same number of perhaps even more excited, chattering parents. The atmosphere was quite different from the last time we were there: all the adults were introducing themselves to each other, and one mum – Lynn, whose daughter Grace had filled the Brigitta gap on the last team list – was passing around a printout of the kids' names for us to fill in our contact details. I was impressed. She was obviously very confident, organised and experienced in the stage mothering department. It was only months later I found out that I was completely wrong. It was Grace's first professional stage role, and Lynn had been terrified at the prospect of meeting the other parents. 'I thought everyone would know each other already and be really pushy,' she told me. Adrianna – the first person we'd met at the first audition we'd been to – had been cast as a Gretl, and had both happy parents with her, and there were a few others I recognised, including Yasmin and her mum Wendy, the people who Dora had invited herself to move in with at the final audition. It was lovely to meet everyone under such relaxed conditions.

Jackie – the mum with two daughters in the show – wasn't there, but had already got in touch with me via www.notapushymum.com. She was very excited, but also anticipating a wearying few months, as her girls had been put in different teams: which meant she, her husband and the other family members who'd be helping out with taking and fetching the girls would be spending an awful lot of time travelling to and from their home in Tonbridge and hanging around waiting for rehearsals and performances to end. But the excitement massively outweighed 'the shock of how my life is over for the forseeable future'. She was at work that Monday – she is a teaching assistant at her younger daughter's school – and her husband Scott, a landscape gardener, had taken a day out to accompany his girls to the sorting.

In fact, the atmosphere in the waiting room that day was rather like the first day at Hogwarts. The Really Useful boardroom was buzzing with the same kind of excitement and anticipation, a similar sense of impending magic as when the witch-and-wizarding newbies are sorted into Gryffindor, Slytherin, Ravenclaw and Hufflepuff, only with more parents and without that sumptuous start-of-term feast. Shame. Still, on the upside, we were provided with compli-mentary tea, coffee, juice and water which, I realised on reflection, were probably more suitable for that hour of the morning.

The kids were called into another room, and when they'd gone, Jo Hawes explained a bit about what would be happening. There was, she told us, a huge buzz around this production, a lot of excitement, and there would probably be a lot of publicity. The Gretls would, she said, get the most attention – at which point I broadened my grin and deliberately crinkled my laughter lines to make sure no one could tell that my stomach had been showered with small sparks of envious regret that Dora had been cast as Marta. Jo went on to tell us that she'd managed to organise it so that she would probably have some – most likely about ten – top price tickets available for parents for each show. They couldn't all go to one family, but would need to be shared around, and we'd have to follow her system to the letter, because she was very busy and was doing it as a favour. She'd set up this arrangement because parents with kids in *Mary Poppins* had ended up having to queue outside the theatre at 8.30 a.m. so as to watch their children perform – 'and I didn't think that was on'. She wouldn't be able to confirm which seats we'd have (or, in fact, that we'd actually get any at all) until the day of the performance, but they would be good seats, ones that the production company would be holding for VIPs.

She also made it clear that whilst the children would have a fantastic time, we parents wouldn't, and that while they were in the show we would have to strictly limit all their other extracurricular activities, so they could save all their energy for school first and *The Sound of Music* second. Tech week – when they're rehearsing the show intensively in the theatre and making sure that all the sound, lighting and stage sets work – would be sheer hell, and before the end of it at least one of us would be on the phone screaming at her about how terrible it all was. 'I want to stress,' Jo continued, 'that I will say "no" if anyone asks if they can go on holiday. So in case you're brave enough to try, please just be aware that I will refuse.' Oh, and could we all please make sure we checked our emails last thing at night, as she might not be able to get vital information about the following day's schedule until the creative team had talked over that day's rehearsal, returned home, eaten dinner and then called or emailed Jo to tell her what she needed to tell us. Any questions?'

Bethany's mum Rachel had told me how the kids in *Les Misérables* finished at the end of the first half and so only got to do the curtain call on their last night. Would the von Trapp children, I asked, mindful of the licence condition saying they had to leave the theatre by ten o'clock or half an hour after the show finished, whichever was earlier, get to take a bow? Yes, she said. They couldn't have a curtain call without them, as they were central to the show. How would expenses be paid? someone else asked. By cheque, in arrears. When would we know the final teams our kids would be in and the dates they'd be performing? 'As soon as the creative team decides and tells me,' Jo responded, 'but it may well change after today.' What was the schedule for rehearsals? She'd let us know as soon as she knew. And so on.

After Jo had finished, we settled down to chatting amongst ourselves: which child belonged to us, what, if anything, had they done before, what part they'd be playing, how old they were – there were, it transpired, some very experienced young actors and actresses amongst the cast: several former Jeremys and Jemimas from *Chitty Chitty Bang Bang*, a Jane Banks or two (*Mary Poppins*). I discovered that Dora was the youngest there by a few months, and worried slightly that all the girls who were playing Gretl were older than her. The team were hoping to cast four or five Gretls as the girls playing the part would be so young, but they weren't planning to cast more than three Martas – and my daughter was the youngest of all. Was she, I wondered, mature enough to cope with doing more shows than some of the older children? We'd soon find out, I thought, and she did look like she had more physical reserves than the sylph-like Gretls.

I found the mum of the girl with whom Dora had had her oval face/round face contretemps and apologised for my daughter's lack of tact. We settled down for a chat. I'd seen Nicky at the final audition with two identical, Gretl-sized girls: one had got in and the other hadn't. How did she – and they – cope with that? 'I've got four kids performing,' Nicky told me, 'the triplets and their older sister.' The *triplets!????* The three girls (two thirds of the triplets and their big sister) had all auditioned for *The Sound of Music*; Haydon, the third triplet and the boy who was, a few months later, in *Cranford*, being too young to try for Friedrich or Kurt. 'If they want to do it,' she said, 'they have to be able to cope with one of them getting a part and the others not. It is tough,' she continued, 'but that's the deal. Otherwise they can stop. It would,' she conceded, 'have been harder if two of them had got in and the third hadn't. But there you have it.'

Nicky seemed extremely nice, very grounded, businesslike and sensible. Not remotely the kind of person I'd expected to meet in this glitzy showbiz world. How, I wondered, had she ended up like this?

'Oh, my eldest was into it and I ended up taking her to Young 'Uns – that's the Sylvia Young Theatre School agency,' she added, realising I wouldn't know what Young 'Uns was. 'Anyway, because the triplets were really young they went everywhere with me. When Kirsty (her oldest, who'd played Jemima in *Chitty Chitty Bang Bang*) was called in for her audition, they wanted to know who was making all the noise in the background, so I explained and apologised, saying they were too young for me to leave behind. They called the triplets in and signed them up as well.'

As we were chatting, the door swung open and Connie Fisher came in, accompanied by her agent, who was busy on her mobile making arrangements. We all looked up and started clapping and cheering. Connie looked slightly taken aback: it's unlikely that anyone had explained to her that the room in which she would be waiting to meet the director and choreographer would already be packed with over-excited stage mothers and fathers. *How Do You Solve a Problem Like Maria?* had only finished the previous Saturday and Connie had spent most of the thirty-six-odd intervening hours being interviewed and recalibrating her life.

Given that I don't like to think of myself as the starstruck type, Connie Fisher's entrance had an embarrassingly strong effect. I suddenly found it very hard to concentrate on my conversation with Nicky and, like most of the other *Sound of Music* parents present, found my attention irresistibly drawn towards Connie. It was the traditional reaction to someone you're familiar with watching on the telly. Having, like everyone else in the Really Useful boardroom that morning, followed her progress through the competition with significantly more involvement than we generally invested in our own job-seeking efforts, I felt as if I knew her. It was the same sensation as being a soap operaholic, bumping into the actor who plays your favourite character when you're out shopping, and accidentally saying hello and asking how he is, before you register that, in real life, you aren't on meet-and-greet terms as he doesn't have a clue who you are. The pull towards Connie was so powerful, I felt like I was about to regress to those bizarre mid-teenage years, when, with some equally hormonal friends, I hung around after the men's doubles finals at Olympia, and, after everyone else had left the arena, collected the plastic cups that the tennis stars drank out of and spat into, took them home, labelled them carefully with the name of the hunk who'd drunk out of and spat into them (I didn't wash them out) and kept them until I was old enough to be embarrassed at having done so. Fortunately, on this occasion, I managed to suppress my inner adolescent long enough to continue my chat with Nicky, who, being a seasoned stage mum, and considerably more sensible than I had just discovered myself to be, had glanced up to see what all the fuss was about, smiled, then returned her full attention to our conversation.

This wound down fairly soon after that, partly because it had come to a natural conclusion, and partly because it was obvious that I was being magnetically drawn to the boardroom table where Connie was now sitting. Shana and Darren – Adrianna's parents – had struck up an easy conversation with her: they had people in common and were discussing their various connections. I sat tongue-tied on the other side of the table, before eventually asking Connie if she'd managed to get any sleep over the past week (I'd thought she looked slightly tired and stressed on the final programme). She shrugged off my concerns. It had, she replied, been a busy time, 'but I always sleep like a baby'.

A few minutes later the kids wandered out of the sorting room. Dora was holding hands with another bunchied little girl wearing a white t-shirt and dungarees. They looked very cute. They let go of each other's hands and Dora came to find me.

'I'm going to be Gretl again,' she announced.

'Are you really?' I asked, suspicious that there was no accompanying grown-up endorsing the change.

'Yes. They made us all stand in lines and I was between the Martas and the Gretls. They said maybe I could learn two parts! Everyone laughed, but I could, couldn't I?'

'Look who's here,' I said, pointing over to where Connie was coping admirably with the swarm of smiley children that had landed around her, all talking at once. 'Why don't you go and say hello while I ask Jo if you're going to be Marta or Gretl.'

Dora looked reluctant, and went to find her new friend before sidling shyly over to stand near where Connie was sitting. I cornered Jo Hawes to ask if it was true that Dora's part had changed. She went off to find out and returned to tell me that Dora's report was accurate. She was, in fact, going to be a Gretl.

I was delighted. It wasn't that I wanted my daughter to play the role that would attract the most attention. At least that's what I told myself. Firmly. I was pleased, the good-parent part of me purred, because Dora was so young, and the change of role meant that she would be doing slightly fewer shows, which would be better for her welfare. However, my inner stage mother was cartwheeling around my vital organs with excitement at the prospect of my little girl getting the part with the biggest 'aaah' factor. I crossed my fingers and hoped that my inner stage mother and inner adolescent never managed to join forces. I wasn't sure that the rest of me would prove strong enough to prevent them triumphing. There was no telling how much embarrassment I might cause myself. Or, more importantly, Dora.

It would be okay, I figured, were I entirely devoid of self-

awareness. Then I could act appallingly without troubling my con-
science. I could boast about my daughter's brilliance, acknowledge
any other child's achievements in a slightly off-hand and patronising
way that made it clear I considered them vastly inferior to my child's,
and blame any ill will generated by my behaviour on other people's
envy of my super-talented daughter. It would, of course, impact
badly on Dora, but hey, I would also be completely unaware of that
too, and when she grew up and either disowned me, or descended
into a hell of drink and drugs, I could just scream, 'How could you!
After everything I've done for you!'

But sadly, because I have some self-awareness – not enough, it's
true, to prevent me saying or doing the wrong thing at the wrong time
and place on an embarrassingly frequent basis – this was not a
practical option. The problem is, every mistake I make generates
acute and extended bouts of guilt, embarrassment and self-
recrimination, which tend to be completely out of proportion with
the wrong doing that preceded them. That's an awful lot of time
spent feeling ashamed. To limit that, I do at least *try* to do the right
thing.

After we'd said our goodbyes and see-you-next-weeks, Dora and I
headed back to Covent Garden station. I wondered vaguely where
they'd found another Marta at such short notice. I guessed it must
have been at the auditions for the last Louisa and Brigitta, where,
apparently, they'd also checked out an additional Gretl or two.
Maybe they'd also done an extra sweep at Sylvia Young's, or
something like that: perhaps the producers had a special relationship
with the stage school, like the one between the US and Britain. As
the Really Useful Group seemed unlikely to invade Iraq, I couldn't
see much harm in that.

It was only after rehearsals started that I found out the answer.
Emily, who had landed the part of Marta, had been begging her
parents to allow her to audition. Her father, David Ian – one of the
show's producers – had, eventually, given in and called Jo Hawes,

saying, 'I've got this daughter who sings and dances, but I don't know how she'll be compared to the drama school kids'. Jo asked him how he wanted to handle it, and David said: 'If she auditions, she does it the same way as everyone else.'

'Emily did two or three auditions,' Jo Hawes told me, 'and then came in to meet Jeremy and Arlene. It was not until she was just about to be cast that they discovered who she was.' Emily had been hoping to join the production with the second cast of kids, in the spring, but was called in early when the creative team were rethinking their Gretls and Martas. According to her mum, Tracy – a former dancer, singer and actress – the director, Jeremy Sams, was a bit surprised that he hadn't known who Emily was during the audition process. 'But it would've been wrong if they'd known she was David's daughter. We were happy for her to be in the show – but only if she was really good enough. Also, we insisted that she didn't get any publicity. She just had to be one of the kids.'

After we'd returned home, I called the Jerwood Space. I explained that my daughter would be rehearsing there and asked if they had a wireless network that the public could access. The man who answered was very helpful. Although they didn't have a public network, I might be able to get on to one of the local ones, but failing that, if I asked very nicely, they'd let me access the Jerwood Space office one. Sorted, I thought. Then I knuckled down to my own work. I was quite busy that week: there was a research report to write up and some training to plan.

The following day, I emailed Jo to ask about what Dora should wear on her feet for rehearsals – I thought trainers would probably be okay, but wanted to check that I wasn't required to provide some obscure variety of dance shoe that I'd never heard of. Trainers would be fine, she responded. That evening, after Dora and I had taken a swift trip to Brent Cross Shopping Centre to kit her out in cheap-but-comfy rehearsal clothing, another email arrived. A rejigged team list was attached – the teams no longer red, green and blue, but now (respectively) Mittens, Kettles and Geese. Dora was still in Mittens, but was now the Gretl, and several of the other members had changed. The Marta in her team was now Molly-May, the little girl whose hand she was holding when they emerged from the sorting. Olivia and Alicia – Jackie's daughters – were now both in the same team (Geese). That'll make her life easier, I thought. Jo wrote, 'I really hope it doesn't change but actually I think it will!' She also told us that they weren't yet sure how the four Gretls' performances would be scheduled across the three teams. And that they hadn't yet decided whether the teams would perform three days on and six days off, or two days on and four days off. The director, she told us, was also very concerned that the children should treat the rehearsal process as a big secret that they kept from us until we saw them on stage. Parental influence on their performance had to be kept to a minimum. On top of that, 'We have been asked not to hang around in the coffee bar there so I am afraid it will be much like the theatre – drop and run!' I needed to find another café to sit and work in.

The next day, another email arrived: Jo didn't yet know which children would be off on which afternoon the following week, but was trying to find out. The next day, another email: the first with the actual address of the Jerwood Space: not all parents had done what I'd done and hit Google the minute we'd been given the name of the venue, and someone had, sensibly, asked Jo for details. 'All children,' she added, 'should come with packed lunch and drinks. Russ and Rebecca will be there to meet the kids.'

Russ and Rebecca would be chaperoning the children. Russ was the smiley man with grey hair, tattoos and a measuring stick who we'd met briefly in the original audition queue outside the London Palladium. Rebecca was the gentle, white-blonde girl who I'd seen taking the three small girls to the loo at the final audition. She was, it turned out, Jo's daughter and used to work in a nursery. Russ – a former brickie – seemed, at first sight, a much more unlikely chaperone.

He and his wife Linda (who also chaperoned on the show once performances were underway) had moved from Middlesbrough to London when their daughter Claire was eight, so she could attend Sylvia's (as those in the biz call the Sylvia Young Theatre School). Claire had started dancing at two and a half, and heard about the school from other children at dance competitions. 'Originally,' Linda told me, 'we didn't intend for her to go full time. We just thought we'd put her on the agency. But we let her audition, because we wanted them to see what she could do, and she was offered a place. And we thought, she's done her bit. We can't disappoint her and say you can't go. So, because we only had Claire to consider, we decided we'd sell up and move to London.'

Linda – then a careers adviser – found a new job down south, and also took in children from the school as boarders. Russ was working for ICI, and the company promised him a transfer to London. But it never materialised, so every weekend Linda and Claire would commute back up north to see him. Until, that was, a year or so later when a ballet teacher at the school noticed a slight tilt to Claire's spine. After a variety of comparatively unintrusive therapies proved ineffective, doctors did a thorough investigation and discovered a tumour in her chest cavity that had broken through into the spinal cord.

'They called us in,' said Russ, 'and sat us down. Then the doctor said, "I must tell you, Claire's going to be a paraplegic. She could possibly die." '

Russ and Linda then had to break the news to Claire (who asked her dad whether he'd cried – 'I said "yes, but only because I've just bought you some new shoes and they'll be wasted" ' – and told her parents firmly that she wasn't going to be paralysed) and also explain to Sylvia Young that Claire would have to leave the school. 'And Sylvia said, "No she won't. We'll fix things up. Even if she can't walk, there's people here, big strong boys, she still comes back to this school",' Russ recalled. 'We thought that was amazing.'

'The school were really very good,' said Linda. 'When Claire was in hospital, the headmistress used to come and massage her feet. Matron would come and brush her hair. Sylvia used to visit and all the kids used to come up and bring her things.'

Claire carried on working in the theatre up until the time of her operation, and then between periods of hospitalisation. Both school and production companies proved hugely supportive. On one show, they even employed an understudy for her – something almost unheard of in live theatre, as the teams of children cover for each other. There was no thought of Claire stopping, either before or afterwards, and today, in her early thirties, she's still an avid performer, with an MA in Theatre Studies and Education under her belt. 'Once she's finished her acting,' Linda told me, 'she'd like to teach special needs children.'

It was while Claire was in hospital that Russ discovered his new vocation. 'That's how I got to love children. I've always liked kids, but it gave me the insight into them. In the cancer ward, where Claire was, I used to sit up with these children till twelve o'clock at night, talking, and they used to ask me about my life up north, I used to have games with them, and persuade them to take their medication. It was hard, because there they'd be going, "Why should I? I'm going to die anyway."' He now works as a chaperone for children performing in film, television and theatre, obviously loves his work, and the kids (and parents) adore him.

'My life's completely changed. If you ever go to the north-east, you'll see. Men: bars; women: lounge. They don't kiss anybody on the cheeks, nowt like that. It just completely opened my mind to theatre, to travelling, food and stuff. I've really enjoyed it. At first, I was homesick. But I would do it again.'

I studied my A–Z to make sure Dora and I wouldn't get lost on the way to the Jerwood Space. It seemed a pretty straightforward journey: out of Southwark station, across the road, then we would be on the right street, keep walking, cross a couple more roads and we'd be there. It would take between five minutes and half an hour depending on the number of distractions en route.

'Can I go in there?' asked Dora, Scooby-Doo backpack bobbing as she held my hand, skipped across the first road and pointed at a revolving door. As it was revolving on the threshold of a very big and swish-looking office block, in direct eyeline of a very broad-shouldered and scary-looking security guard, I said 'no'. Her pleading stopped when she noticed that some of the building, supported by concrete pillars, overhung a strip of cobblestones next to the pavement. Because the road sloped slightly upwards, the overhang sloped down to meet the ground. If you were quite small, and into that kind of thing, you could walk underneath, crouching lower and lower, and get as close as possible to the point where overhang and ground intersected, ignoring your mother while she hissed at you to come out quickly because you had a rehearsal to get to when what she really meant but was too embarrassed to say, because the rational part of her knew that it wasn't going to happen, was 'come out quickly because I'm anxious that the sticky-out bit of that building's going to collapse on top of you, because I can't see enough things holding it up'.

Then there was a boring stretch, until you came to the café attached to the little theatre under the railway arches, where, if you were desperate for the loo or a chocolate muffin, you could get both. A bit more walking and you were on the stretch of Union Street where the Jerwood Space is. On that corner we found something else interesting to look into: an open-plan basement office, where several of the desks had cuddly toys or model cars on them. Dora had great fun counting how many desks had toys on them and, later in the month, moved on to trying to see what snacks the workers had brought in with them: 'Ooh. Look! She's got *two* packets of crisps. And a banana. Can I have a packet of crisps, please?' Then, a few doors along, there was a French horn shop. When that was open, you could peer through the dusty windows and see lots of French horns hanging on the basement walls. But the best thing about it was the door handles. These were brass and mini-French-horn-shaped.

We crossed Union Street and entered the Jerwood Space. The reception area was light and airy and opened on to two gallery spaces – one to the left that you had to go through a doorway to get into, and another on the right, which was part of the same room. Diagonally to our right was a café with a glass roof. We spotted a couple of other *Sound of Music* kids and their parents in there, and went to join them. Rebecca was sitting at one of the tables and she ticked off Dora's name as we said hello.

The glass-roofed area was soon buzzing with excited children and parents. Dora was feeling slightly shy and snuggled into my lap. I was feeling slightly shy too, but made small talk with Nicky, whose daughter Lauren was another Gretl, and who was even earlier than we were. There were two other doors out of where we were sitting: one led outside to a walled-in patio, the other into the serving area of the café, where there was more seating. Peering through, I wondered if, amongst the people sitting chatting, were some of the adult cast members and creative team. I didn't recognise anyone, but then I didn't expect to.

Once Russ had appeared and he and Rebecca had whisked the children, their nutritious packed lunches and extra drinks off into the rehearsal rooms, some of the parents had to rush off to work, but others amongst us started getting to know each other. Shana stayed around, as it would take too long and be too expensive for her to return to Southend and then come back again to collect Adrianna. Carol, whose son Michael was one of the Kurts, also stayed, as did Lynn. There was another woman who, like Shana, was pretty, with immaculate shoulder-length brown hair, and beautifully turned out. She turned out to be Molly-May's mum, Helen. Because travelling home and back again to collect Dora would have eaten another two hours out of my working day, it made more sense for me to find somewhere local to sit and get on with it. That way I would still lose two hours, but much more enjoyably. Wendy had brought Yasmin in, and offered to come with me on the hunt for a suitable café that could, for the next month, serve as my temporary office. Before heading off in different directions, a bunch of us wound up our conversations outside the Jerwood Space. 'Oh look,' said someone. 'There's Andrew Lloyd Webber.' I turned for a quick stare. He'd gone. The door was still swinging.

It wasn't long before we discovered Café Arlington round the corner on Southwark Bridge Road. Along with reasonably priced food and drink, it offered – the clincher – that irresistible combination of comfy sofas and free wifi. Result! We settled down for coffee and a chat. Later, I got down to some work, and Wendy went off for a wander. Then I was joined by Lynn, Carol and Shana and we talked some more. At one point, Helen popped in. Then they left, and I did some more work. I now knew what they all did: Lynn was taking a year out after being made redundant from her human resources job. Wendy, I already knew, worked as a teaching assistant at Yasmin's school. Shana and Helen were very busy and dedicated mothers and housewives. And Carol – a lively and abundant redhead with a huge laugh – was one quarter of a Lincolnshire-based ABBA tribute band. *Lincolnshire?*

'Yes. I must be bonkers,' she laughed. 'When Michael got the part, I bought this tiny flat in Harrow. It's so small, I put the hoover away almost as soon as I've got it out! The freeholder lives upstairs and is really weird, never smiles. And once a month I'll be getting the train back up to Cleethorpes so I can see my older son and do some work.' We laughed, and I wondered if I would ever go so far as to move across the country to make it possible for Dora to chase her dreams before she was old enough to follow them under her own steam. I decided I probably wouldn't, but then she was only six. Maybe I'd change my mind when she was in her teens and a hundred per cent certain. Have to wait and see.

Molly-May had also travelled quite a distance to take up her part

– she lives with her mum Helen and teenage twin sisters near Harrogate, but while she was rehearsing and performing would be staying with her dad, who lives in west London, where she would be tutored by a family friend.

Soon after 4.30, an email arrived from Jo, providing a rehearsal schedule for the rest of the week. Dora was due to be there Tuesday, Wednesday and Thursday afternoons and Saturday morning. I dutifully emailed through the details to Dora's school even though everything was 'subject to change, of course', and a little later I packed my laptop away and moseyed back to the Jerwood. I hadn't got through half the work I'd planned to, but I'd started to get to know some of the other stage mums, and been pleasantly surprised. None of them seemed to be the viciously competitive, fiercely pushy, cheerfully two-faced, hissy-fit-prone types I'd been expecting. Of course, this was only the first rehearsal, and it was possible that they were all just very good at being two-faced . . . As Russ commented, eyes twinkling, 'Oh, you're all good friends now. But we'll see when they pick the kids for the opening night. That's when the true colours come out.'

Early back, I strolled round looking at the artwork on display, and picked up an information sheet about them, which I didn't read. Soon, other parents arrived, and we sat and waited in the glazed café area, some making small talk, others reading newspapers.

Then Russ and Rebecca brought the kids out. 'I'm hungry,' said Dora, who was struggling with her backpack, lunch bag, jacket and two thick manuscripts whilst simultaneously trying to hold Molly-May's hand. 'Can I go to Molly-May's house?' Realising that I'd only given her the same amount of food as when she went to school, I was hit by a sudden pang of guilt. Usually by this time she'd also have demolished a snacky tea (*if* she'd eaten all the healthy food in her lunch box) and be asking what was for supper. I wrestled the wodges of paper into her backpack. 'We need to put them in a file. And I have to bring a pencil and a rubber so I can make notes,' she told me. I promised her something for the journey home, hoping that would distract her from her request for a play-date, which I completely ignored. We walked back to Southwark station with a few of the other kids (back under the overhanging building, me controlling my anxiety), said goodbye, then crossed over The Cut to find a snack.

On the train on the way home I looked at the manuscripts – script and score – and asked Dora about what had happened. I found out that they'd all been in a big room, and Andrew Lloyd Webber (who had really been there this time) and David Ian had welcomed them and shown them some pictures of what the stage would look like. 'But we're not allowed to tell you because it's a secret.' Then they'd started on the songs. It had all been very exciting, except that someone had been wearing the same trousers as Dora.

After making a round of phone calls to let people know how the first day had gone, I stayed up late that night browsing the script and looking at the musical score. An email from Jo Hawes arrived at twenty past midnight, saying that the following day's rehearsal would finish half an hour earlier than she'd previously told us, confirming Dora's need of pencil and rubber (I thought she'd better take two pencils and a sharpener as well, and also another rubber) and asking us to make sure that the children arrive at the rehearsal 'having eaten so that they can give their best to the job in hand. Also,' Jo added, 'looking ahead, when we are in the theatre and they are coming in for an evening show, it is really important that they have a decent meal in between school and arriving at the theatre. They will fill up on junk otherwise and that is not a good way to do a performance.' Quite.

Next day, Dora had school in the morning and I picked her up before lunch to make sure she ate a proper, balanced meal. And then, ring-bindered script and score, pencils, rubber and sharpener in her back pack, laptop and *Harry Potter* in mine, we trundled off to the Jerwood Space. The noise in the glasshouse seating area was even louder that afternoon – some of the children already knew each other from school or previous theatre performances, but those that didn't had started to make friends and were chatting and laughing noisily with them. Or playing tag and shrieking in happy disregard of all the Jerwood Space's other customers. A few of us headed off to Café Arlington together for a drink, a gossip and a laugh, and I managed to squeeze in a token stab at some work.

That afternoon, another email from Jo, confirming the following day's rehearsal. On Wednesday (same routine), three emails. The first confirmed Thursday's times, the second had, in the subject field, 'A whinge from Jo!!' Oh no! What had I done wrong? What had Dora done wrong? Was there a packed lunch problem? Had she bitten someone? Had I bitten someone without realising? No. It turned out that Jo was cross because a couple of the parents with older children in the production had asked if their kids could be allowed to make their own way home. These teenagers were accustomed to travelling long distances to and from school, as well as embarking on all kinds of solo adventures in their spare time. But whatever degree of freedom young people are permitted in normal circumstances, it's different when they're working in the entertainment industry, under licence. Then it's against the law for them to travel alone. If, Jo pointed out, she and the chaperones allowed any of the kids to slope off by themselves and got caught in the process, it could lead to all the licences being revoked 'and bingo – Captain von Trapp has no children!' Which would, obviously, be a bad thing.

The third email told us that Saturday's rehearsal would last all day, instead of just the morning as we'd been told. The children would be singing in the morning and blocking in the afternoon. Very nice, but 'blocking'? What was 'blocking'? It sounded more like rugby than musical theatre . . . I emailed Jo. Blocking, it turns out, means staging. Oh, right. I adjusted my diary and added a new word to my lexicon of theatrical jargon.

Thursday, same routine: school, lunch, journey, *Harry Potter*, noisy wait at the Jerwood, coffee at the Arlington, followed by a half-hearted attempt at getting on with the research and report-writing I was supposed to be doing. The trouble was, everything else going on around me was so much more interesting. Even Café Arlington, with its own art gallery and its community projects. Concentrating on what I was supposed to be doing wasn't easy. Still, there was always Friday, when Dora's team weren't in, she would do her first full school day of the week and I would have a whole day at home to catch up on my work. And things like washing, shopping and spending time with my husband. With a little bit of luck – and an impressive amount of multitasking – I could fit all of that in between nine and three thirty. In my dreams.

Jo's email arrived at six o'clock, with the subject line 'Lots of things – sit down with a drink!', but I didn't. She confirmed Friday's rehearsal times. The following week there would be rehearsals every day from ten in the morning until eight at night. The children wouldn't be required all the time – that would be illegal – but Jo thought the timetable would be very different from the first week. Also, we or our agents (Dora was one of the minority who didn't have one), might be contacted by the BBC, who would be making a documentary about Connie and filming during rehearsals. And – because the show was likely to finish 'the wrong side of 10 p.m.', the performance schedule had to be two days on, four days off, in order to comply with child labour laws. So it would look like this

Monday	Geese
Tuesday	Geese
Wednesday	Kettles
Thursday	Kettles
Friday	Mittens
Saturday	Mittens
Monday	Mittens
Tuesday	Mittens

Wednesday	Geese
Thursday	Geese
Friday	Kettles
Saturday	Kettles etc.

The Gretls, because four of them were being divided into three teams, would be dancing to a different beat, one that was yet to be decided. Jo was planning to do a draft schedule for everyone else, which would exclude the first couple of weeks, because it would be a while before the creative team decided which team – and which Gretl – would be performing on press night. This meant that everyone apart from those with Gretls in the show would soon be able to book tickets, at least for their children's later performances, but we wouldn't.

And finally:

We have been asked by the Jerwood Space to ask you all not to take the children into the Glasshouse while you are waiting for the chaperones if you arrive early. If you would all wait just inside the main entrance doors that would be great. Also on Saturday the building itself does not open until 10 a.m. so if you arrive early please don't think that you have got it wrong and that the rehearsal has been cancelled.

Later on the Friday, another email arrived from Jo, this one asking us to provide our kids with a small tape recorder so that they could record the music. Great, I thought, after begging Laurie to let Dora use his old Sony handheld tape recorder. I'll be able to find out what's going on.

We were early on Saturday, Dora was desperate for the loo, and the Jerwood wasn't yet open. Fortunately, the pub across the road was, and the woman behind the bar let me sneak Dora in for a quick visit. Most of the parents headed home to enjoy a slightly quieter than usual day with the rest of their families. A couple stayed up to shop. As Laurie – being a children's party entertainer – works most weekends, I headed off, with my trusty laptop, to the Arlington. Much to my dismay, it was closed. Situated as it is in the midst of officeville, Café Arlington doesn't do Saturdays. I wandered up to the South Bank to find an alternative.

On Sunday, I sat down with Dora and listened to some of the rehearsal recordings. The singing parts were cute, and whilst they didn't actually make me feel like I was in a privileged fly-on-the-wall position, they did give me at least the sense of being an ear at the door. 'That's me!' said Dora, when it came to her part. 'That's Molly-May. That's Adrianna. That's Emily.' 'What I want to try and stress today,' I heard Ros, the children's music director, tell the von-Trapps-to-be during a run-through of 'Edelweiss', 'is that you don't have to sing loudly all of the time. It's all about emotion in this piece, isn't it?' There were parts that just sounded like a lot of muttering. From what I could tell, Frank, the children's director, was working out a scene with them: 'Let's walk and talk it through,' I heard him say. 'Molly-May, show me your curtsey. And you, Dora.'

'Were you supposed to record this?' I asked Dora. 'Don't know,' she said. 'But we weren't doing any singing.' She also seemed to have accidentally taped lunchtime, but at a distance, so all I could hear were muffled voices and doors slamming, followed by a discussion of Christmas, which seemed to be dominated by Dora shrieking about her visit to Santa Claus at Brent Cross Shopping Centre, and finding an orange in her stocking. I could hear Russ's voice, but not what he was saying, and then one of the boys announced that they'd just had surround-sound installed and it was 'wow'. I strained my ears to try and catch something revealing, but to no avail.

Over the next few weeks, we settled into an all-consuming, haphazard kind of routine. Dora would be rehearsing four out of five weekday afternoons and generally all day Saturday. We parents – okay, almost exclusively the mums – would sit there nattering.

Within a few days, we had bonded. We were routinely telling each other our deepest secrets, information that we either hadn't yet divulged to our partners or our best friends, or that we didn't intend to. 'I don't know why I just told you that. I haven't told anyone else,' was a common refrain. It was wonderful. We'd expected to be having an awful time, but here we were, looking forward to seeing each other and becoming completely absorbed in each other's lives and stories. We heard tragic tales and triumphant ones, listened to each other, dispensed, took and ignored advice and guidance and frequently laughed until we couldn't breathe. Several of us also found we had a weirdly visceral reaction to each other's children. Part of the reason they'd been picked for the show was that they looked like each other, like part of the same family. They all looked like part of our families. And the sight of the whole chattering mass of them pouring out of rehearsals provoked an unexpectedly primordial kind of recognition: a gut-level impact based, it seemed, entirely on appearance.

As these new bonds deepened, my grip on everything else – i.e. real life – started to slip. I had stumbled into a whole new world, and whilst I was as disoriented as Alice in Wonderland, I was also as full of wonder. And at least as busy. The trouble with this whole performing child thing is that it eats your life. Aside from the essentials, everything else had to be put on hold. It was actually a positive thing that my friends had stopped answering my phone calls because they were tired of me wittering on about *The Sound of Music*, as there was no room left in my brain for anything except managing the complex logistics of getting Dora to where she was supposed to be with a (nutritious) packed lunch and no nits, and almost keeping on top of the work I was being paid to do. I've no idea how I would have managed if I'd also had to deal with the guilt and consequences of neglecting other children. Dirty washing hung out of the laundry basket, and no matter how hard I tried to shove it all in, there was no way I could get the lid on. The clean washing piled up, creased and uncared-for, on the chaise longue that I'd bought off eBay, planned to work on and never have, until it fell off, gathered dust on the floor and needed to be washed again before it could be worn. Meanwhile, the new life-forms growing on forgotten leftovers in my fridge had evolved so far that they'd held democratic elections and invented a cure for Ecover, as I discovered on the occasion when I tried, much against my better judgement, to find and deal with whatever it was that was making it smell like that. Neglect had prompted a fit of creativity and our house had transformed itself into a Tracy Emin art installation.

I couldn't imagine Lauren's mum Nicky's fridge being anything like as rank. Or at all rank, in fact. It would be spotless, and full of fruit yoghurts, cherry tomatoes and other sensible salad stuff – lettuce, cucumber, spring onions, but nothing pretentious like frisee or radicchio. There would be a cold, neatly roasted chicken, with one breast carved off, covered in cling-film, a giant pack of thinly sliced ham and a four-litre bottle of semi-skimmed milk. Her freezer would be well stocked with pre-prepared meals, plus a couple of packs of fish fingers, a big bag of healthy oven chips and plenty of peas for emergencies. Washed clothes would be instantly ironed and either hung up in wardrobes or folded and stacked on shelves or in drawers that were full, but not to bursting. Nicky always looked perfectly turned out and was always on time – even though she had three other children to look after and get to the places where they were performing or rehearsing. Graham, her husband, also mucked in whilst simultaneously working as a plumber. On one occasion, after Nicky had described the intricacies of her timetable, which involved getting Kirsty (her oldest) to Southend, where she was filming, while Hayley (the other girl triplet) was making a commercial somewhere on the other side of London, Haydon (her son, the other triplet) had to be got to school, and Lauren needed to be at the Jerwood Space, I asked her how on earth she managed. 'Oh, I'm just permanently stressed,' she told me. In awe, I told her I thought she could segue straight from this to heading the UN, or single-handedly protecting Gotham City, diplomatically, humbly, with sense of humour intact whilst modelling a perfectly pressed cape sparkling with sequins she'd sewn on herself. 'No way!' she laughed. 'I don't sew. And if you want to know what I'm really like, you should ask the kids. They'll tell you how Mummy's always shouting!'

I've just realised that I might have given a false impression here, attributing the state of my house to Dora's involvement in *The Sound of Music*. Whilst it's true that it was worse than usual, I have to admit that my house is always a bit disgusting. In fact, it may have been a mistake having the floors stripped. The old boards do look nice all stained and varnished, but carpet – even carpet with yucky brown swirly patterns on it – absorbs dust much more effectively. These days, it just gathers in corners on the stairs, until it's reached a critical mass, at which point it bowls down into the hall like tumbleweed.

Then there are all the things that I haven't got round to putting away, because I can't decide where to put them. In all other aspects of my life I'm a ferociously decisive person, subscribing to the point of view that in most situations it doesn't really matter which option you choose, so long as you choose one and follow through. Time management is no problem, the files on my computer are all carefully organised, my work backed up. My diary is accurately planned and I never forget an appointment. But I have a problem with objects. The problem is that they don't have minds of their own. This is very inconvenient, as it means that I have to make all their decisions for them, and that just doesn't come naturally.

In my defence, about once every six months I do have a flash of inspiration and it suddenly becomes clear how to solve a particular storage problem, at which point I visit IKEA, morph into the Flat Pack Queen and it gets sorted in a flurry of manic activity and everything looks much better. Then my back starts hurting, I have to lie down for a month and by the time I've recuperated everything doesn't look much better any more.

Every night, just before I went to bed, along with all the other *Sound of Music* parents, I'd check my email, just in case something important had come through from Jo Hawes, breathlessly hoping that she'd write. Most nights she did, even if it was just to confirm or amend the following day's 'call'. On the nights where there was no email, I'd find myself feeling anxious, neglected and out of the loop. It would be difficult to get to sleep. I'd keep my laptop by the bed, and if I did doze off, would wake at varied intervals in the night and check that she hadn't sent something after midnight. Had other people been receiving emails when I hadn't? Was there something going on that I didn't know about? It was like having a love affair; that on-tenterhooks feeling of waiting for a communication from someone you feel you can't contact first, unless you have a very good reason or a plausible excuse.

On a very wet 1 October, Jo emailed round to say they were making a change to the teams. The Martas from Mittens and Kettles were swapping round, but for some reason not for another week. Cue four crying girls – two Martas and two Gretls who had all bonded passionately and were gutted to be parted in what felt to them a rather arbitrary way. I comforted Dora by pointing out that she would still get to see Molly-May because one of the brilliant things about being a Gretl was that she would get to work with all three teams. I promised to arrange a sleepover with Molly-May and reminded Dora that she liked Yasmin a lot too.

Two days later, another email announced an outbreak of nits in the group, together with Jo Hawes's suggested treatments (she recommends either a combination of tea tree oil conditioner and white vinegar – you leave the latter on overnight, and repeat several days on the trot – or Hedrin). I checked Dora, who, I was relieved to discover, had escaped infestation. I knew that at some point it was inevitable: most of her friends had already had them, and I was dreading the hours I'd be forced to spend sitting on the toilet seat in our tiny bathroom, combing them out of her long, excessively thick, conditioner-soaked hair, while she whinged bitterly and yelled 'ow' every time I hit a tangle and sometimes, just for effect, when I hadn't.

The next day another email arrived.

Just to let you know that there will be a photocall on Tuesday at the Palladium for all the children with Connie. The arrangements are TBC but I think they will need to arrive at the Palladium at 9.30 and when they are finished they will be minibussed with the chaperones back to Jerwood to rehearse in the afternooon. You will be able to collect them from Jerwood time TBC. Apparently they will be given *SOM* t-shirts to wear.
More news as I have it.

That was exciting. But also worrying. The previous day I'd been at a meeting with one of the organisations I work with, the Reading Agency, who coordinate inspirational and enjoyable reading pro-motions in libraries. We'd been looking at the company's child protection policy. I'm slightly cynical about child protection policies, many of which seem designed to protect the adults looking after children from allegations of abuse, rather than actually protecting children from abuse and neglect. I've seen policies and procedures followed in a way that proved extremely distressing to a young child and watched someone's life turned upside down when a cocked-up CRB check credited them with an offence they had not committed – one which was so out-of-character that it would have been laughable had the consequences been less devastating (they also mixed up the person's name and date of birth). Child protection policies can incul-cate an atmosphere of fear, in which children are encouraged to view all unrelated adults with suspicion, rather than learning to dis-criminate between those who are trustworthy and those who aren't: an inexact science, obviously, but a necessary part of all our emotional development. How, otherwise, can we bond properly with other people? And personally, I would prefer a trusted teacher, chaperone or other carer to apply sun cream to my small child than just leave her to burn in the sun, because the child protection policy prohibits touching the children being cared for. I would also like someone she turns to for comfort to cuddle her if she's distressed and I'm not there to do it.

That said, child protection policies are there for a purpose. And one aspect of the policy that the Reading Agency was working on caught my eye: the section on photography. The guidelines stated that even where parental permission had been given for the child to be photographed and for that photograph to be displayed, the Reading Agency wouldn't use the child's name with the photograph, or provide any information about the child's whereabouts. We'd discussed this point at some length: one of the organisation's managers had had a strange man turning up on their doorstep offering, bizarrely, to cut their child's hair after a photo of the child had appeared in a local paper, with their name as the caption. It is standard stuff in child protection. You don't let people who might want to do something horrid to a child know where that child can be found – even though the majority of people who do horrid things to children know where they are, because they are either related to the child or close to their family.

Anyway, here I was, doing one hundred per cent the wrong thing child protection-wise with my daughter. The short biog I'd sent in with Dora's photo for *The Sound of Music* gave details of the area we live in and the schools – primary and dance – she attends. I couldn't think of anything else to write. Putting her on the stage at all goes against the first principle of child protection: guarding a child's anonymity. But how big a risk was it really? After all, several of the other children had been doing this for years with no obvious ill-effects.

I spoke to Mark Williams-Thomas, one of the country's leading child protection consultants and a former police detective specialising in major crime. He feels there is some risk, in that theatres are places where people who want to abuse children can gain access to them (it's more of an issue with amateur productions, where companies tend to use volunteer chaperones rather than professional ones). But whilst he is very keen on limiting potential abusers' access to children, he does not believe that you should try and eliminate risk from their lives. 'The simplest way to protect children is to ensure that they are educated about being able to protect themselves. In other words, make them aware that there are some horrible people out there. Make sure they understand that if they feel uncomfortable about something, then the chances are it's probably wrong. So talk to somebody about it. Make sure that there is communication on a two-way basis. But give children privacy, give them respect, help them to grow up in an environment that enables them to be safe, but at the same time allows them to take a certain amount of risk.'

The next few days' emails were mostly concerned with rehearsal and costume fitting schedules, with the odd googly bowled in. As she didn't possess any I found myself dashing round all the children's clothes shops in Brent Cross trying to find a pair of black trousers for Dora to wear with her *SOM* t-shirt at the photo shoot. They were, obviously, out of fashion (in other words, nothing suitable in H&M), and something in me baulked at paying over a tenner for a polyester school-uniform pair that didn't look remotely Dora-shaped and that she'd never wear again. After about an hour of fruitless searching, I fetched up at Zara, where a rummage turned up a pair of plain black cotton leggings with a little lace trim. Perfect! 'Couldn't she just wear jazz-dance trousers?' asked one of the other mums the next day. Well, she could've, if she did jazz dance and had any.

In the same email that provided the details of the photocall at the Palladium came the following ADVANCE WARNING.

The kids are working very hard and everyone is very pleased

with how it is going. Could I ask you please to make sure they get plenty of rest when they can. Half-term week is the first week of technicals and it is going to be intensive and the most difficult of all the rehearsal period. It is especially important that they sleep well that week and if they do have a day off (which they must) please don't rush off on a busy activity day. They really will get tired especially the little ones with a lot of evening calls.

Dora didn't seem that tired yet. She appeared – the Marta swap aside – to be taking it all in her stride. Her first sleepover with Molly-May – great excitement! – took place at Molly-May's father's house while he was away, and Molly's mum Helen was down from Yorkshire looking after her. When I went to collect Dora, the two girls announced that they were going to put on a show, and promptly performed a Reduced Shakespeare Company version of *The Sound of Music*, playing all the roles themselves. Where they'd been unable to decide which of them should play a particular part, one of them mimed while the other sang or spoke. They performed studiously, sang and spoke perfectly and only occasionally dissolved into girlie giggles. Meanwhile, Helen and I were hysterical and lamented the lack of a video camera that we would, undoubtedly, have been laughing too hard to operate.

There was more great excitement for Dora. A couple of weeks into rehearsals she was handed her first payslip and cheque. The payslip was more exciting than the cheque, because it had three perforated edges which needed tearing off in order to open it, and also because it told her not only how much money she'd earned that week, but how much she'd earned so far. 'Is that enough for a bike with gears?' she asked, jumping up and down. I assured her that it was, but suggested that we didn't go out and buy one until spring as she wouldn't have much opportunity to ride it before then. A few weeks earlier, we'd emptied her piggy bank and lugged the contents – five notes and a ton of small coins – to our local bank to open a savings account. To my annoyance, she could only have the kind of account that required me to queue up and hand the money in over the counter.

Every day I'd drop her off at the Jerwood reasonably neatly dressed with either almost equal bunchies or, if time was short, an acceptably tidy ponytail. Every day I'd pick her up, and although her clothes would still be more or less in the same order, her hair wouldn't: she'd emerge looking more like a disarmed Edward Scissorhands than a Gretl von Trapp. And she'd be bursting with tangential and incomplete information, setting half a scene for me, or bubbling out stories shiny with the kind of gloss that only six-year-olds can broadbrush across their world. She told me all about the Big Boys in her team – Jack Montgomery, nearly fifteen, the oldest member of the children's cast, who was playing Kurt, and John McCrea, just about to turn fourteen, who was playing Kurt's older brother Friedrich. John's mum Jane had taken him, aged eight, to the local drama club after the teachers at his school had called her in and begged her to find something to channel his energy: 'He was really naughty. Never anything malicious or vindictive, but just naughty. Used to moon at his teachers. Things like that.'

'I have to protect Jack,' Dora informed me. 'John's always fighting with him and I have to look after him.'

'Do you think they're pretending?' I asked, picturing Dora standing in front of Jack, chin stuck out, eyes blazing, one hand on her hip while she waggled her finger at John, more than twice her age and over a foot taller than her, and shouted at him to stop it at once.

'No,' she replied, rolling her eyes and tutting at both the naughty boys and her dense mother. 'They really mean it. They're really fighting! And no one else does anything about it, not even the chaperones, so I *have* to.'

The Big Boys were one of the wonderful things about the whole *Sound of Music* experience. Here were two of them, thirteen and fourteen years old at the time, playing happily, gently and generously with a six-year-old girl. And their attitude persisted throughout the run of the show and even beyond. This was not at all what I expected. Perhaps I was being horribly prejudiced, but I would have expected boys of that age to ignore her completely, while discussing the minutiae of football matches, violent video games and the best of YouTube. Months later, the mothers of several other teenage boys confirmed my suspicion that I was horribly prejudiced. Contrary to the negative press they regularly receive, most teenage boys are, most of the time, lovely, caring creatures.

Some time after Dora had left the show, at the end of the summer holidays, I watched – along with Grace's mum Lynn and John's mum Jane – as John, Grace and Dora played on the trampoline at Lynn's house, cycled together, along with Grace's younger brother Joe, to the local park and later performed a selection of hilarious and beautifully executed musical numbers. When it was time for Dora and John to be taken home, the three of them parked themselves on the floor, announced that they were holding a 'sit-down' and sang 'We Shall Not Be Moved' in perfect three-part harmony. That's the thing about the youth of today. They might not know what a sit-in is called, but when they do one, they do it very tunefully.

The Big Boys looked out for Dora and for all the little ones. They involved them in their games and even cuddled them, in what I considered a most unteenage-boy kind of way. It was a real eye-opener and made me think that every child should have the chance to be in something like *The Sound of Music*.

In fact the relationships amongst all the children seemed to be remarkably good. There was the odd grumble, the occasional falling-out, but considerably fewer and much more minor problems than you'd encounter in the average playground. It's not always like that: in productions involving large groups of girls all of similar ages it can, apparently, get quite bitchy. But as Jo Hawes had told me when Dora was first cast, the kids usually have a wonderful time, often making friendships that last a lifetime. And by all accounts, and to all appearances, the children were bonding beautifully. The gorgeous harmonies that I heard on the practice tapes that Dora brought home from the rehearsals seemed to be reflected in their relationships with each other. The people who'd picked the children had chosen well: here were nineteen kids who seemed to be natural team workers and full of fun. As a number of them attend the Sylvia Young Theatre School, it occurred to me that, rather than being the kind of places that produce poorly educated young people with monstrous egos and superb tap-dancing skills, stage schools might, in fact, be a very good thing indeed. I had to sit down for a minute.

After I could stand up again, I talked to Sylvia Young about the image people have of stage schools and confessed my own prejudices. 'The idea of eyes and teeth and all that came about because all the original stage schools developed from dance schools,' she explains. 'The dance world is different, it's quite competitive, with the festivals. And they focus on making you look traditionally pretty for the stage.'

It's not like that at Sylvia's. 'I never had a dance lesson. I came from a drama background, and for me, acting is the number one. I was the first person to call it a theatre school. Theatre, as opposed to stage. Before me, Anna Scher called hers the Anna Scher Theatre. Wasn't school, or classes – she was part time – but I liked that idea. Theatre.' Sylvia enunciates the word very clearly. 'I liked that. Theatre school.'

She asks senior teacher Maggie Melville-Bray to call in a couple of nearby children. One of them is Caroline Riley – the Brigitta in Kettles – who started at the school after she finished in *The Sound of Music*.

'What is it that I tell you you must never be?' asks Sylvia.

'Stage school brat,' Caroline shoots back, without having to think about it. Then she says hello, gives me a hug, asks how Dora is and tells me to send her love.

'They learn communication skills,' Sylvia tells me. 'The ability to understand what work is, discipline, being able to work with adults. They're at ease, and I think that's really important. They're confident, but not overconfident. They have the ability to converse.'

Sam Keston, head of drama at Redroofs Theatre School (also an agent and Molly-May's auntie), agrees. She thinks theatre schools are good for lots of children.

'Those who are clearly lovers of all things creative,' she said. 'The kids who love to dance, to perform. Also life's eccentrics who don't really fit in with what the state system offers, aren't good in groups of thirty. Children who are particularly bright who need the challenge of a dual curriculum, and can also cope with the added pressure of castings and performance schedules. Children who have low self-esteem can be turned around. Theatre schools love individuality.'

Both agree that they're not for everyone. 'Academia versus shuffle-hop-step,' says Sam. But there's a lot to be said for a small school bursting with highly motivated children working hard at all their lessons – even if their academic curriculum is somewhat circumscribed. 'Basically,' Sylvia tells me, 'they're here because they have an aim: it's theatre and it's performance.' Maggie nods and adds 'This kind of environment is geared to what they want and can deliver. So they work hard.'

Okay. I'm converted. Theatre schools are a good thing. I ask Sylvia, Maggie and Sam what they think the state school system could learn from the Sylvia Young Theatre School and Redroofs. Not a great deal, is the answer. 'State schools can't cater for specifics in the same way,' Sylvia explains. 'It's hard unless you can offer the children what they want, and when you've got the wide diversity of interests you get in a big state school, I can't see how you can.'

I'm not so sure.

HIGH ON A HILL

A large part of *The Sound of Music* magic was probably down to the work itself. Along with its terrific, memorable songs and worthwhile based-on-the-truth story, it has – as a couple of my most sensitive and aware friends pointed out – an extraordinary air of innocence about it. It is a musical in which you can happily leave your six-year-old daughter without worrying that she might learn about things it would be better for her not to learn about until she's a few years older: a play from which she might learn something about human-kind and her place in it. It is wholesome without being preachy, gentle and layered with meaning. It is about standing up for the truth, for what you believe in, and not cooperating with evil. It's a love story that isn't just about the attraction between a man and a woman, but about a whole family. It tackles serious moral and spiritual dilemmas in a genuinely heart- and mind-opening way. As director Jeremy Sams once pointed out, it is about the healing power of music. It is, in fact, as pure as the air in the Austrian Alps, and nigh on fifty years after its first Broadway production, still feels as fresh as the water cascading down an Alpine waterfall. So it's no more surprising that being involved with something like this seemed to bring out the best in so many people than it is to find that sitting with your feet dangling in a mountain stream and your face turned towards the warm summer sun makes you feel good.

Dora and I arrived at the Jerwood Space one afternoon, and as she was peckish, we popped into the café area to buy her a snack. Arlene Phillips, the choreographer, was sitting at a table. She called Dora over, hugged her and, grabbing her loose ponytail, redid her hair so that it wouldn't disintegrate. 'Please can you do it like this?' she asked me. I nodded, embarrassed, and uncertain whether I would actually be able to do it like that. 'Otherwise she fidgets with it while we're rehearsing. She's one of my little fidgets,' she added affectionately, which came as no surprise to me whatsoever.

Just before we picked the kids up that evening, I confided my lack of hairdressing nous and confidence – especially where partings were concerned – to Helen, Molly-May's mum. We were in the pub across the road from the Jerwood, where we often congregated and where, the barmaid informed one of the mums, many of the cast and creative team came after the rehearsals. Especially the nuns, who would, she reported, get drunk and sing. Not only did Helen always look fab, but so did Molly-May, who, when Mum was in charge, invariably turned out in perfectly matched French plaits which hung one each side of an immaculately straight parting and, in a final flourish – which had even been noticed by the show's director, who'd asked Helen how she did it, as he was considering having all the Martas' hair like that – did so in elegant Austrian-style loops, secured with neatly tied ribbon. In fact, even when Dad was in charge, Molly-May's hair was always neater than Dora's.

'It's easy,' said Helen, who'd learned to do her own hair when she was a child performer and was now on her third daughter and so had had lots of practice. 'Use a comb.'

A comb? I went out and invested in one. It made a massive difference, as did the fact that I was, after my gentle rap on the knuckles from Arlene, trying harder. Dora's partings still weren't perfect – I'm always stumped by anything involving straight lines – but they were adequate, and my plaiting and bunchying improved dramatically in terms of both equality and neatness. French plaits, however, remain to this day completely beyond me, and Dora is resolutely unimpressed by my hairdressing skills.

On Tuesday, 10 October, Dora and I left the house bright and early. Her hair was plaited and I was proud. She was wearing her new black leggings, which were only slightly too long, with a bright orange embroidered top: a gift from my dad's friend Elfi. She was looking forward to getting her *Sound of Music* t-shirt. We walked to Willesden Junction station – I carried Dora's backpack and lunch – caught the train, read *Harry Potter* all the way to Oxford Circus, bounced out of one of the Argyll Street exits and walked down to the Palladium.

A broad and low black stage had been erected outside the front steps, and an enormous *Sound of Music* sign, featuring the mountain-top and an ecstatically arms-raised back view of Maria, dominated the entrance almost as much as the herd of press photographers, cameras poised and ready, did. We skirted photographers and stage to head up the steps at the side and enter the foyer. It was buzzing with children, parents and activity. Company manager Nick Bromley was rushing round trying to find the t-shirts. Dora dashed off to meet Molly-May and I hung around, watching. Then the big bundle of t-shirts arrived, and all the kids formed a massive, giggling huddle around Nick, scrambling to get theirs. The t-shirts were plain white cotton, with the *Sound of Music* logo emblazoned across the chest. Dora's was age 5–6 and I worried for a few seconds that it might not be big enough. Connie arrived, trailed by her BBC camera crew, and Dora and Molly-May bounded over to say hello and show her their t-shirts. She was lovely with them. 'Do you ever talk to Connie?' I'd asked Dora after one rehearsal, curious to know whether the friendly, open demeanour she'd displayed on *How Do You Solve a Problem Like Maria?* transferred into real life or was just good acting. 'Lots,' she said. 'She's nice.'

'What do you talk about?' I probed, keen to get some insight.

Dora shrugged. I gave up.

I managed to pluck up the courage to approach Nick Bromley to ask if it was okay to watch the photocall. 'Of course,' he replied, beaming broadly. So as soon as Russ and Rebecca had taken our kids off to get ready, a few of us shuffled outside and took up positions across the street. We waited. And waited. We chatted to each other. Then we got bored and wandered up the road to Costa Coffee and queued for drinks, at which point the mum who'd been deputised to keep watch dashed in and told us that the kids were marching down the stairs and out on to the stage. We paid for our coffees and hot chocolates, promising to pick them up as soon as it was all over, and dashed out again, realising as we did that it hadn't occurred to a single one of us pushy stage mums that it might be a good idea to actually bring a camera. Fortunately, Mike Riley – Caroline's dad – was both sensible enough to come equipped and assertive enough to get himself into a position where he could take photos, which he later emailed out to the rest of us.

Later that day a big photo appeared in the *Evening Standard* over a small article mostly about Connie, but also about why there were so many von Trapp children. There were snippets on the lunchtime news programmes, which didn't only feature Connie, but also showed the kids, a few of whom did little interviews. The next day, there was half a page in the *Telegraph*. And lots of other papers and online media outlets ran stories and photos. Dora beamed proudly out of them, holding leading man Simon Shepherd's hand. Molly-May sat next to Connie. A week or so later, most of us mums were doubled up with laughter after someone noticed a picture of our children – with poorly corrected red-eye – featured in *Hello!* magazine. In some publications the children were name-checked, in others they were just grinning von Trapps. It was all good, high-profile fun.

When I collected Dora from the rehearsal that afternoon, she was full of excitement about the photo shoot, the most thrilling aspect of it being the free bar, where she had been allowed *as much lemonade as she wanted*. I heard her out and agreed that it was all fantastic, before saying, 'You do realise, don't you, that in a few months this will all stop, and things will be back to normal?'

'Oh no,' she replied, instantly. 'I need to keep my life going like this.'

I was slightly taken aback by her conviction. 'I think not,' I said. 'I'll need a holiday.'

Dora was equally clear about her needs: 'I won't.'

That night I headed off to York to run a training course for librarians, leaving Laurie and Dora at home. Dora had a day off rehearsals while I was away, and on the Friday we had a photocall with the Mittens team, as I'd written a newspaper article about accidentally becoming a stage mother, and they wanted some photos of me failing to get into rehearsals. This translated into the photographer standing me on a box, and making me pull faces through an outside window, holding my breath so as not to mist it up, while the kids inside performed 'So Long, Farewell' dressed in their black trousers and *Sound of Music* t-shirts. Then they came and did it again outside – so I got a privileged preview of one of the routines, which made the whole mortifying process almost worthwhile. In the end, the paper used an innocuous picture of me brushing Dora's hair together with one they took of the kids in full costume a couple of weeks later.

During my journey back from York, I had picked up an email from Jo Hawes. It was headed '23 October Week' and was all about the first week of technical rehearsals. The children would have to be at the Palladium Tuesday to Saturday 1.30 p.m. to 10 p.m. Please, Jo asked, could we all take advantage of the fact that they were on half-term to make sure they got plenty of rest. We were to ensure they were well fed before turning up, and told that they would be taken out for a meal in the evening.

From previous experience, at some point next week at least one parent will telephone me to complain loudly that their child was called all day and spent the entire time in the auditorium! I can tell you right now that there will be times when your children will not appear to be doing much, but we have a very short time to tech the show and we have to tech in all three sets of children and four Gretls. We must have the children available and it is wearing and tiring for everybody. I have sat in the Palladium in the past watching it take two days to tech the first 10 minutes of a show. It is a process that has to be endured and it is at times frustrating but also the most amazing and exciting part of the procedure! Please stick with us and know that we are all doing our very best! The tech week will be the most difficult week of all for everyone with sudden changes of schedule and I promise it will drive you to distraction. Look past it to the time when the show is in previews and settling down – not long now!

Thanks for everything up to now – it has been lovely so far and all the kids are fabulous!

I am hoping to get a schedule for next week tomorrow.

And then, in red, the details

Week commencing October 23

13.30	Company into costume/wigs/mics (except Tuesday when children should come at 1 p.m. please)
14.00	Company on stage
17.45	Company out of costumes, etc.
18.00	Company break
19.00	Company back into costume/wigs/mics
19.30	Company on stage
21.45	Company out of mics
22.00	Company break

I emailed back

Thanks Jo.

Aaarrggh.

Any tips for extra stuff I should send in with Dora that week –
e.g. books, comics, colouring accoutrements, espresso?

On the up side, I was hoping that this might initiate Dora into the joy of lie-ins. These hadn't been a feature of her life to date. In fact, on the one occasion before then that she'd slept beyond 8.15 a.m., I'd found myself checking that she was still breathing . . .

While Dora and two of the other Gretls were each attached to one team throughout the whole rehearsal period, Adrianna's schedule was now changing weekly. She'd done the first couple of weeks with Geese and Alicia, the next one with Kettles and Lauren and was now about to join Mittens and Dora for the next week. Dora was pleased. As far as she was concerned, the more the merrier. Shana, however, was a bit worried. Did it mean, she wondered, that Adrianna was the spare Gretl? Number four of four? I thought it unlikely. It was more probable, I felt, that they were making sure that she could work with all the teams and preparing her to do the opening night. It made sense. She was the oldest of the four Gretls, with the most experience of live theatre, and I was certain – especially as she skipped out of rehearsals looking as gorgeously pristine as when she arrived – she was the least fidgety and, consequently, the most likely to be where she was supposed to be when she was supposed to be there.

With one more week to go at the Jerwood Space, I was starting to wonder where I'd set up my temporary office near the Palladium. I would, I knew, miss Café Arlington, where I was happily ensconced for much of the time that Dora was rehearsing, even though I knew there would be much more to do around Oxford Circus and many more opportunities to spend money. And then I started wondering *whether* I would be setting up a temporary office near the Palladium. I'd be taking Dora in on the Bakerloo line, but couldn't imagine doing the return journey with an overtired, over-excited six-year-old after ten o'clock at night. I would, I realised, be dropping her off, hopping back on the tube, and driving back into town again to pick her up. Oh well, once performances started, it would only be twice a week at most, and then only for a few months. It didn't seem like too onerous a commitment if I thought about it quickly. And I was sure that Laurie, my dad and my Auntie Ruth would help out from time to time.

The final week of rehearsals at the Jerwood opened, with me and Dora dashing in after school so that she could have a costume fitting, as they had been arranged on the one day that week that she and Mittens weren't rehearsing. It didn't take long and we headed back home in time for dinner and an early night. The rest of the week went past in a blur of packed lunches. On the Tuesday, Jo emailed round to ask if we would be willing to let our children stay on for an extra month, so instead of finishing at the end of February or beginning of March, they would finish at the end of March or beginning of April. I checked with Laurie – as this would only bring Dora up to the beginning of the Easter holidays, there was no problem: even he wasn't planning a break before then. Everyone emailed back to say yes. So we had to fill out more forms, and get another letter from Dora's school, and one from her doctor.

On 18 October, Jo emailed with details of which teams would be performing when from Monday, 20 November. So, with the exception of the preview period and the first few nights, parents could now start booking tickets. Unless, that was, like me, they were the parents of a Gretl. The show would open officially on Wednesday, 15 November, with previews starting on Friday 3rd. As yet, the creative team hadn't decided what to do with the Gretls: 'Because of their age/their various strengths and weaknesses, etc. etc. minds keep changing!' So we still didn't know whether they'd each do one show in every four, or whether they'd follow a different pattern, let alone which among them would be performing on opening night. And frankly, despite Russ's contention that 'that's when the true colours come out' – in other words, that was when we parents would all stop being best buddies and morph into bitchingly jealous rivals – none of us were particularly bothered about that. Whilst we all felt that in some ways it would be nice for our kids (and us) to bathe in the glory of attention, there were caveats. What if the show bombed? If the press hated it? After all, *The Sound of Music* has, in the past, garnered some terrible reviews. Or what if it was all fabulous – with the exception of my child, who said, sang or danced the wrong thing in the wrong place at the wrong time in front of all those watching critics and celebrities, then burst into tears and developed sudden, unprecedented stage fright at the worst possible moment?

And to be honest, who got to do press night paled into insignificance in the face of our concern that we might not be able to watch them whichever night they started on. I wondered whether the four Gretls' families should get together and each book two tickets for one of four consecutive performances. But this wouldn't work for Jackie and Scott, who had two daughters in the show who might – or might not – be performing on the same night, and who would want to take Olivia to watch Alicia if they weren't. So in the end, we just had to wait.

There was, that week, an extra buzz of excitement. The proofs of the children's entries in the programme had arrived. I checked ours to ensure that the meagre details were correct. They were. Dora's entry read:

Dora Gee
Gretl
Dora is six and lives in Harlesden, north-west London. She attends Leopold Primary School and learns ballet at Adele's School of Dance.
This is Dora's first acting job.

To the left of the text was a photo that my father had taken of Dora in his garden. She was wearing an enormous gappy grin, and an even bigger silk flower in her hair, and appeared against a leafy background. Everyone else's photos were devoid of both hair decorations and foliage. It looked as though they had all had professional portfolio pictures taken – although I later found out that Jackie had simply whisked Olivia and Alicia off to the local passport photo studio.

Dora was off school from that Wednesday – half-term was extra long as the staff were doing their training days then. This gave her the opportunity for slightly more rest than she would otherwise have had, although, being her, she didn't really take advantage of it. She had been to stay with Molly-May a week earlier and had a fabulous time, so I organised a return visit for the Saturday after the final rehearsal at the Jerwood. Molly would go home on the Sunday, and I'd make sure Dora had a quiet day on Monday before starting at the Palladium on Tuesday. I picked them both up from the last rehearsal that afternoon. They sang on the train all the way home, rehearsing numbers from the show. 'They're really good,' said a man sitting near me. 'They could really do something when they're a bit older.' My inner stage mother took over. Instead of just smiling and saying 'thank you' quietly, I told him exactly what they were doing right now.

There is, I'm sure, a knack to knowing when it's okay to talk about what your child is doing, when they're appearing in a major West End show, and who it's okay to tell, but I never managed to get the hang of it. I knew that it shouldn't be the first thing she or I told everyone we met, but there were some friends I never got round to telling, who wished I had told them, and several strangers whom I told inappropriately. On the other hand, talking about what Dora was up to led to other people telling me about their – sometimes surprising – showbiz connections. After I'd been describing the extent of the child-ferrying involved, one colleague said, 'Yes, but imagine doing all that for a dog.' Turned out her friend's pet was playing Snowy in *Tintin*. Meanwhile, Boyd Tonkin, the super-erudite literary editor of *The Independent*, told me about the years of Sunday afternoons – 'for some reason I always associate those rehearsals with winter twilight. I don't know why . . .' – he spent singing with the Finchley Children's Music Group. 'It was, and is, one of the leading secular, as opposed to church-based, children's choirs in London. There are a couple of others, but in north London, the Finchley Massif is the one that rules.' He was taken there by his parents when he was six or seven. 'At that age you don't really take decisions for yourself. My parents decided that I would go along to do an audition. To join, I just had to not make a sound horrible enough to spoil the entire effect.'

Whilst a member of the choir – which he was until his voice broke – Boyd sang at the Royal Albert Hall in what is regarded as the seminal performance of Mahler's 8th Symphony, conducted by Leonard Bernstein, and on records made at Abbey Road studios. Although the Sunday afternoon rehearsals could feel penitential, the big events were thrilling. 'Those hours of boredom purchased the ability to do the exciting things. We were aware, from a very early stage, that this was leading up to the buzz of performance. And that was exciting. Everyone around you is hyped up, and it's contagious'

Boyd feels that he gained a sense of discipline – 'it was a very well-run choir, they were pretty good at making sure that everyone knew that everyone had a role to play, that everyone was important. And therefore, you couldn't chat at the back. Of course, if you tried chatting at the back at the EMI Abbey Road studios, the ferocious studio engineers would descend on you.' He also believes it gave him an early grasp of the concrete relationship between effort and reward.

'Most of the time when you're a kid and adults say do this very boring thing for a long time then something great will happen, it's all to do with passing exams. And unless you have parents who give you enormous presents when you pass exams, even doing well is slightly abstract. It's very easy to feel "what was all that about?" But when you go on stage and there is the instant feedback of audience appreciation, you do sense that there is a point to this long period of sustained effort.'

Something else I never got a proper handle on was how to manage an extremely tired and tetchy six-year-old. Dora is not, and has never been, a difficult child. Like any other small person, she has her moments – sometimes at impressive volume – but because she's bright, communicative and straightforward, dealing with them is, usually, comparatively simple.

During this intensive rehearsal period she was claiming more of my attention than usual. This, in a way, seemed fair. Not only had she been doing a paid job at an age when most children don't even get pocket money, she'd also, as per legal requirements, been going to school whenever she wasn't rehearsing, as well as doing extra homework to ensure that she didn't fall behind and, when she could, attending her two dance lessons and keeping up with friends and family. She was managing to keep up with all her work, but in her down time she was knackered. I had to tread carefully, trying to ensure she was okay to do her job, but also avoiding becoming over-solicitous and over-attentive. It was hard, but the only thing worse than being told what to do by a small child is, as I discovered, finding yourself doing it. Again.

Tuesday, 22 October. The first technical rehearsal. We stuffed Dora's backpack with colouring things, a book to read and a pad to draw on. As usual, I read Harry Potter to her on the train – we were now on to . . . *and the Chamber of Secrets*. When we arrived at Oxford Circus, we took the first of many walks down Argyll Street, past the front of the theatre – which now, as well as the massive *Sound of Music* sign, was also displaying larger-than-lifesize photos of Connie Fisher, Simon Shepherd and Lesley Garrett – turned left past Café Uno on to Marlborough Street, where, between the newsstand and Café Libre, we found the Palladium stage door. The gates were open, revealing a couple of gigantic wheelie bins, some steps and a slope down to the stage door itself. Kids and parents were milling around, chatting excitedly. Dora clung to my hand, temporarily shy and uncertain. I looked around and thought about how I'd be spending a lot of time standing here over the next few months. It wasn't so bad at that point, just before one o'clock on an October afternoon, but I could imagine that the wheelie bins would provide meagre shelter on a wet and freezing winter's night.

As I was a 'new mum', Wendy, whose daughter Christine had previously worked there in *Chitty Chitty Bang Bang*, and was now the Louisa in Mittens, had helpfully emailed me a warning of exactly how not-nice the experience could be:

> The Palladium drop-offs and pick-ups are even less parent-friendly than the Jerwood. We have to stand outside the stage door (by the lovely wheelie bins) and not set foot inside. There is an outside loo, which is usually okay for an emergency! If you're collecting Dora by car, beware the wardens, who magically appear at the end of the show and do slap a ticket on any car parked on yellow or zigzag lines.

Meanwhile, as many of us parents who could manage to – in other words, those of us without full-time jobs or lots of other children – arranged to get together on the Wednesday afternoon for a treat. We all felt that we'd been working hard to support our kids and deserved a bit of fun. We hadn't booked anything in advance, because there was a good chance that the rehearsal times would, at the last minute, be changed and we'd have ended up forking out for tickets which we couldn't use as we suddenly had to pick our kids up halfway through the show we'd paid to watch. After much discussion – *Avenue Q*? No matinee on Wednesdays. *Mary Poppins*? No, those of us who hadn't yet seen it wanted to watch it with the kids – a herd of us, eight mums, plus Caroline Riley's teenage brother, sat in a long row to

watch *Cabaret*. It was darkly gripping, beautifully designed, choreo-
graphed and performed, shocking, sexy and included a lot more
nudity than *The Sound of Music*. I felt embarrassed for Caroline's
brother watching it from the middle of eight mothers.

Dora found the technical rehearsals actually rather fun. She was
especially excited about the 'Lonely Goatherd' routine, which
involved the Gretls being pushed on to the stage in a wheelbarrow:
this was particularly enjoyable when there were two Gretls being
rehearsed simultaneously. 'It was *so* funny mummy. Alicia was in
the wheelbarrow and Frank [Thompson, the children's director]
carried me in next to her. I think we should do it like that all the
time!' In fact, in Dora's opinion, the whole performance would be
massively improved if there were twin Gretls on stage throughout
the show – or, ideally, all four of them performing at once. She also
enjoyed bounding across the sofa during 'Do-Re-Mi': 'Sophie
[Bould – Liesl] and Connie were supposed to carry me, but that
was too hard, so Sophie puts me on one side of the sofa and Connie
picks me up and puts me down at the other end', and being given
a piggyback by Sophie when they're playing cowboys and Indians,
wearing play clothes made of curtains in the scene where their
father meets them for the first time on his return from Vienna with
the baroness.

But, being six, by ten o'clock at night she was over the top and
exhausted. So she quickly settled into the routine of coming out of
the Palladium, climbing into the car and babbling out her news
which was, in line with Emily Dickinson's famous dictum, generally
told slant. Because I was really curious to know, I would gently ask a
couple of questions, trying to tease out exactly what she was talking
about. This would exasperate her (why didn't I get it from her first
telling, which was, to her mind, completely clear?) and provoke a
brief but intense tantrum, at the conclusion of which she'd pass out.
When we arrived home I was usually able to find a parking place
pretty close to the house, but even so, I couldn't carry her from the

car to her bed, so I had to wake her up again. She often lost it and, frankly, who could blame her?

I was also pretty tired by this point, but usually managed to stay calm, and not do anything to up the ante. Even so, it was hard to get the right balance – and I can't claim that I always did – and to judge when and where to draw the line. It's easy to see why children who do this kind of thing can end up being over-indulged. Even though Dora was having the time of her life, I certainly felt there were moments when I needed to compensate for the pressure she was undoubtedly under: moments when I let behaviour that in other circumstances would have been completely unacceptable pass without comment, because she was so far past her sell-by date that there was no point trying to discipline her and I didn't really feel it was her fault anyway. There were, however, also moments when – like any child – she took full advantage of the extra latitude she was allowed.

Although the kids were now being taken out to restaurants to eat between sessions, we were asked to send them in on the Saturday of the technical rehearsals with a packed tea, as they still had so much to get through. As *The Sound of Music* was a period piece, Jo warned us, the boys would, one by one, be whisked off to the wigs department for a short back and sides. There was still a possibility that the girls who didn't have one might need to have a fringe cut in. If Dora had to have one, I'd have to grin and bear it, but I really hoped she wouldn't. I didn't fancy going through that annoying, hairclip-laden process of growing it out over the next year.

On the Saturday, Jo also reminded us that although it was all very exciting, the theatre was a place of work. She'd had a couple of complaints about the children's behaviour. Could we please, she asked, 'remind the older ones to set an example and the younger ones to do their best to listen'. And wished/instructed us to have 'a restful weekend'.

It wasn't only the children that hadn't been behaving. My

previously reliable iBook had, for the past couple of weeks, also been playing up: freezing in a way that the operating system was, according to the marketing blurb, supposed to prevent. So, sadly, because Laurie was out entertaining other children, Dora was forced to give up part of her restful Sunday and accompany me to Brent Cross Shopping Centre, where someone at the Apple Store, whose job title was 'genius', would use technical brilliance to stun me by fixing my computer within the twenty-minute time slot the Apple website had allotted me.

The sign in the window said, 'At 4 p.m. today, Julie Andrews Edwards will be signing copies of her new children's book *The Great American Mousical.*'

We had parked up with minutes to spare before my 1.30 appointment and I'd made Dora run out of the multistorey car park into the shopping centre and walk down the escalator to ensure that we'd arrive not on time, but a bit early. She had complained, with some justification. As we sped up to W.H. Smith, I noticed a couple of queue control barriers outside and a few people sitting by the shop window, waiting. Must be a celebrity book signing, I thought, skidding to a halt to investigate, even though I suspected either Jamie Oliver or Jordan, neither of whom were of the remotest interest.

But I was wrong.

I blinked. Julie Andrews? At Brent Cross Shopping Centre? This afternoon? Now, I'm not usually remotely interested in meeting famous people, and wouldn't go out of my way to do so. But there are exceptions – and right then, with Dora about to be in *The Sound of Music*, Julie Andrews was definitely one of them.

'Do you want to stay and say hello to Julie Andrews?'

'Who's Julieandrews?'

'Maria in *The Sound of Music* film, Mary Poppins in *Mary Poppins*. And in *The Princess Diaries*.'

'Where is she?'

'She'll be here. At four o'clock. We'll have to buy her book.'

'Can we do it now?'

'No. I have to get my computer fixed first. Besides which, I don't want to sit in a queue for over two hours just to get a book signed.'

'I want to.'

'Well, I have to get my computer fixed.'

'Awww.'

We reached the Apple Store and I hopped on to one of the high stools at the Genius Bar and told someone I was there. Dora struggled up on to the stool next to mine and watched while I got my computer out. A couple of minutes later, my name was called, and a Genius with a crew cut and a goatee beard took my computer and listened while I told him what was wrong. Then he pressed a couple of keys on my computer that I should have been able to press by myself and said, 'I think that should do it. If it doesn't, bring it in again. All I had to do was empty the ©©$f\partial ß$® and then clear the $\Sigma®f†·\sqrt{}ç≈\Omega f\partial$.'

'Thank you,' I said.

I'm usually fairly on the ball where computers are concerned, and if there hadn't been someone tugging at my sleeve asking whether it was time to go and see Julieandrews yet, and telling me she was bored and hungry, I might have been able to make sense of what the '©©$f\partial ß$®' and '$\Sigma®f†·\sqrt{}ç≈\Omega f\partial$' were so that I'd be able to empty and clear them myself in the future should the need ever arise. I was also rather hoping that it would take a bit longer to fix the laptop, so we wouldn't have as long to wait in the Julie Andrews signing queue: I don't enjoy window-shopping at the best of times, let alone with a bored six-year-old in tow asking repeatedly whether we could go and meet Julieandrews yet and demanding a good reason for my refusal to buy her a bag of chocolate-coated brazil nuts. Or almonds. Or raisins. She wasn't fussy.

So I stuffed my laptop into my backpack and we moseyed on back to W.H. Smith. Here, I bought two copies of *The Great American*

Mousical and, as Dora wanted to start queuing straight away, and I couldn't think of anything better to do, a cheap Barbie colouring book that came with four felt-tip pens, *The Observer*, a packet of crisps and two bottles of water. We took our places in the queue, after I'd read a notice that informed us that we could only have one book per person signed and that Ms Andrews Edwards wouldn't do dedications, just sign her name. 'How many books do you have?' asked the man from Smith's who was patrolling the queue, before giving us two pink raffle tickets: Ms Andrews Edwards was only going to sign 200 books, so we all had to be numbered.

'Can we see her soon?'

'No. We have to wait for almost two hours. Why don't you colour in one of these pictures and give it to her? You could write her a letter too, if you like.' I wanted to read my newspaper.

Dora set to colouring in with a level of enthusiasm that would have been appropriate if she hadn't been planning to hand the result to Julie Andrews: i.e. not very much. Although entirely capable of doing so, she didn't bother to keep inside the lines, or pay much attention to whether the colours she was using were appropriate to the Barbie body-part she was applying them to. I couldn't entirely blame her. Maybe colouring in does enhance the development of hand–eye coordination, but it has always struck me as a singularly futile activity, one designed merely to absorb little girls' attention and stop them bothering their parents. Which would be okay if it actually worked, but it doesn't, because it's boring.

When Dora had finished her desultory colouring, she started writing a note to Julie Andrews on the picture. 'Hello Julie Andrews,' she scrawled, in thick black, largely illegible felt-tip. 'I'm going to be Gretil in *The Sownd of Myoosick* at the Paladyum. I hop you are well, love Dora.'

I've finished,' she announced, ripping the sheet carelessly out of the book and crumpling it slightly. 'Can we see her now?'

'Have some crisps,' I said. 'Do another picture.'

'How much longer do we have to wait?'

'Another hour and a half.'

'I'm bored. Can we go back to the shop and get something else to do?'

'No.'

I turned back to my newspaper. I was quite enjoying sitting on the floor outside Smith's with nothing much to do. Dora was semi-occupied with her colouring and her crisps. I browsed the paper and flicked through *The Great American Mousical*. It looked sweet and rather jolly and the illustrations were very cute indeed. At the end of the story there was 'A Glossary of Theatrical Terms' which I thought might come in handy over the next few weeks. I read Julie Andrews Edwards's biography on the flyleaf. 'While she is perhaps best known,' it ran, 'for her performances in *Mary Poppins*, *The Sound of Music* and *The Princess Diaries*, she has also been an author of children's books for over thirty years.' I didn't know that. Above her biography was a photograph, in which she looked as perfect as ever, wearing a pink sweater and looking sensibly, grown-uply beautiful. Beneath her biography was a brief paragraph about Emma Walton Hamilton: 'Julie Andrews's daughter as well as her co-author', and then another about Tony Walton, the illustrator, Emma's father.

I started wondering about what she'd be like in person and whether we should tell her about what Dora was doing. Given that we'd have, at my reckoning, about thirty seconds in her company, would it be rude to mention it: 'Hello, Julie Andrews, how are you, my daughter's going to be in *The Sound of Music*. Thank you for signing our book. Bye.' Or should we just say hello quietly, smile mysteriously, and hope she had enough time and interest plus a degree in cryptography with which to decipher Dora's note? Or would that be silly? Would it actually be doing the right thing to tell her? And why was I devoting so much time to thinking about the rights and wrongs of the situation when it mattered so little?

'How much longer?'

'Not long now. Look, the people at the front of the queue have started to go in.'

'What numbers have we got?'

I handed her the tickets, and told her to hold them carefully. 'If we lose them, we can't get in. We have to give them to that man at the door. Give me your colouring book and pens,' I added, trying simultaneously to fold my newspaper and pick up two bottles of water, an empty crisp packet, two copies of *The Great American Mousical* and my backpack in a quixotic effort to avoid holding up the queue. There was now a sizeable gap between us and the people in front as the queue was moving at the speed of a highly efficient production line. With a final effort, I managed to stuff everything into my backpack and, beckoning Dora, we caught up. Then I realised that I shouldn't have put the books in there, as we needed to keep them out for signing. So I struggled down into the bottom of the bag, where they were nestling happily underneath everything else, and pulled them out, only just preventing newspaper, bottles, crisp packet and computer from cascading to the floor. Then for a moment I panicked, thinking I'd dropped, packed or accidentally eaten the pink raffle tickets.

'I've got them, Mummy,' Dora said calmly, holding them up for me to see as I looked round wildly and broke out in a sweat.

'Well done,' I said, trying to zip up my backpack.

A couple of minutes later, we'd handed in our raffle tickets and were at the front of the queue. The staff had constructed a little booth for Julie Andrews to sit in, so she was shielded from view. Only the person whose book she was signing and the next in line could see her. There was a small and rather jolly man assisting, making sure only one person went up at a time, with their book open on the right page. He beckoned Dora over. She looked up at me and I nodded. She walked up to the table where Ms Andrews Edwards was sitting, looking exactly like her photograph, quietly beautiful, skin flawlessly unlined, smiling, hair elegant. She said 'hello' to Dora. In reply, Dora held out a felt-tippy hand and proffered the picture she'd coloured.

'Is that for me?' Julie Andrews asked.

Dora nodded.

' "Hello Julie Andrews",' read Julie Andrews, smiling, then she put the picture down.

Dora smiled and said nothing.

Julie Andrews signed Dora's book.

She didn't tell her, I thought. I looked at the organising man quizzically. He nodded. I went over.

'She's going to be in *The Sound of Music* at the Palladium,' I announced, without slipping in anything polite and civilised first like, say, 'hello', or 'how are you', or 'I'm really looking forward to reading your book'.

'Are you?' Julie Andrews asked Dora.

Dora nodded.

'Who are you going to be?' Julie Andrews asked Dora

Dora fidgeted.

'Gretl,' I said, proudly.

'You'll be perfect,' said Julie Andrews, smiling sweetly into Dora's eyes, and quickly signing her name in the book I'd put in front of her.

'Thank you,' said Dora.

We left.

I cringed all the way back to the car and for most of the rest of the day. And then some more in quiet moments during the following weeks. Oh no: Julie Andrews must have thought I'd tracked her down, queued up and bought the books just so I could tell her that my daughter was going to be in *The Sound of Music*. It was all wrong. It was an accident. I shouldn't have said anything except 'hello', 'how are you' and 'thank you'. I should have just smiled mysteriously. The cool thing to do would have been to meet Julie Andrews and not tell her that my daughter was going to be in *The*

Sound of Music. It would, I thought, have been all right if Dora hadn't suddenly gone uncharacteristically tongue-tied and had excitedly blurted it out herself. That would have been sweet. But she hadn't, and I had opened my big mouth, allowing my inner stage mother to pop out, clear her throat gently, bat her heavily mascara'd eyelashes and declaim. Must acquire more self-control, I thought. Must develop sense of dignity. Must not think too much about developing sense of dignity after what happened that time when I was eighteen and running to the station in Brighton chanting to myself 'I must be more dignified, I must be more dignified', only to skid in some dog poo and end up sitting in it.

'Julie Andrews is nice,' said Dora.

Dora was named after my beloved maternal grandmother, Dorothy. I'd hoped and prayed for a little girl I could name after her, but didn't want to give my baby exactly that name. Dorothy just sounded too grown-up for a wriggly bundle of noise and smiles, and although I loved the diminutives my grandmother answered to – Dottie, Dot and Dolly – they didn't feel like the sort of thing that should appear on a birth certificate. Whilst I was pregnant, I'd come across the name Dora when writing about Hartley Coleridge (Samuel Taylor Coleridge's son, also a poet) and his relationship with the Wordsworths: it was William Wordsworth's daughter's name. It felt gentle, soft-sounding and easy for a small child to learn to say and, eventually, spell. It was uncommon, but not outlandish. Even though Dora is already a diminutive of Dorothy, she could still choose to call herself Dot, Dottie or Dolly, if she so wished. The name is originally Greek and means 'a gift of God'. I'd waited a long time for her to arrive, and she is.

Dora was born and named some time before the children's programme *Dora the Explorer* hit British TV screens. She enjoyed the programme, identified with her namesake and counted proudly to ten in Spanish along with her. What she didn't enjoy, however, when she got slightly older, was being called Dora the Explorer by kids at school. Even though I could understand how annoying the constant repetition could be – especially once she'd grown out of the show's target demographic – it struck me as being way up at the friendly end of the playground name-calling spectrum.

During the breaks at the technical rehearsals, some of the other *Sound of Music* kids started doing it too. Dora didn't find this quite as annoying as at school, partly because the *Sound of Music* kids did it, over dinner, in perfect multi-part harmony, which sounded much nicer: 'Dora, Dora, Dora the Explorer, -orer, -orer', they'd serenade her, barber-shop-quartet-style. It sounded like the kind of exercise Dora told me they had to do for vocal warm-ups, both at the beginning of rehearsals and then, later, before the shows. They had to sing tongue-twisters – 'Red lorry, yellow lorry', 'Six thick thistle sticks' and 'Licky sticky toffee pudding' (that was my favourite, for obvious dessert-related reasons) up and down the scale, getting faster and faster and also 'Rubber duck, rubber duck, rubber duck, duck, duck' to the tune of the *William Tell* Overture. They were also supposed to practise them at home, which Dora did diligently, in the back of the car, any time we went anywhere. She also made me do it sometimes – 'Come *on*, Mummy, you *have* to!' – which I couldn't. Six thick thistle sticks seemed to be the hardest. Those 'th' sounds did it for me every time.

Dora was enjoying being taken out for dinner. The kids went to Garfunkels, where she always plumped for spaghetti bolognaise, to the Plaza – where they could choose from a variety of exciting and unhealthy junk food options – and, very occasionally, to Wagamama. It meant she could eat and drink the kinds of things she wasn't often allowed at home, but very sensibly and well-behavedly (although mostly, she recently informed me, because she doesn't like it) stayed off the Coke, which she's not allowed. Dora does not need caffeine.

On the Monday before the show was due to start previewing, Alicia, not Dora, rehearsed with Mittens and Dora rehearsed with everyone else later. On the Tuesday everyone went in at the same time, all day. An email arrived from Jo Hawes telling us what would be likely to happen on Wednesday, 1 November (to be confirmed later), with the addendum:

If you are all tearing your hair out / hurling the computer at the wall / cursing that you ever got involved in this at all – please remember that I did tell you these two weeks would be awful! Once we are running it will all be lovely!! There will be rehearsals on some afternoons during previews, though, I am afraid.

Actually, the technical rehearsals hadn't been that bad. Tiring, yes, and tantrum-inducing, but nowhere near as boring as we'd been warned. Dora had, however, been slightly miffed at missing out on the Hallowe'en trick-or-treating experience. Immediately – and rather previously – she started thinking about which Harry Potter character she'd dress up as for next Hallowe'en, and continued to do so over the next twelve months. The following September she was still vacillating between being Hermione Granger and professors Dumbledore, Snape or Umbridge. By the middle of October 2007 she'd made up her mind and we started planning her Professor Snape outfit.

Anyway, I had a lot of fun during tech week. The mums had been hanging out together. We'd colonised Café Libre, which was next to the stage door, and spent lots of time and money eating, drinking and gossiping. We swapped stories our children had told us, shared the funny things our kids had said about each other – particularly useful for those of us with smaller children – and giggled at their small naughtinesses. We didn't only do this when we met either. Phone bills were rising. There just seemed to be so much to talk about – and for some reason no one else we knew wanted to go into quite the same level of detail, quite as often, as most of us did. We expended a great deal of time and energy speculating about who would do opening night – my money was on Kettles and Adrianna – and about whether we'd get to go to the party. Having been swotting up a bit, I reckoned we wouldn't be invited. But when I asked Russ, it turned out I was wrong. 'Do you really think,' he asked, 'that I want to be chaperoning your children that night?'

There were other highlights too. One day during the technicals, Pippa, Piers' mum (he was the Kurt in Kettles), and I were walking up Argyll Street, heading for the underground and deep in conversation when we heard music. The children – all of them – and the orchestra were rehearsing together for the first time and someone had, accidentally, left all the windows open. Sheer exuberance poured out. The singing sounded heavenly: extra delicious because unexpected. Pippa and I held on to each other, squealed with delight, and stood there transfixed. 'I don't think we're supposed to be hearing this,' Pippa whispered.

At a quarter to one on Wednesday morning, Jo emailed through the first hints of who would be doing what and when. Mittens and Adrianna were to arrive early the following morning, to be joined by everyone else at lunchtime. The early arrivals were to break at 5.30 p.m. 'and have an early night'. She then gave an educated guess at the timetable for the rest of the week, including the first two previews. Twenty minutes later, she sent through the first scheduling information. There were still a lot of gaps on the Gretl front, but at least we now knew when our daughters' first few shows would be. Mittens and Adrianna were to do both the first preview and the opening night. Dora was slated to do her first show four days later, with Kettles – 'Fantastic!' I told her the next day, to counter the slight disappointment she felt about not doing her first shows with the team she'd been rehearsing with. 'You get to be with Molly-May!' The electronic press kit would be filmed that night, which meant that when clips of the show appeared on TV, it would be

Kettles and Dora that everyone would see. Then she was due to do a show with Geese on the 17th, which would be preceded by filming for *Children in Need* at the BBC. There were a lot of dates where the Gretls were still to be confirmed.

Early that evening Jo sent through the first full schedule, which had the Gretls filled in for the first couple of weeks, and Alicia was now timetabled to do the *Royal Variety Show* with Kettles. 'Hi to all!' Jo wrote. 'Attached is a schedule with all sorts of publicity etc. on it . . . You will find lots of things to look forward to – the Royal Variety, the EPK, the press photocall, *Blue Peter*, *New Year Live* and *Children in Need*. These are all being fairly distributed amongst the children which is great.' And it was. On some shows, Russ told us, one team gets to do everything, which, inevitably, affects relationships between children – and between parents.

Dora was now due to start on the 6th, still with Molly-May's team, and would do several more shows. Also included in Jo's email was the news that everyone whose children weren't doing press night would – assuming that there were any left for the night we wanted to go – receive a pair of top-priced complimentary tickets to the show of our choice (one that our child was performing in, obviously). That was a bit of unexpected munificence on the part of the producers – and not something that happens on many shows. We would also be given two tickets to the opening night, one for our child and one for a parent to chaperone, plus two invitations to the party. The people whose kids were on for press night would receive one ticket for the show and two invitations for the party, one of which was for their child.

Although this was great for those of us whose kids weren't doing press night, it seemed unfair on those whose kids were – as if they were being penalised because their children were the best. We would get three tickets to their one. Jackie and Scott, having two children in the show, merited four opening night tickets and invitations to the party, as well as two sets of comps for other shows. They tried to act in solidarity with their friends and offered one set of their opening night tickets and invitations to the opening night families, but got told off by Russ, who said they both needed to be there to ensure Olivia and Alicia were properly chaperoned.

Being picked to perform on opening night is an amazing coup for a child – and also for their parents. Especially if you're deeply immersed in the world of performing children – which, by then, most of us were. If you zoom out and manage to keep a proper sense of perspective, it's not. All people need food, drink, shelter and love. Some people – children included – are driven to perform and, like anyone else, are happiest when they're doing the thing they love doing. But no small child needs to be in a West End production, let alone opening it. And even though so many of us parents were completely obsessed with the show to the point of neglecting our homes, partners and jobs, no one lost that sense of perspective. Lynn, whose daughter Grace played Brigitta on press night, was surprised. 'I was expecting animosity,' she told me. 'But everyone was lovely.' It helped that we liked each other and were genuinely happy for each other's children. A couple of the parents of the older ones reported their kid being miffed that their team wasn't chosen. But as one of them said, 'I told her, "They pick their bankers for the first night. The ones they're certain of. And this time it wasn't you. Tough, but that's it."' Russ said that one of the reasons he loves working with the little ones is that they don't care who does press night. 'The first time they're on it's their first night and they're just really excited about that.'

I was neither surprised nor upset that Dora hadn't been chosen for the opening show. As the youngest Gretl, with the least performing experience, I had never expected her to be, and had I been responsible for choosing, I wouldn't have picked her. She'd never done any live theatre before and was a whole year younger than the oldest of the four (Adrianna). At six and seven, that's a big difference. Irrespective of how good any of them were compared to each other –

and later reports from the parents of older kids who saw all the Gretls perform suggested that although they all brought their own style to the part, there was nothing to choose between them in the talent stakes – there was no knowing if a child that young, who had never done it before, would actually deliver on the stage, in front of an audience, the first time she got up there.

Naturally, my inner stage mother disagreed with the rest of me. She was adamant that Dora was the best Gretl and the dead cert for opening night and couldn't understand how the responsible parties could consider anyone else. But on this occasion, because she was so obviously wrong, I was in control. That's not to say I wouldn't have jumped up and down, shrieked and been hugely thrilled and proud if Dora had been picked. I would. I also wouldn't have slept the night I'd found out, or for a few nights before the actual event, partly from the excitement and partly from the worry about all the things that could possibly go wrong: how wonderful the experience could be and also, should Dora get something wrong, how humiliatingly awful and scarring it could prove.

The fact that Dora wasn't doing opening night didn't mean that I was sleeping soundly, though. There was plenty for me still to feel anxious about. Getting tickets, for instance. On the Thursday (my birthday), I ordered a pair of comps for me and Laurie for the following Monday, which would be Dora's first night. There was, as yet, no news on whether the people who'd ordered theirs for the Friday and Saturday previews would get any. I'm not very good at waiting for things to happen, especially if there's a chance I might miss out. So I emailed Jo anxiously to say that if she thought she wouldn't be able to get them for me, I'd buy some from the box office. She replied to say that I wouldn't be able to get any from the box office. Fortunately, I'd already checked online and knew that there were still a few seats available. Because the thought of not being able to watch Dora on her first night was unbearable, I bought a couple in the upper circle. After that, I could sleep. Even if all we would be able to see was a tiny speck on the stage, at least we'd be there.

The previews turned out to be more eventful than anyone had anticipated. Dora had the Friday off from the show – she was at school – so I had to rely on the other mums for news from the dress rehearsal and the first preview. The dress rehearsal turned out to be open to the public, who were allowed in gratis. If only I'd known . . . Unfortunately, the set broke down, so they could only run half the show.

Although they didn't find out until Friday afternoon, which was when the unused VIP tickets were returned for resale, all the parents whose kids were on that night and Saturday managed to secure the seats they wanted. I figured I'd probably be safe for Monday night and so rang my Auntie Ruth to ask whether, if my complimentary tickets were forthcoming, she would like the ones I'd bought. I warned her that she'd probably have to be on standby, as I was unlikely to hear until the last minute whether I'd be getting my comps. She was delighted. Meanwhile, I'd also booked to sit in the upper circle with my sister, her husband, Dora's two cousins and my father on Dora's second night, the 7th. This would mean rushing back from Birmingham, where I would be running a training course for librarians – but it couldn't be helped.

The first preview went off without any technical hitch, the kids were, by all accounts, brilliant, and Connie Fisher proved herself, silencing almost all the critics who'd been disdainful that she was cast by a reality TV show. Whilst the private auditions that West End theatres rely on generally, but not inevitably, guarantee a high quality of performance, they make it very hard for new young performers to break in. Connie, as Andrew Lloyd Webber has pointed out, would never have won the role of Maria going through the traditional route. She had – despite her first-class degree from the Mountview

Academy of Performing Arts, a top music theatre college – been unable to find work in her chosen profession and had been languishing in a telesales call centre for months prior to getting her big break. I didn't attempt to say more than 'hello' to her on more than a couple of occasions. But she endeared herself to me by being genuinely kind to and fun with Dora and by responding lightning-quick when I said I liked one of the photos on her CD case: 'It's the best bit.'

Saturday morning, kids and parents congregated outside the stage door. When we arrived, a gaggle of kids were posing while a small man was taking photos on his mobile phone. I glanced at him and thought he looked slightly odd – not quite all there – but harmless enough. Dora ran to huddle in with the other children, and I joined a couple of the parents for a chat. The man carried on taking photos. And on and on. It started to feel a bit uncomfortable and increasingly inappropriate. 'This isn't right,' said Piers's mum Pippa, to Lauren's dad Graham – the biggest dad there. 'Do something.' Graham did. He asked the man to stop, and when he became difficult, grabbed his phone and, having deleted all the pictures of our children and checked through what was left of his photo gallery, performed a citizen's arrest and marched him off to find the nearest policeman. When he returned a few minutes later, Graham told us that elsewhere in the gallery were pictures the man had taken when he was following young girls round and sticking his phone up their skirts. 'I had to use reasonable force,' he said ruefully, rubbing his hands, 'otherwise he wouldn't have come with me.' The man was taken to a police station and released on bail the following day pending further investigation. No charges were ever brought. 'If a licensed chaperone had been there,' Jo Hawes later told me, 'it would never have happened. They wouldn't have allowed it.' In fact Pippa – the parent whose antennae were finely enough tuned to get the man stopped – does sometimes work as a chaperone. 'It just goes to show,' said Mark Williams-Thomas when I told him about this incident, 'these are people who are part of your community. People who children will talk to.'

We all became much more vigilant after that, much less inclined to let anyone take photos of our kids outside the stage door, although I did once make an exception for Sister Mary – a bona fide nun, in full regalia, all the way from the American Midwest – who watched the show with me one night. '*This* is a wimple,' she whispered, gently waving a corner of hers at me while Lesley Garrett and her co-nuns trilled the relevant line of 'How Do You Solve a Problem Like Maria?'. It also made me think about all the dangers Dora and her friends would face working in the theatre. As they were being so well looked after by the chaperones, actual physical assault seemed highly unlikely, but accidents didn't. Theatres are hazardous places. There are orchestra pits to plummet into if you get over-excited when you run forward to take a bow. There are concrete staircases to fall down. Lots of electric things and complex machinery to get your limbs excruciatingly caught in – which happened to one of the adult actors during the previews of *The Lord of the Rings* when it opened a few months later and the set tried to eat his leg – and props and scenery that can fall on top of you. Injuries happen. People – even sensible grown-ups – get hurt, badly, working in theatres.

On Sunday Jo emailed us with the schedule for the next couple of days. She also included a thank you for the kids – and for us.

I would like to say that I think the children have been fantastic especially during the last two weeks when things are difficult, slow, boring for them and generally trying! So well done to them! I am also fully aware of the way that this sort of commitment turns family life upside down so thank you to all of you as well. You get all the hard bits, travelling, sudden changes of schedule, midnight emails, tetchy children (and children's

administrators!) etc. and the kids get all the glory! It will now
start settling down and we can look forward to a period of
relative calmness!

The same day, having been told by a helpful parent that it was
traditional to give cards and/or small first-night pressies to other cast
members, I bought some blank craft cards from Smith's and
'encouraged' Dora to design something to go on the front. We
discussed whether it should be a picture or some words. Eventually
she settled on 'You're brilliant' in coloured-in bubble writing. I
checked after she'd done the first, pencilled words, and made her rub
out 'Your' and replace it with 'You're'. She didn't grumble too
much. I scanned the finished design into the computer and printed
out lots of copies. In our spare moments over the next few days, we
glued them on to the fronts of the cards and added blobs of glitter,
and with the tip of her tongue poking sideways out of her mouth as
she attempted consistently legible joined-up messages, Dora wrote
her good luck and love to her co-workers.

On the Monday, Jo sent through an email on 'a sensitive issue'.
Turns out some of the children had been gaining weight. What with
all the sitting around during rehearsals, the snacks that they'd been
sneaking into the theatre, the dinnertime trips to McDonald's, not to
mention the fact that they were doing less physical exercise than
usual because they didn't have the time or the energy, it wasn't
surprising. And could they please abstain from wearing mascara?
Even though I felt she was a highly unlikely offender, I checked
Dora's eyelashes, just in case she'd sneaked into my ill-equipped
make-up bag. She hadn't, and was justifiably annoyed that I might
have entertained the suspicion.

All the children were due in that Monday at 1 p.m. for a press
photo shoot. As we were slightly early, on the way to the stage door,
Dora and I popped into the box office to see if my tickets were there.
They weren't, so I asked the nice man behind the counter if he

thought they might be forthcoming, and if so, when. He didn't know, but helpfully informed me that they would be COBO'd a bit later. I asked what that meant. 'Care. Of. Box. Office,' he enunciated slowly and carefully. I wondered if I ought to write it down. Or maybe I should just keep a copy of *The Great American Mousical* with me so I could, at times like this, surreptitiously consult the glossary of theatrical terms and appear slightly better informed.

I took Dora round to the stage door, where she skidded off to join her friends. I chatted with a couple of other parents. Mixed in with the buzzing excitement of the show opening was a slight sadness, as there weren't many more occasions when the kids would all be together: once the show was up and running, except for the Gretls, and if a child had to cover for another who was ill, they would only see the kids in their own team. They would, we thought, miss being together. We would miss being together.

Once the chaperones had channelled the children down the ramp and through the stage door, a tableful of parents settled ourselves down in Café Libre for a drink, a giggle and some gossip, anticipating the upcoming 'period of relative calmness' that Jo had promised us. Then Carol, Michael's mum, looked down and checked her phone. When she looked up again, her eyes were round with shock. 'Oh my God!' she exclaimed. 'Michael's just texted me to say that Simon Shepherd's left the show!' Simon Shepherd was Captain von Trapp. A couple of the parents had reported back from the first two previews that he didn't look particularly happy in the role. But still, we were all stunned. You don't expect the leading man to go after two previews. Was it true? Or had Michael misheard or mistexted? If it was true, who would step in and replace him as our children's father? Were they upset? Would they be able to relate to another actor in the same way? And, most significantly for me – much more so, I'm ashamed to say, than 'Is Simon Shepherd all right?' – would my daughter's first performance that night be cancelled? Jackie (Olivia and Alicia's mum) headed off to do some shopping and phoned through to say that Simon's photo had already been removed from the front of the theatre. I pulled out my trusty laptop and checked my email. There was one from Jo, telling us that there were going to be more rehearsals over the next week than had been anticipated, but she couldn't yet tell us why. Then I Googled, but couldn't find out any more information. After about half an hour, when I could no longer cope with the suspense, I called Jo to check whether that night's preview was still going ahead. 'Yes, of course,' she told me. 'The show must go on!'

On the way back to the tube, clocking the *Sound of Music* posters that had been hastily put into the frame at the front of the theatre that had previously housed Simon's photo, I popped into the box office again, just in case. The tickets were there, which I was very relieved about, as the heady combination of excitement and nerves was bubbling up inside me already, and having the tickets in my hand meant one less thing to worry about later – by which time I knew that I'd be frothing over in a fidgetingly childish, unable-to-stand-in-a-queue sort of way. I also asked the staff if they knew anything about who'd be Captain von Trapp now, and what had happened – did he jump or was he pushed? – but they didn't. Then I apologised for being a nuisance, which I hadn't really been yet, but suspected I would become over the following few months.

I headed home to prepare for the course I was running the next day, but found it impossible to concentrate. So I stopped trying, rang Auntie Ruth to confirm that she and her friend could have the two upper circle tickets, and arranged to give them to her outside the front of the theatre at seven o'clock. I managed to sort out what I was going to wear that night (nothing too smart) and what I'd wear for the course (semi-casual), but couldn't really get my head around anything more intellectual than that. Every so often, the phone would ring: Simon Shepherd's departure had made the news, so friends and family wanted to know if I had any inside information, which I didn't, although I was happy to speculate. I surfed a bit more and discovered, from a press release posted on the Really Useful Group's website, that Simon would be replaced by someone called Alexander Hanson – a famous and established actor with a lot of musicals under his cravat. Even though I'd never heard of him, I thought he sounded promising. But would Dora think he was nice?

Then, as Laurie and I would be driving into town, I paid the congestion charge online, carefully noting down the receipt number in my diary. This led me on to worrying about parking. By the end of the technical rehearsals, I'd managed to work out where the best single yellow lines and the spaces where you only had to pay for parking until 6.30 p.m. were. The trick was to arrive just before then, when you were almost certain to find a space, then sit in the car, listening to Radio 4 until the 6.30 comedy show started, when you knew you could safely lock up and go. The only difficulty would be chivvying Laurie out of the house in time to make sure we got there early enough to get a space – and today that felt very important.

It's not that Laurie tends to the tardy. Well, not especially. It's just that I am slightly neurotic about getting to places early. Consequently, when he takes a bit of time deciding which shoes he should wear, asks me, makes a decision on the basis of my recommendation, gets in the car, changes his mind, gets out of the car, goes back into the house, changes his shoes, remembers something else he's forgotten and can't manage without, answers the phone, deals with the call, picks up the shoes he was previously wearing and one other pair just in case he changes his mind again, then stows the two spare pairs of shoes safely and neatly behind the passenger seat before getting back into the car, I get a bit ratty. This is usually entirely unnecessary, as I will have begged, nagged and, on occasion, dragged him into the car half an hour before we really need to set off. It is always counterproductive. One day I'll learn.

I drove us into town and we arrived just in time to find a place to park. I walked round to the front of the theatre to find Auntie Ruth, while Laurie headed off in search of a couple of bottles of water and a bar of Green & Black's milk chocolate with almonds for us to squabble over during the show. The pavement outside the theatre was packed and noisy. People, mostly smartly dressed, were milling about in the road, while the odd taxi tried to inch past. Theatre staff in red and black uniforms were standing up at the theatre entrance yelling, 'Stalls to the left, please, royal circle to the right, thank you.' Everyone – with the exception of the odd few best-dress-wearing little girls – was taller than me. How on earth was I going to find my aunt? Or, for that matter, Laurie?

In fact, there weren't *that* many people there. We all knew what each other looked like, where we were due to meet and when. We all had mobile phones and knew each other's numbers. The potential for disaster was, barring the sudden intervention of a freak tornado (don't laugh, a month later there was one near where we live), severely limited, which could only mean that I was experiencing a stress- and excitement-induced over-reaction. Never let reality get in the way of a good panic, that's what I say.

A few minutes later I spotted Auntie Ruth, handed over the tickets, said I hoped she and her friend would have a fantastic evening, hooked up with Laurie, and dragged him into the theatre about half an hour before we needed to be there. Laurie and I rarely shell out on theatre programmes. Although I often feel like I need to read one during the performance, because I'm very nosy and generally want to know as much as possible about the people up on the stage, I can never decide whether to keep them or throw them away afterwards. Keeping them is a waste of space as, under normal circumstances, I never look at them again. But throwing away something made of paper that thick and luscious feels like a bad and wasteful thing to do. Also, there's always the possibility that *this* time I might want to look at it again . . . Better not to give myself that dilemma in the first place. Tonight, however, was different. Obviously we would buy a programme, treasure it, admire it frequently and force lots of other people to look at it too.

I skipped off to buy ours the moment I got into the theatre and, in an unaccustomed feat of self-control of which I'm still very proud, managed to restrain myself from telling the programme-seller that my daughter was that night's Gretl. Then we found our seats. We were right in the middle of the front row of the royal circle, in two of the best seats in the theatre. We would have a terrific view. I begged Laurie for some chocolate, whilst flicking through looking for Dora's picture. I was too excited and nervous not to eat. While I gobbled down as much of the Green & Black's as I could wrestle out of Laurie's grasp, I wondered if Dora was feeling as nervous as I was and hoped she wasn't.

At 7.30, the lights went down, and we were invited to turn off our mobile phones and welcome Simon Lee, who would conduct *The Sound of Music* orchestra. I bounced up and down on my seat, squeezed Laurie's hand too hard and grinned at him. Simon Lee lifted his arms and the music swelled into the auditorium, Lesley Garrett's voice soaring over the top as she knelt at the front of the stage before a curtain with a clear oval window in it, through which a golden religious icon shone. A chorus of nuns filed past her, carrying nightlights in jars, and harmonised their way off stage up through the stalls. The icon lifted, the lighting changed and suddenly there, visible through the window where the icon had been hanging, was Connie, singing 'The Sound of Music', lying on what looked like a grassy hillside. Then the curtain lifted and the hillside was revealed as an oval disc, clothed in wild astroturf with a few rocks peeping through, and tilted at an alarming angle ('We call it the mouldy pitta bread,' one of the box office staff told me). The disc untilted gently as Connie – now thoroughly Maria – danced, sang and twirled around it, her voice gloriously pure, pitch-perfect, the orchestra exuberant. It was wonderful, captivating, enchanting, and a smile stretched itself across my face in an instant – ages before my daughter made her first entrance.

I had, fortunately, stocked up on hankies. In the run-up to the previews, anticipating the show's effect on us, several of us mums had, jokingly, considered approaching Kleenex for sponsorship, but hadn't got round to it. *The Sound of Music* has lots of Kleenex moments.

Still, I got through the opening dry-eyed. I got through 'How Do You Solve a Problem Like Maria?' and 'I Have Confidence'. And through the scene where Maria meets the captain – Christopher Dickins, the understudy Georg von Trapp, did an excellent job in very difficult circumstances, although he didn't look quite old enough to have heroically captained ships in the First World War and then fathered seven children.

Then he blew his whistle and the kids came marching on, dressed in sailor suits and in height order. People cheered. And that was it. Out came the tears and tissues and they stayed out for the rest of the show. I couldn't see a lot of the second half properly because by the interval, my contact lenses had salted up. But while I could still see, it was obvious that all the children looked inexpressibly sweet and gorgeous. Their singing was spine-tinglingly good, their acting convincing. 'It's an amazing feeling,' Wendy, whose daughter Christine was the Louisa in Mittens, emailed me, 'seeing your child on that stage, isn't it?' Yes, it is – especially when it's the first time. It is very easy to see how you could get hooked on your child being up there. It's not as amazing as when they're born and you first get to hold them – but it's a lower-intensity version of the same sort of feeling. You suddenly see your child from a completely different perspective, with most, but not quite all, of the familiarity stripped away. It was breathtaking and awe-inspiring. There she was, a person entirely in her own right, doing something I could never have done, not at her age, or since.

I was also very nervous (much more so, it turned out, than she was). *Please let her not make any noticeable mistakes*, I prayed. *Let her enjoy it, let her do her best, let her best be good enough.* But what was uppermost, as the scenes changed, the lines were spoken and the songs sung, was a sheer heady joy and a dizzying sense of wonder. This could, I realised, not only be addictive, but also distort my sense of reality. Theatre is, of course, a work of illusion: you buy into that illusion when you pay for your ticket. But when you're watching your child doing it, the boundary between reality and illusion feels, somehow, muddied, and your gut-level response is different. And it's hard to remember that what you're feeling isn't only because it's your child up there on stage, but is also, to a great extent, down to the power of the words and music and the performances and creative skills of the actors, musicians, directors and the rest of the team around them.

It is extraordinarily easy to lose that perspective when your child is on the stage, very easy to lose all sense of proportion. Not only does your attention – at least the first time you watch her in the show – home in on your child, but everything outside the glorious technicolour of performance fades to grey. Nothing is as interesting as the show your child is in: no one else is as interesting as your child. Consequently, you become incredibly narrow and boring. I'm sure it's not only stage mothers who are tempted in this way. It must be the same for parents whose kids excel at sports. Or when they take to anything in a living, breathing, eating and sleeping kind of way – providing you can get as excited about it as they can. Your view of the world shrinks and skews, your child – and everything brilliant about him – looms ever larger in your field of vision. Interesting, isn't it, how the activities and situations that bring out the best in your child can bring out the worst in you? It matters not a whit if your child makes it through the auditions and fetches up in *The Sound of Music* at the London Palladium. It's nice, it's fun, and it means that you don't have to give them pocket money while they're doing it, but that's it. Frankly, it doesn't matter if they don't turn out to be particularly brilliant once they're up there. It doesn't matter if they never go to another audition again. But it really, really feels like it does. When your child is doing something like this, you feel like you're that close to the centre of the universe and that this is where you want to stay for ever and ever and ever. Especially as that's how your child is probably feeling too.

'Sometimes,' Paul Petersen told me, 'you just get caught up in the life. We've all witnessed it, particularly with beauty pageant mums, sitting there and doing their children's routines and grimacing and mouthing the words to the music, as if they're up there. And,' he continued, 'it amazes me to see auditions these days, where five hundred children will show up for a one-line role in a marginal television show. Five hundred! And there are five hundred parents or more in the immediate environment too. All of this time, all of these resources, which might be better spent on something else, concentrated on one line of dialogue, which might have had a union rate of $750. You spread that $750 out between those five hundred adults who weren't at work at that particular moment and we're talking pennies. And the icky part is that the employers know very well that there will be no lack of hopefuls. That outer office in the auditioning process will be full.'

If you're that way inclined, being up on the stage is addictive. It's possibly even more addictive watching your child up there. And even if you're not the addictive type, it's unlikely that much else in your life will match up to the buzz of a West End musical. Certainly not going to Birmingham the morning after and running a training course. Unfortunately, for the duration of the course, my mind was more on getting back to London that evening in time to catch Dora's second night than it was on the job in hand. The day was not a success and it was, consequently, the last one I was asked to run. On the up side, I made it back to the Palladium in plenty of time.

Still smiling, Laurie and I filed out of our seats. As we were leaving, Lynette, who I'd met when she measured Dora for her costumes and who had been sitting near us, caught my eye and smiled. I said 'hello'. She said 'You made me laugh. I was watching you mouthing along with the show. You know all the words, don't you!' I hadn't realised I'd been doing it.

Still smiling, we went to collect Dora from the stage door after her first ever professional show. There was a small crowd there – which wasn't only made up of parents. Those of us who did have kids to pick up, and had watched the show (most but not all of the parents had been in to catch their child's first performance) shrieked, jumped up and down, hugged and told each other how much we'd enjoyed the show and how brilliant each other's kids had been. About twenty minutes later, to applause from all assembled – most of whom were waiting for Connie Fisher and Lesley Garrett – Russ led the children out. A few people asked them to sign autographs. Some of the older children added 'with best wishes', or 'love from', or 'x' by their photos. Dora carefully wrote 'Dora'.

'Mummy,' she asked me once she was safely strapped into her car seat, 'why did those people want me to write my name when they've already got it in their programmes?'

I didn't have a good answer. Once I'd finished being a teenager, I'd started feeling slightly bemused by the tradition of meeting famous people and asking them to write their name on a piece of paper. Why do we do it? What does it mean? Especially the part where they ask you for your name, so they can address it personally. How personal can a dedication be when it's written by someone who has to ask you what your name is before they can write it? Fair enough if you were lucky or prescient enough to garner all four of the Beatles' autographs on the front cover of *Please, Please Me* – or to inherit a precious copy from an older, cooler relative: you could now sell it and take a few months off work to go traveling, or update your kitchen. I did, it's true, queue up to get Julie Andrews's autograph. But that was so Dora and I could meet her, not so we could have her name written down in the space under where it was printed. I do also generally get books signed by authors when I meet them, because a long time ago a writer told me that they like being asked to do it.

Some time after the children had finished their stint in *The Sound of Music*, three of the mums took theirs into town to shop together for school uniform (two – Yasmin and Grace – were just about to start at Sylvia Young's; John had already been there for several years). After a trip to John Lewis, they decided to take them to say hello at the Palladium. Outside, they bumped into Connie Fisher, who was pleased to see the kids and hugged them all and chatted. An elderly couple asked the three mums who the children were. 'They were in the original cast,' they explained.

'Were you?' the couple asked.

'Not us, the children.'

'Can we have your autographs?'

'Not us, *them*.'

'Which one were you? Liesl? Can we take your photos?'

The mums gave in, signed their autographs and posed for pictures.

I enjoyed Dora's second night more than her first, partly because I cried less and my contact lenses stayed transparent throughout, which meant I could actually see the show, but also because I was much less anxious. Dora was obviously enjoying the whole experience. 'I was *so* nervous, I nearly *threw up* before we marched on that first time!' she'd announced bouncily on the way home from her West End debut. It was perfectly clear from her untroubled cheerfulness and her first ever use of the phrase '*threw up*' that she was simply parroting what some of the older kids had said and hadn't felt remotely nauseous. She might, I conceded, have had slight butterflies, but the idea of 'stage fright' was, for her, evidently oxymoronic, and so I assumed she was unlikely to suffer a paralysing second-night bout of it. And I knew – objectively – that the show was terrific, that you didn't need to actually be related to someone on stage to be utterly entranced.

Tuesday night found me sitting with my sister Nikki, brother-in-law Richard, my niece and nephew Millie and Freddie (aged five and three respectively) and my father (aged seventy-three) right at the back of the gods. It gave me a completely different perspective from the previous night. On the up side, you get a much better overall view of the action, a much better sense of how everyone and everything on stage – people, scenery, props – jigsaw together to create the whole effect: it's more like watching a film. On the down side, from where we were sitting, when Maria first appeared behind the oval window in the curtain, it looked as if she'd been decapitated. But as it was only a matter of seconds before the curtain was raised, this didn't spoil our fun. And even three-year-old Freddie sat happily through the two-hour show, thumb in mouth, index finger up nose, occasionally extracting them to point and shout, 'Look! Dorwa!', which ensured that everyone sitting near us soon knew that we were connected to someone on stage.

When other people in the audience find out that you've got a child in the show, nine times out of ten their response is 'You must be *so* proud.' Even though the standard reply is to nod equivocally, laugh and say, 'S/he is having a very nice time,' one or two mums were irritated to distraction. 'If one more person says that to me . . .' fumed one, through gritted teeth. But it's the natural response. Except that it isn't exactly pride that you feel. I felt proud when, one day, waiting in the school playground for the bell to ring, I overheard Dora stick up for a friend of hers who was being teased by some other children. I felt proud of her when another mother at school told me that her daughter had said that Dora was always kind. I felt proud of her when, despite going out to work two nights a week at the age of six and not getting to bed until eleven o'clock at night, she still knuckled down at school and also got her homework done. I didn't feel proud of her for doing something that felt, to her, like the most fun she could possibly have, ever.

What I did feel when I saw her on stage was different and also had the potential to be more damaging to our relationship. Pride in your child is something you feel partly because of your closeness – and your proprietorial relationship – to her. The awe and wonder you experience as you watch her singing, dancing and acting her little heart out up there in front of the audience that you are part of are distancing. On the one hand, this can help you step back from your child and view her as an individual in her own right, rather than as a mini-me (or mini-you). But it can also tempt and encourage you to put your child on a pedestal, to see her as – and treat her as if she is – more grown-up, more worldly-wise than she can possibly be.

It is, in fact, very easy to forget that these small people, who've learned their lines, music and moves, and are strutting their stuff on stage with the confidence of seasoned professionals, are, in real life, children. That although, because they are good at what they do and are being paid, they can be described as actors, actresses, singers and/or dancers, a child's real job is – to paraphrase what Lizzie Maguire's mum says during one episode of the children's comedy series – to hang out with friends, do well at school, and be good. There's a big difference between treating a child as an individual and allowing her all the rights, privileges and responsibilities of adulthood – especially when she's only halfway between nappies and puberty. But in circumstances like these, it's a fine line to locate and keep on the right side of. You don't have to be an evil pushy stage mother, Machiavellianly planning your six-year-old's ascendance to superstardom to end up on the wrong side of it. Being temporarily dazzled will do just fine. Or simply enjoying the guilty pleasures of reflected glory a little too much. After all, spotlights can feel too bright and exposing. How much more pleasant just to bathe in the gentle light of the moon, instead of the fierce burn of the sun. Especially when that someone else is your child and you can, almost legitimately, claim some of the credit. After all, if your child's doing something that brilliant, you must have done something right, mustn't you?

Nancy Carlsson-Paige – a child psychologist and professor at Lesley University in Massachusetts, who also happens to be Matt Damon's mother – told me that she feels there are risks to sending children into the entertainment business at a young age, some of which are down to parental attitude. 'Honestly, I often observe that the motive to do this lies more with adults than with children. What kids want to do is play creatively and this is their best foundation for going into the creative arts later on. I do know that some kids have a wonderful time being in plays and seem to thrive doing it. I hope when this happens such children also get a lot of time creating their own characters, scripts and scenarios in imaginative play.' Dora certainly did: to the amusement of the chaperones and some of the older kids, she and Molly-May devised their own 'horror film', called *Greenaway*.

But a firm line needed to be drawn between backstage playtime and backstage work time – and when you're six years old, it's not one that's easy to recognise. When he brought the children out after Dora's second preview performance, Russ took me aside. There was a problem. Towards the end of the show, there was a tricky scene change to negotiate, when the children had precisely sixteen seconds to come off stage, change out of one costume into another, and file back on again. It was a tense moment. And Dora had been bouncing around excitedly, delaying the process unacceptably. The dressers – under pressure to get six kids and three adults changed in an impossibly short time – were, understandably, not happy. Could I, Russ wanted to know, have a quiet word?

On the way home, I asked her what had happened. 'Mummy. It was brilliant! On the quick change, we all did it in the right order!' she shouted excitedly. 'Liesl first, then Friedrich and me last!' I understood. She had wanted the von Trapp children to be ready for their next entry in age order – which meant she had to be last and had done what she could to slow her dresser down. Exactly the kind of thing that would feel thrilling to a child that age, but completely inappropriate in the circumstances. I had a lot of sympathy for her point of view and so explained gently:

'They need you to stand still. Otherwise you might be late for the concert scene.'

She didn't want to be late.

Not only do the children have to behave in a very grown-up way, but they are also catapulted into what is, very much, an adult world. That doesn't mean that they're suddenly surrounded by shocking levels of sex, drugs and rock 'n' roll – at least not when they're working on *The Sound of Music*. But it does mean that they're spending a lot of time around adults, going about their business in an adult way. This has its moments. 'Mummy,' Dora said seriously, during a morning walk to school, 'once while we were rehearsing, me and Liesl and Brigitta come in and Uncle Max is supposed to say "We're in the Salzburg Festival", but he said the F word. He said "We're in the F-u-k-i-n-g [*sic*] Festival." Then we skipped straight to "The Hills are Alive".' She was slightly shocked but, mostly, amused. 'Naughty Uncle Max,' I replied, only just restraining myself from correcting her spelling. Nothing much out of the ordinary there: Dora had already heard plenty of swear words and showed no inclination to repeat them. But it did get me thinking. Not every show is as upliftingly innocent as *The Sound of Music* and not all chaperones as good, as on–the-ball, funny and compassionate as Russ and his team. What happens to kids who are working on shows or films that they're not old enough to be allowed to watch themselves? Where there are no other children working with them?

While Dora and her friends were prancing around being cute and Austrian, over in the US, twelve-year-old child star Dakota Fanning was filming *Hounddog*. Her role included portraying the victim in a rape scene. Paul Petersen of A Minor Consideration contends that 'for a gifted child actor asked to portray a difficult, emotionally loaded scene, *over time* there is NO difference between reality and pretend'. That is, the child may appreciate the difference between acting and reality while she's acting the scene out, but later on the memories of filming will become jumbled up with the memories of having watched the finished movie, and with the audience reaction to it. Before *Hounddog* was released, despite the director's insistence that the scene was filmed bit by bit rather than in one take, done sensitively, and that the child was wearing a bodysuit and had her parents' consent, Petersen condemned it. He wrote on A Minor Consideration's website that it was likely that Fanning would fetch up with 'memories' of being raped: memories which would be reinforced by the way people responded to the images of her being violated during the film: 'The internal workings of a child on the threshold of womanhood who has been raped . . . and raped for public consumption . . . cannot be predicted, nor can her encounters with people exposed to that image be guaranteed to be in any way "uplifting".'

There's quite a sophisticated argument going on here, one that separates the making of the work from the finished product and marks a clear division between the way the child actor is treated during the creative process and the way in which they are seen, by themselves and, crucially, by their audience, afterwards. It's not such an issue in stage work, where what the audience gets to watch *is* the creative process, the realism is tempered by the medium and the images only last as long as the production. But with film and television it's different. A child can be treated fantastically during filming, and not be remotely troubled by the experience of making something quite hard-hitting. That doesn't mean they'll be able to cope with watching themselves in the finished product. But even assuming they can, that they are clever enough to differentiate a realistic on-screen illusion from off-screen reality, and aren't adversely affected by their involvement, that doesn't mean that their audience will be able to do the same.

'That's the downstream day of reckoning,' Petersen told me. 'It's one thing to participate in a project that has an edge to it. It is entirely possible to have a child in a highly charged emotional scene and, in terms of the work, the kid gets through the day. They know the adults are not really mad, they're not really screaming and the child's not in fear of their life. The water may just roll off your child's back. But what doesn't roll off the back is the way the audience suddenly perceives you. When the audience sees it, their reaction, and subsequent dealings with the real child, is what changes.' Look at the men who stalked Jodie Foster and Brooke Shields – the former shooting Ronald Reagan, the latter plaguing his victim for twenty years before he was caught. And much more recently, the Afghani boys who were chosen from 2,000 Kabul schoolchildren to appear in the film of *The Kite Runner* have had to be relocated to the United Arab Emirates for their own safety. Ahmad Khan Mahmidzada, whose character is raped, has claimed that he and his family weren't told about the shocking, though not explicit, scene in advance and feared attacks or kidnap attempts if the film was shown in Afghanistan. He and his family are worried that people in the audience will believe that he really was raped. There are also concerns that showing a Hazara boy being raped by a Pashtun will inflame ethnic tensions. The film company, whilst insisting the content of the film was fully explained, has arranged and paid for the move and is putting the children and their parents and guardians up in luxury hotels until they can be found more permanent accommodation. They are unlikely to be able to return to Afghanistan in the near future.

Shirley Temple famously made her film debut in the Baby Burlesks, hour-long parodies of grown-up movies, with all roles played by pre-school children, clothed waist up in adult dress, waist down in oversize nappies. Titles included *Polly Tix in Washington* – the story of a call girl attempting to corrupt an honest politician. Today the makers would almost certainly be arrested on kiddie porn charges – if not for child cruelty: small actors and actresses who misbehaved were shut in a big dark box with only an enormous block of melting ice to sit on. In her autobiography, Miss Temple Black describes the films as 'a cynical exploitation of our childish innocence and . . . occasionally racist or sexist'. Aside from Marilyn Granas, who became Miss Temple's studio stand-in, used for setting up shots, until her mother refused to bleach her dark hair to match

Shirley's, none of the other children are known to have gone on to other acting roles. Miss Temple turned out just fine. But one wonders about her co-stars.

The fact that both Dakota Fanning and Shirley Temple were supported by their parents when they appeared in what were, arguably, entirely unsuitable ventures is not that surprising. Mrs Temple Black explains that the producers of the Baby Burlesks made all kinds of promises to her mother – about the nature of the films, the professional training she would be given and the care she would receive. 'Mother,' she explains, 'had no cause to disbelieve the promises nor presume a mean-spirited character to the films.'* Russ told me that when he's been chaperoning on film and television sets, children attended by their mum or dad are often given permission, by their parents, to continue working beyond their legal hours, even when they're exhausted. Parents are less likely to be willing to stand their ground against a production company than a professional chaperone, because they worry that they'll be perceived as difficult and affect their child's chances of getting more work. Also, we get carried away.

On the way home after her second performance, I asked Dora if they'd filmed the show, as they had been scheduled to do, for the electronic press kit, and also if they'd had their photos taken the day before. I'd imagined that with the change of leading man, this would be delayed until Alexander Hanson was up and running. I was wrong. Photos had been taken on the Monday, and they'd filmed earlier that afternoon with Alexander Hanson (Christopher Dickins was still being Captain von Trapp that evening). 'We had to smile more when they were filming,' said Dora, 'and look at the camera instead of where we're usually supposed to look.'

'Where do you usually have to look?'

'Lots of places.'

*Shirley Temple Black, *Child Star*, pp. 13–14.

The rest of that week was comparatively quiet. Dora was only needed to rehearse on Saturday; otherwise, she wasn't required until the following Monday, when she was back on stage. I didn't book tickets for her third performance: I wanted to watch the show more than a few times, but definitely not every day she was on. However fabulous it was – and like thousands of other audience members, I was genuinely, deliciously swept up in it – too many viewings and not only would I have to declare myself bankrupt, but the magic would undoubtedly pall. Faced with boredom, my brain turns pedantic, which can be as inappropriate as jumping up and down excitedly while a frustrated dresser is trying to get you changed. It was okay when Dora was young and we watched TV together and I became expert at spotting continuity errors in *Bear in the Big Blue House*, but I really didn't want to find myself analysing the differences between the plot of *The Sound of Music* and the true story of the von Trapps. Or trying to work out the mathematics of making a theatre carbon neutral. Or deconstructing 'The Lonely Goatherd'. The whole *Sound of Music* experience felt enchanted and I wanted to keep it that way.

That said, my inner stage mother was having the time of her life and didn't want to miss a single moment. She was stamping her foot on several of my vital organs and complaining bitterly at my failure to fork out for a front-row ticket for every single performance starring Dora Gee as Gretl. She wanted to be right up by the stage, wearing a t-shirt with GRETL'S GREAT AND I'M HER MUM! emblazoned across it in huge dayglo letters, whilst clutching a programme held permanently open to display Dora's photograph, which she would spend every interval shoving up the nose of anyone lucky enough to be sitting near her, whilst booming out, 'That's *MY* daughter up there. The littlest one. Isn't she cute? Isn't she just the best thing about the show? Yes, she *is* fantastic, isn't she? Yes, I am proud – it's like a little bit of me up on the stage.' But I kept her firmly under control. Most of the time.

During this quieter, calmer time, we mums started discussing what we were going to wear to the first-night party. I am not good at clothes. When I was a child my mother used to despair at the speed with which any outfit she dressed me in 'came apart at the middle', my hair's refusal to do anything neatly girlie and the fact that one of my knee-length socks would, inevitably, hang gaping around my ankle, revealing a tragically hairy shin. Since my late teens I have been the humble recipient of a stream of hand-me-ups from my much more style-aware younger sister (in fact I'm sitting here writing in one of her cast-off cardis, and very nice it is too). Not being under any illusions about my ability to dress for such an occasion without significant guidance, I emailed Jo: 'For the sartorially hopeless amongst us (i.e., me), is there a dress code for press night/the party?' She replied that she hadn't seen the invitations yet, but thought it would be 'quite posh'.

I had neither the money nor the energy to shop for a new outfit. Scouring my wardrobe, it became clear that 'quite posh' narrowed it down to two possible dresses, both of which, by some fluke, I'd managed to buy in the Voyage closing-down sale several years earlier. Voyage was a very trendy boutique, which didn't let just anybody in. In fact they were so selective about their clientele, it's rumoured they once refused to admit Madonna. Anyway, I was, for some reason, pushing Dora's buggy down South Molton Street when I saw a sign with the magic words 'Final Day! Closing Down Sale! Everything At Least 70% Off!' The shop was being considerably less fussy about who they let in – and even opened the door to me. I bought two dresses: one simple black one, and one that the shop assistant forced me into, that I'd never have picked for myself in a lifetime of shopping trips. It was knee-length, all green and gold sparkles, with a big green-and-gold rose thing slap bang in the middle of my belly. The dresses were thirty quid each. I kept the original price tag from the green and gold one. It had been reduced by £969.

That was what I was going to wear for the opening night, so all I needed to do was buy a wrap, an evening bag that would carry my phone, a credit card and a bit of cash, and some boots to go with it. T K Maxx and John Lewis and I was sorted, although that makes it sound a lot quicker and less painful than it was, especially as I also trawled the department stores around Oxford Circus with a few of the other mums, several of whom took the opportunity to invest in new frocks for themselves. Dora, she and I decided, would wear her bridesmaid's dress from our wedding, although as it was now November, and it was a strappy, floaty, summery number (with gold beading), I popped into Marks & Spencer and bought her a little golden bolero thing to go over the top. Then to H&M for some new gold pumps and grown-up tights. And that was more than enough clothes shopping, thank you very much.

Dora's Monday night performance went fine. It was her first with Alexander Hanson, who had debuted the previous Thursday. The word on the stage mother grapevine was that not only was he right for the part, but – big bonus! – he was also 'a good thing for mums', i.e. sexy. Dora, however, was still a bit cross that she hadn't done a show with Simon Shepherd – 'It's not fair, Mummy. Mittens and Adrianna got to do one, but the rest of us didn't.' She continued to feel the unfairness of this for several months, and would still occasionally complain about it even after she'd left the show. Some of the other things that Dora considers unfair are 1) that children aren't allowed to go into outer space; 2) that February – her birthday month – has fewer days in it than all the other months (not sure if she thinks it's unfair to her or to February); and 3) that when she tries to 'imperius' me it doesn't work and I still don't do what she wants me to do.

That night, she came out wearing a huge grin and grasping an extra carrier bag. Because she'd stood so nicely and been so good during the stressfully quick quick change, and the creative team had decided on a slightly different costume, they'd given her the nightie she had, until then, been wearing in one of the scenes. She was very proud of herself and loved it so much that for six months I had to do the whites wash first thing in the morning so that her precious nightie was dry and ready to wear again by bedtime. Now it's too small, we've hung it on her bedroom wall.

After a bit of excitement about her nightwear – 'Can I wear it tonight? Please? *Please? PLEASE?*' she begged, drowning out my yesses – she strapped herself into her car seat and found an excuse (I think I accidentally clicked on to Radio 4 instead of a CD) to have a short yet intense tantrum and then passed out. When we arrived home, she woke up and watched while I unpacked her Scooby-Doo backpack. Big shock! Somehow one of the blue elasticated ties that the boys wear during the party scene had ended up coming home with her. Dora was distraught. What if they didn't have enough ties for the next performance? They might not be able to do the show. Supposing they thought she had stolen it? On purpose? Who had put it in there and why? 'Mummy, you must take it straight back to the theatre now. You *have* to.'

'Er, no. I don't.'

I explained that everyone would be gone by the time we got there, that no one would be cross with her, that they would almost certainly have extra ties and if, by some fluke, they didn't, we could get it there the next day in plenty of time for the show. But I promised to call Jo first thing in the morning, just to make sure. That sorted, I took her up to bed, gave her a cuddle and she fell asleep. I spoke to Jo, who promised to call the people responsible for the costumes (actually, she promised to call 'wardrobe', but I assumed she meant a person rather than an item of furniture). She emailed back later telling me (and Dora) not to worry, that they thought it was funny, and just to drop the tie off at the stage door next time we were in.

As the opening night approached, the publicity for the show took off. There were lots of photos in the newspapers – and Dora appeared in a lot of them, looking cute and sometimes, but not always, facing the camera. On the day the show opened, all the news programmes ran stories, featuring clips from the electronic press kit. She and her friends 'Do-Re-Mi'ed tunefully on breakfast news, and 'So Long, Farewell'ed at lunchtime. I watched much more TV than usual, my finger hovering over the record button. Dora began to think it was quite normal to have her picture in the newspaper and to see herself on telly, but didn't seem overly affected by it all. I told her that after press night it would stop, and all the pictures would be of some of her other *Sound of Music* friends: Mittens team and Adrianna. She wasn't bothered, being much more concerned about the opening-night party, specifically exactly how late she'd be allowed to stay up.

'Can I stay at the party until eleven o'clock *at night*?' she asked.

I explained that as the do wouldn't be starting until after then, she would be allowed to stay up after eleven o'clock.

'Until *midnight*?'

I nodded. Dora widened her eyes and mouth into big Os. This must truly be something special if she was allowed to stay up *that* late. Helen and I had decided to share a cab home. The party was due to end at two and we'd decided to book the taxi for one o'clock. This was on the decadent side for children of Molly-May and Dora's ages, but we figured that this was a once-in-a-lifetime experience and excitement would keep them going. Or at least, keep Molly-May going. Dora, I knew, would experience sudden-onset exhaustion, loudly and inconveniently, but what the heck. She'd coped with the technical rehearsals, and one night wouldn't kill her. Also, even though it would probably slash years off my life expectancy, and it wasn't really my party, I wanted to make sure I had enough time to have some fun too.

All we knew about the party was that it would be quite posh, it would be at Old Billingsgate Market, and the kids who weren't performing that night, plus one parent each, would be taken there from the theatre along with all the other guests by double-decker bus. This wasn't really much information, but did allow plenty of room for speculation. Once us mums had got through the 'what are we going to wear?' phase, we moved on to 'who do you think will be there?' Would Julie Andrews turn up? Would we get to meet Andrew Lloyd Webber? Would Graham Norton be there? Jonathan Ross? The other Marias from the television show? Who else?

The debate raged, and not only when we met. Phone bills soared. We gossiped for hours on the phone, much to the annoyance of husbands, partners and children, and occasionally to the detriment of our work. In one incident, John's mum Jane, who works for a vet, was supposed to be bagging up a dead cat, ready for incineration. Unfortunately, by the time she'd spent an hour on the phone to Grace's mum Lynn, rigor mortis had set in. Her gossiping hadn't so much let the cat out of the bag as made it impossible to get it in there in the first place, a problem she only managed to solve by snapping one of its legs in two.

Dora and I went on the tube to the show. I couldn't fit a Harry Potter book into my evening bag, so we had to entertain ourselves, which essentially involved me hissing repeatedly: 'DON'T DO THAT: you'll get your hands/dress/face/bolero . . .'

'What's a bolero?'

'The gold cardigan thing you're wearing . . . filthy and your lipstick will come off on that window.'

In fact I wished I'd managed to find an evening rucksack: it was a struggle to fit the essentials – tickets, invitation, Oyster card, cash, credit card, door keys, mobile phone, a few tissues, lippy, eye pencil and foldaway hairbrush – into the little beaded purse I'd bought specially for the occasion. My inner stage mother thought I should also have packed a few business cards to hand out to famous people, but I ignored her. Anyway, no matter how violently I shoved in everything I needed to take, the catch still kept popping open. Eventually I realised I'd have to leave the tissues out and either sniff disgustingly, use toilet paper or both. Under normal circumstances I'd have taken a bigger bag, but tonight it felt important to make the kind of effort that seems to come naturally to most women, but leaves me feeling confused and inadequate. Partly, I suspect, this goes back to my mother's exasperation with my untidiness. Partly it's down to having enough self-awareness to know that I am genuinely clueless. As a student, I landed a Saturday job in a posh Brighton shoe shop. I was not a success and ended up being sacked, because, as the manager's report made clear, I was the worst salesperson he had ever had the pleasure of trying to train. Alongside my inability to persuade people to buy shoes they didn't really want and that didn't fit them, there was the problem of my dress sense. I had been caught wearing lipstick that clashed with my shoes.

My skills hadn't improved much over the intervening decades, so it was fortunate that the week before Laurie and I got married, the sixteen-year-old daughter of a friend had patiently explained eye make-up to me in the ladies' loos at a function. 'You put on the lightest colour eye shadow first. No. Not like that. *Before* the mascara, otherwise the eye shadow gets stuck in it. Then you put the darker colour on top. And *then* the mascara.' Oh. If only she'd been there to advise on veil-fixing techniques, I might have looked okay during our wedding.

I managed to remember my make-up lesson while I was getting ready for *The Sound of Music* opening. The only make-up I had was the stuff I'd bought for the wedding. It didn't go that well with my outfit, but as it didn't clash with my boots, I didn't think it really mattered, so long as I made a bit of an effort – no one would be looking at me anyway. I hadn't, after all, been invited on my own account, but to make sure that nothing untoward happened to my child and that my child didn't happen untowardly to anything or anyone else. And in case she did, so that I would be on hand to apologise and mop up afterwards.

We arrived at the theatre early, but there was already a crowd milling around outside and a group of children dressed as the von Trapp family singing to the camera crews and snappers who were hovering on the steps outside the entrance waiting for all the famous people to arrive. Dora was very excited. So was I – and I also surprised myself by feeling genuinely glad that she wasn't performing that night. It meant that we could both just concentrate on having a good time. That didn't mean I didn't experience a hint of wistfulness: of course I did, but it was nowhere near strong enough to count as envy. And I certainly didn't envy the way the opening-night parents – most of whom were rigid with nerves – were feeling at that moment. 'I felt *sick*,' John's mum Jane told me later – and John was one of the more experienced performers that night. 'I could only hope that he wouldn't have an attack of nerves. He'd never had one before, but there's always a first time. And also that they'd all be as good as they had been during the previews.' On the up side for the first-night parents, a day or so day beforehand, some seats in the upper circle had been released for sale, which meant that the per-forming kids' dads could also watch the show, as their mums had bagsied the tickets and party invites – although the more egalitarian amongst them had, previously, been planning to watch half the show each.

I carefully extracted our tickets from my microscopic bag, wrestled it closed and, clutching Dora's hand tightly, wobbled around on my high-heeled boots to Café Libre, where the parents of the children performing that night were waiting. They were, understandably, even more excited than I was, but it was hard to tell as they'd also gone uncharacteristically quiet with nervous tension. And then it was time for the show, so, heads down, whilst surreptitiously keeping an eye out for anyone famous, we braved the crowd and cameras and made our way to the theatre.

Excelling myself, I managed to recognise several Marias from the TV show, and Cilla Black. Also David Ian – but that was mostly because he was with his daughter Emily (a Marta) and his wife Tracy, who I'd met by the stage door wheelie bins. Amongst others, I completely failed to spot Andrew Lloyd Webber (again), John Barrowman, Martha Kearney and, most gut-wrenchingly for the few cells that remained of my teenage self, Bob Geldof.

All the parents with kids were sitting together in a block at the back left-hand side of the stalls. The parents whose children were performing were just as far back but closer to the centre, seated a little away from the rest of us, but near enough to wave and make thumbs-up signs at. On our seats were the special opening night programmes, black covers instead of the usual white.

We all trooped over to the pile of red velvet booster seats and snaffled at least one for each child – two for the smaller ones. Most of the children chose to sit together, but Dora wanted to stay with me – or, more accurately, on me. The lights went down, the conductor, Simon Lee, waved his arms expressively, the orchestra burst into music and the curtain came up. And for the first half of the show, an over-excited Dora fidgeted all over me while delivering a loudly whispered running commentary.

'Some of the nuns are boys!'

'Sshhh!'

All my attempts to get her to sit still and quiet failed abysmally. She simply couldn't contain herself. It was just as exciting watching her friends perform as it was to be on the stage herself, with the added bonus that she could talk about it while it was happening; something that she was banned from doing whilst actually performing. There was so much she had to tell me, mostly to do with what was going to happen next – 'Look! The wheelbarrow! I get to go in that too!' – but also about what had happened when they were rehearsing. Whilst this was merely mildly inconvenient for me – I had already seen the show twice – it annoyed the woman sitting behind us, an actress who evidently hadn't and who eventually leaned forward and informed Dora that if she wanted to act when she was older, she needed to learn to sit still and be quiet. Now. She didn't actually say *now*, but her tone of voice and face did. It worked for about five minutes, but then all the information Dora needed to impart started bubbling up inside her and eventually her lid popped off and the wriggling and whispered explanations recommenced. Fortunately, by then, Lesley Garrett was launching into 'Climb Ev'ry Mountain', Dora decided she was desperate for the loo, and when we returned to our seats, it was time for the interval.

We all chatted amongst ourselves and congratulated the now much-more-relaxed parents of the kids on stage, who'd been absolutely, delightfully brilliant. Over an overpriced ice cream, Dora elected to join her friends. I smiled at the woman sitting behind me and apologised quietly. She ignored me stonily. Dora, I noticed, glancing over to check on her, was now behaving impeccably. Away from me, she sat still and quiet throughout the second half of the show, completely focused on watching. No wonder they ban mothers from backstage.

At the end of the performance we all trooped outside. I held Dora's hand firmly as we made our way through the crowds to the fleet of double-decker buses blocking Argyll Street. Instead of a number, the buses were displaying *Sound of Music*, and the route was: London Palladium–Austrian Border. We were about to be whisked off on the 'Salzburg Express'.

Aside from the performing children – who would be brought along later in a minibus along with their accompanying parent and the rest of the cast – and Emily, who travelled separately with her parents, all the children, mums and the odd dad got on to one bus together and made for the back of the top deck. Here the younger ones shrieked over-excitedly, while the older ones wound them up, until they all got bored and burst into song. They sang exuberantly and tunefully all the way to Billingsgate. One or two of the mums thought they ought to quieten down a bit – but it was their night and, after all, they sounded fabulous. None of the other passengers seemed to mind, and why would they? Occasionally Dora would pop over for a cuddle. When she went back to the other kids, I sat looking out the window, watching the city lights and listening to the a cappella harmonies, while Alicia (Gretl) bopped Michael (Kurt) over the head rhythmically with an empty plastic drink bottle.

When the bus stopped, we filed down the stairs and out on to the chill east London street, walked around a big building and, having shown the smartly dressed bouncers our invitations, filed into a large, plain lobby. Here, those of us with coats to leave left them at the cloakroom. The children piled up in front of a curved temporary wall which was repeatedly branded with the *Sound of Music* logo, and the waiting photographers took a few photos, although they were really waiting for the cast that had performed that night. Then we were all herded into the party proper.

To enter, you passed through a tunnel housing an artificial snow-fall, which proved especially popular with the younger children, who caused a traffic jam by wanting to stay and play in it. Once through, on the right was a glühwein bar, the drink served in *Sound of Music* mugs. I failed to snaffle one, although several other parents managed. And then . . . well, the entire enormous space was Austrian- and *Sound of Music*-themed. There were almost life-size model cows (complete with cow bells) and sheep, standing in neat lines and confined to an astroturf paddock, and a oompah band, clad in green jackets, black britches and long white socks, playing oompah music. There was a mini Alpine chalet, picture perfect on the out-side, but spookily dark and unfurnished inside; and a picnic area featuring enormous hampers filled with a combination of fake and real food set amongst enormous silky black scatter cushions and gigantic potted silk daisies. Electric 'stars' shone through a black cloth night that covered the walls. Towards the middle of the enormous space was a gigantic circular bar from which staff served drinks to about twenty double-decker-bus-loads of glamorous guests. It was very, very noisy and very, very exciting. I felt dazed and dazzled.

Dora didn't, and along with a gaggle of her friends started disembowelling the picnic hampers and sorting the real food from the fake by either taking bites out of it or throwing it at each other. There was a tall round table by the side of the picnic area and a group of us parents set up home there with our glasses of champagne and pretended we weren't with our children. Food was served: small bowls of – you've guessed it – schnitzel with noodles. Canny catering that: one small bowl of schnitzel with noodles is, usually, enough. There was also sauerkraut and, apparently, crisp apple strudel, but I failed to spot that. There was plenty of champagne and glühwein but no Almdudler. Andrew Lloyd Webber had missed a trick there. Or perhaps not. I kept half an eye on Dora, who seemed to be enjoying herself loudly and uncontrollably, and realised that I should have brought my camera. Most of the other parents had. Unfortunately, there was no way I could have fitted one into the little beaded bag which was dangling open on my wrist, even if I'd left everything else out. There must be a way of being simultaneously elegant and well equipped. You probably need either staff or a tardis of a bag, like the one Hermione Granger has in the last Harry Potter book.

Jane, John's mum, and Lynn, Grace's mum, came over. The opening night children had been photographed and interviewed by the press and hugged by Graham Norton, and their parents were now relaxed and basking in the reflected glory. But Jane was particularly excited about something else. 'I snogged John Barrowman!' she shrieked. 'He said, "You're a yummy mummy, aren't you?"' John (her son, that is) was only slightly embarrassed. Grace's dad Patrick had managed to sneak in – along with all the other dads who'd wanted to come – and was lying low, in case he got caught gatecrashing. Adrianna's dad Darren took a different tack. He had brought his camera and was working the room with his daughter, taking photos of her snuggled up to every available celebrity. There were a lot of celebrities. He took a lot of photos.

Meanwhile Dora and her friend Alicia had got bored of dismantling the picnic and decided to 'collect' Marias from the *How Do You Solve a Problem Like Maria?* television programme, irrespective of whether or not they wanted to be collected. They shot off at a run, giggling, arms around each other's shoulders. Brandishing an empty glass and toppling off my out-of-character high heels as my viscose pashmina flapped dishcloth-like in my wake, I hared off after the pair of them, taking my chaperoning duties very seriously. Their Maria quest saw them charging through the kitsch mini Alpine chalet, up and down the stairs, past the glühwein bar. I apologised a lot, not only to the Marias, but also to all the other guests the girls cannoned into during their single-minded high-speed chase. Most people smiled back at me, but not like they really meant it.

I caught up with them when they were accosting Helena Blackman.

'Do you two want to be Gretls?' she asked them.

'We *are* Gretls,' they chorused back.

'We won!' they shrieked, having amassed a full set, and immediately decided to start all over again. The Marias' smiles grew increasingly fixed each time they were 'collected'. Eventually, after dragging poor Helena around for a while, they gave up and headed back to the picnic area, which was now being transformed into a dance floor. I was shattered. My feet hurt and the lining of my dress was hanging visibly below the bit you're supposed to see. It was midnight, and although I had apologised to several famous people, I had only managed the odd snatched conversation with my friends. I had drunk one glass of champagne and eaten one bowl of schnitzel with noodles. It had been quite interesting, but perhaps I'm not really a party girl. Dora, on the other hand, evidently was, but by then she was demonstrating clear signs that she was about to turn into a pumpkin. There were tears for no reason, followed by dancing, followed by moaning collapse on my lap on the scatter cushions that had previously been part of the picnic scene and were now piled into a small Alpine range that some of the other children, still full of energy and, probably, Coke, were scaling and jumping off. I hoped she'd last until the cab was due to arrive, but had my doubts.

At a quarter to one, after a quick chat with Helen, we decided to go and wait in the lobby. Molly-May was still awake and functioning, but Dora was exhausted and behaving exactly as you would expect an overtired, over-excited six-year-old kept up hours past her bedtime to behave. I called the cab company and the driver told us he'd be there in twenty minutes. I sat on the floor. Dora fell asleep, grumbling, on top of me, while I watched people (including Graham Norton) leave and lost all sensation in my legs. I didn't dare move them in case I woke Dora. Twenty minutes later, wondering where he'd got to, I called the cab driver. He had got to New Billingsgate Market, which was miles away from where we were at Old Billingsgate Market, which he didn't know how to get to from where he was.

This was not good. I realised that I should have learned my lesson and not used that cab company after our honeymoon experience, when their driver arrived late and, en route to Stansted airport, tried to drive us in completely the wrong direction round the North Circular Road, whilst simultaneously sweating profusely, fondling a stripy towel and muttering strange incantations to himself before announcing that he didn't have enough petrol to get us there anyway.

After another fifteen minutes had passed and the driver still didn't know where he was, let alone where we were, we gave up and decided to try and catch a black cab outside. This was easier said than done, as Dora was no longer remotely compos mentis, my legs were numb and there were 300 other, more nimble party guests also intent on flagging down taxis. We had a long, cold, miserable wait, but after much moaning and wailing, and many fruitless attempts, managed to find a cab driver who took pity on us and drove us home to bed.

The following morning we woke late, but keen to see what the reviews of the show would be like. Dora was particularly excited about seeing the pictures of her friends in the newspapers, so we popped to the corner shop and checked through a few of them. Leafing through *The Guardian*, I was surprised to find, on page five, a photo not of the opening night team, but of Kettles and Dora – more of the same that had been appearing in the papers since the press shoot the previous week. My inner stage mother was delighted, but the rest of me wasn't. We checked through some more newspapers. Same thing. It wasn't fair.

There are all kinds of issues around PR with children in the theatre that don't apply to adults – and that's even before you get on to the advisability or otherwise of turning children into celebrities. The most difficult of these for the people managing the press relations is the fact that whereas an adult role is undertaken by one person, a child's part is shared between several. This is not something that's easy for a media that aims to simplify everything into soundbites. They can't use three – or even four – photos or film clips to illustrate one review, so either one child becomes publicly identified with a role, which is often what happens, and the others end up feeling like second-tier performers, and relationships between them (and between their families) deteriorate, or journalists get confused and end up using pictures of one child to illustrate a story about another. Which is what happened on *Newsnight Review* when they were discussing Adrianna's performance and the subsequent press coverage. To demonstrate exactly what the panel were talking about – and how good Adrianna's performance was – they showed some electronic press kit footage of Dora singing their 'So Long, Farewell' solo.

So, instant dilemma. If you're responsible for the show's PR, do you ignore the children's sensibilities and give one team, the team that opens the show, all the exposure, or do you try and share the custard more fairly? On *The Sound of Music*, the company went for the fairer, sharing approach, but this carried its own problems. Mittens and Adrianna did opening night, but to anyone who hadn't been there, because Kettles and Dora had done the press shoot and the electronic press kit, it looked as if they had. And what about the other children, the Geese team, Alicia and Lauren?

Jo Hawes had warned us on the morning we took our kids to the Really Useful offices to get sorted into teams that the Gretls would get the most attention. But none of us realised quite how much attention until the day after the opening night, when the articles about Adrianna started to appear. After I'd dropped Dora off at the theatre for her rehearsal, I started noticing the billboards in front of the *Evening Standard* newsstands. They read '*The Sound of Music*'s 7-year-old Star'. My stomach lurched with what might possibly have been envy. Then I bought a copy of the paper. Adrianna's photo was on the front, next to a headline about Prince Charles telling his staff to ride bicycles. She looked cute, clever and beautiful. The caption read: 'Girl aged 7 who is making a brilliant *Sound of Music* . . .', and in smaller text, 'Triumph: Adrianna Bertola, aged seven, is being hailed a star today after her first night performance in *The Sound of Music*.'

On page three was a sweet article, with a picture of Adrianna standing in front of 'so proud' parents Darren and Shana ('at home today after she stole the show at *The Sound of Music* alongside Connie Fisher and Lesley Garrett'), two of her costumed up for earlier, local to where she lived, performances: in one she was dressed as a bee (aged four), in the other as a princess ballerina (aged five). In the fourth photo, she was shown taking her triumphant first-night bow with Connie Fisher, Lesley Garrett and Alexander Hanson. As I read, feelings that definitely weren't envy started bubbling up inside me. Foremost amongst these was relief that it hadn't been Dora on that stage on the opening night and that it wasn't her and us on page three of the *Evening Standard*. Although I read the article and thought 'how nice for them', I was aware that I would have felt it too exposing. I also wouldn't want my child hailed as a star that young – that would feel like tempting fate to treat her in the same way that it has treated so many child stars over the decades. I wouldn't want anyone to say that she stole the show from the adult cast, let alone see her singled out from the friends who were on stage with her, or who were playing von Trapp children on other nights. I wouldn't want journalists coming to my house, taking photos of me looking strained amidst our characteristic untidiness (just to be clear, Adrianna's parents didn't look remotely strained and neurotic: Shana looked perfect and Darren looked proud, and their house, I know, always looks spickly and spanly clean and tidy), and then calling social services because everything was so messy, dirty and generally unhygienic. Perhaps I just feel like I have more to hide . . .

Incidentally, in case you think I'm protesting too much, I will admit to being deeply envious that Adrianna was picked for the cast recording and Dora wasn't. And that means me, not the stage mother within. She would, obviously, have loved Dora to be on the receiving end of all the attention that Adrianna and her family were getting, and secretly fantasised about having her photo in the paper too. I, on the other hand, would happily have traded all the pictures of Dora in the press and the electronic press kit video for the sound of her voice on the CD, but it wasn't to be. Actually, I'd have loved all the children to have been on the CD: it would have sounded gorgeous and been a fabulous memory for us all.

But production companies don't decide which child is going to do what on the basis of what their mothers would like, and nor should they. I swallowed my disappointment and reminded myself that Dora was only six years old and really didn't need to be on a CD.

The next day (Friday), Adrianna's photo was on the front page of the *Daily Mail* and then on Saturday the paper ran a long feature on her, complete with more photographs. Adrianna seemed more or less unaffected by all the attention. By the weekend, Shana said she was finding it all a bit much, but didn't feel she could say no as it was all good publicity for the show. On Sunday, she phoned and then she and Darren sent an email round, apologising for Saturday's *Mail* article. It had, apparently, offended some of the other parents. I hadn't read it, so wasn't remotely offended. Nor was I after reading it, although it was quite clear that, despite it being perfectly complimentary about Adrianna, it didn't portray her parents quite as kindly as it could have done. They had, Shana and Darren told us, been thoroughly misquoted.

On the Friday, when *Newsnight Review* covered the show, Martha Kearney talked about how *The Sound of Music* had moved her to projectile crying. Both Mark Kermode and Paul Morley admitted to 'manly moisture'. Morley – to his credit, the only person reviewing the show to raise concerns about the way the entertainment business and the media use children – also commented that 'When the little girl comes out, I'm on the verge of walking out, really. Because you can see the next few days. She's going to get as much [publicity] as the leading lady. No! Please don't do that to us.'

I emailed Paul, asking him to elaborate on his comments.

'This was a reaction to the fact that the whole production, and the search for Maria, after all that, was going to sink under basic, perspective-shattering cuteness, and then the tragic fallout that seems to come with the child performer. Also, there was just a hint of something a little unsavoury, the inevitability that the little girl was going to be hyped and glamorised in the newspapers in a way that doesn't seem quite right, and has nothing to do with talent or dreams.'

He continued: 'I wasn't really ready for it on the night, because I was just thinking of the Maria, of how this had been a new way of finding the adult star. As soon as the little one performed all her moves so perfectly and sang with such conscientiousness, I felt cornered by the . . . cuteness . . . and by the sure knowledge that even if it ended more Drew Barrymore or Aled Jones than Lena Zavaroni or Jack Wilde, it would still not be a very normal story. Perhaps that's what it was – in the middle of something quite middle-of-the-road, something definitely designed for all the family, there was this hint of something abnormal, and there is something abnormal about encouraging children to work inside such a factory, inside such a money-making organisation.'

Also, reviewing a show centred around children presents particular issues. 'How could we be negative about the production when there were such keen, confident kids at the heart of it? It's like using children – even though there is no way around it, because this show needs kids – creates a kind of immunity. However poor the show might be . . . there was this sense that whatever else was going on, the cute factor, the near showbiz miracle of seeing really young children get everything right, would dominate any emotional reaction. You end up not watching a grown-up piece of musical theatre, but falling for the little ones.'

My suspicion is that had the production been poor, had Connie Fisher not been great in her role, it wouldn't have been so easy to fall for the little ones.

From what I've seen, read and researched, even in those instances where the child is acting out something that would be illegal or terrible in real life, it's not the actual acting part that's damaging to a child performer. That can – as it was for the kids on *The Sound of Music* – be both enormous fun and a superb learning experience. It's the attendant publicity, the individual's growing attachment to media attention and the public's perception of them that have, time and again, proved destructive. It's hard enough coping with fame when you're grown up. No one should have to deal with it when they're still too young to cook their own dinner.

'Doing the work,' says Mark Williams-Thomas, 'is the fun bit, the bit that's not exploitative. It's all the rest that goes with it. That becomes exploitation. There is now no cutoff between adult and child. As long as a child's parents say yes, they are interviewed and spoken to in the same way as an adult would be.' It's the way the kids are featured in newspapers, magazines and television programmes designed to be read or watched by adults. 'They are,' says Mark, 'in quite a vulnerable position, because they are entering an adult's world.' Paul Morley concurs. 'As soon as child performers are commented on in a grown-up context, they become grown-ups, they're in the same competitive zone.'

In some senses, we've come a long way since Noel Coward, commenting on a stage production of *Gone With the Wind*, recommended cutting both the second act and the child actress's throat. Most journalists these days try to be kind to the children they write about. At least while they're children. When they hit their late teens, it's open season. 'Having warped their entire character by indiscriminately celebrating them when they were too young,' says Paul Morley, 'we abuse them when they cannot cope with the pressure, and the strangeness, and the fact that they were famous before they really knew what that meant.'

It's a tough call because on one level it's nobody's fault. It's not like an evil entity is sitting in the wings, cackling, twiddling its moustache and planning to destroy the innocence of defenceless children. When kids go out on stage to perform professionally, they do so because they want to, because they love doing it. If they didn't, they wouldn't get the job in the first place: to win a part, as well as lots of luck, you need talent and, crucially, enthusiasm. And it's partly because the children on stage are innocently and enthusiastically enjoying themselves that people in the audience get an entirely innocent pleasure from watching them. It's also natural for the people who watch these children doing something fantastic on stage to feel curious about them, to want to know what they're like. It's also natural for the media to want to celebrate talent and innocent enthusiasm. After all, talent and innocent enthusiasm (not to mention hard work) should be celebrated, just not *indiscriminately*. It is, I think, the ultimately cruel lack of discrimination that implicates us all, collectively – however innocent we may be as individuals – in the failure to protect these children. There should be boundaries. For starters, headline writers could stop describing performing children as 'stars'.

One of the reasons that it isn't usually the doing of the work that is damaging to children is that, in the UK in particular, children are very well looked after when they're working in professional theatre productions.

Some concerns have been raised. The law, says Paul Kirkman of the National Network for Children in Employment & Entertainment, is open to too many varied interpretations. Theatre school Stagecoach is campaigning for the government to provide councils with more guidance on licensing and for the law to be changed so that employers, not individual children, are licensed. There is also some disquiet, Russ explained, about the varying levels of assessment different local authorities apply before licensing chaperones. In some areas they interview and test chaperones face to face every year before granting or renewing their licence, in others it's a paper exercise, and licences are granted on completion of a form, provision of a medical letter and a CRB check. The latter, Russ feels, is not enough. I tend to agree with him.

But overall, in the UK, the work children do in the entertainment business is very well and appropriately regulated, certainly compared to the US – where, despite the presence of a child welfare officer and/or teacher, an unpaid parent or guardian is legally required to be within sight or sound of their child. Here there are strict limits on the hours they are permitted to work and controls on the conditions they are permitted to work under. Child welfare is paramount, and in my, albeit limited, experience treated seriously as such by everyone involved in working with the children.

On the publicity front, it's a different story. Because parents are almost always present when their children are interviewed, they – not the production company – are responsible for their child's welfare. Under most circumstances this would be entirely appropriate: after all, you only need someone to be *in loco parentis* if there are no *parentes* around at the time. The problem is that most stage parents are not wise to the ways of the press (why would we be? Is anyone, for that matter?), and that it's no one's job to hold our hands when we come face-to-face with the ladies and gentlemen of it. The production company's responsibility is to look after the children working for them, not the children's parents.

Also, there is no part of the Press Complaints Commission Code of Practice that limits and circumscribes coverage of children who do something interesting, exciting and worthy of celebration on their own account. The Code of Practice does, of course, have a section on how the press should deal with children, but its focus is on ensuring that their school life is not intruded upon, that they are not interviewed or photographed without parental consent where 'issues involving their own or another child's welfare' are concerned, and that victims of and witnesses to sex offences retain anonymity. Also on ensuring that celebrities' children can be protected from the attention their parents attract. You could argue that the celebritisation of a child per se affects their welfare, but then all that's required is a parent or guardian's consent before this takes place, and it's oh-so-easy to be seduced by the glamour and flattery of it all into making bad decisions where the media are concerned. And none of us whose kids are likely to be on the receiving end of that kind of press attention are overly sensitive about privacy. If we were, we would never have let our children go on the stage in the first place. We are the kind of people who tend to say 'yes' where others might not, and to say it with big, eager grins.

It wasn't so bad for Dora. Although her picture appeared in several newspapers, and clips of her performance were shown on lots of television programmes, she was always in character and never named. She did do a couple of little interviews with *The Jewish News* and *The Jewish Chronicle*, the former by email, the latter over the phone, during which she rolled around on the floor, hummed and cheerfully answered 'dunno' to every question. But we didn't have to deal with anything that felt intrusive, thank goodness. The tidying up would have killed me.

On Friday, 17 November, I delivered Dora to the BBC, where she met up with her friends in Geese team and off they went, with Russ chaperoning them, to pre-record 'Do-Re-Mi' with Connie for that evening's *Children in Need* broadcast. I left happily, looking forward to watching them on telly and also looking forward to not having to travel to the Palladium until I picked her up after that night's show. It wasn't that I resented all the schlepping: I didn't. Yet. But it was nice to have the time free to try and find the floor underneath all the stuff that, to my new husband's understandable dismay, I'd just been dropping carelessly on to it.

That evening, Laurie and I settled down in front of the TV to watch (and video) *Children in Need*. I knew they'd be on sometime fairly early in the evening, probably between 8.30 and 9.00 p.m. I was all fidgety waiting, video recorder recording, while I watched the show, not daring to quit the sofa for the loo in case I missed them. And then, at around nine, there they were. The sofa from the set had been transplanted to Television Centre, and they performed their routine with customary gusto. I hadn't seen that team perform before and it was always fun to see the small idiosyncrasies that each person playing a role brought to it. I rewound and watched again. Several times.

When I went to collect Dora from the Palladium, she excitedly showed me the cuddly Pudsey bear that she had been given at the show, and told me that she kept falling over while they were filming. There's a bit during the 'Do-Re-Mi' sequence when the Gretls have to stand on one leg, and I'd noticed that she was a tad on the wobbly side. During one take she'd keeled over. During another, while they were running round the sofa, she'd skidded on the slippery floor and ended up on it. She was, she said, glad they were filmed and not live on the show.

As this was her first performance after opening night, she wasn't only clutching Pudsey, but also a carrier bag of gifts and cards from the cast and production team. There was a pair of pretty and snuggly warm woollen mittens from Connie, some fruit-shaped scented soaps from Poppy, the Louisa in Kettles, enough chocolate to induce a year-long sugar rush (can't eat all those herself, I thought greedily) and one shiny little silver box, tied up with string and marked 'Dora, love Arlene'. It was filled with sparkly artificial snow and little pink, red and white foam hearts, one of which had the number '10' written on it. It took me a while to puzzle out that the 10 was a top *Strictly Come Dancing* score, but once I'd got there I was hugely touched that someone so busy and high profile had gone to the trouble of making rather than buying.

In fact a lot of the cards that the *Sound of Music* people gave each other were homemade. Ian Gelder ('Uncle' Max Detweiler) had Photoshopped a picture of his face on to the body of a dirndled figure with its arms outstretched on a gently rural backdrop, and captioned it, in yellow, 'The hills are alive with the sound of Maxschtick'. Molly-May had carefully drawn a beautiful and intricate picture of all the von Trapp children in their sailor suits, along with the captain, Maria and Franz the butler, all introducing themselves, which had been copied on to shiny photo paper. Adrianna and her family had printed the *Sound of Music* poster image on to beautiful quality cream card with 'Good Luck' in curly gold script on the front and Adrianna's neat pink handwriting inside. Amanda Goldthorpe-Hall (playing Frau Zeller, wife of the Nazi Gauleiter) produced something truly spectacular: a card with two stand-uppable pictures of snow-capped mountains – a BONSAI MOUNTAIN KIT (contemporary Tiroler edition), which came with the following 'Care Instructions:

Plant your mountains in a south-facing granite and limestone outcrop, and prune regularly. Guaranteed to become one of your favourite things . . .' This all went slightly over Dora's head. 'Uh?' she said, scratching her scalp Stan Laurel-style as I fell about laughing and tried and failed to explain a) what a bonsai tree was and b) why the idea of a bonsai mountain was so funny. She finally got the joke when, making sure that she was happy with what I had written about her, and that I hadn't left out anything significant, we read through this book together in manuscript.

When Dora returned to school the following Monday, a lot of her fellow pupils had seen her on the programme. 'I saw you on telly!' they yelled at her in the playground. She wasn't sure how to react, so mostly just smiled and nodded. 'Are you famous?' several of them asked. Dora wasn't sure about that either, so she looked at me questioningly. 'No,' I said. 'You're not.'

'Yes she is,' a couple of children chorused back.

'Am I a little bit?' she asked. I conceded that she might, in fact, at that precise moment in time be just a little bit famous, but that it would pass and that she didn't really want to be famous anyway. 'Don't I?' she asked. 'No, you don't,' I said.

After six-year-old Connie Talbot didn't win the final of *Britain's Got Talent* (she has since gone on to record and release a CD), writer Andrew O'Hagan – the author of *Personality*, a novel based on the life of Lena Zavaroni – wrote an impassioned and sensible feature in the *Telegraph*. Under the headline 'Celebrity is the death of childhood,' he wrote, 'What a mercy Connie Talbot, aged six, was not allowed to win . . . It would have made a lot of people happy for five minutes, and a little girl sad for the rest of her life.' It's a sentiment that the US organisation A Minor Concern, led by people who were famous TV stars as children, would echo. Childhood fame is rarely a precursor to a happy adult life.

Earlier in the article, O'Hagan described how, when doing some background research for *Personality*, he went into a classroom full of girls and asked them what they wanted to be when they grew up. The girls responded very differently from how girls of his generation – the same as mine – would have done: 'Ordinary girls once wanted to be nurses or hairdressers or, heaven forbid, that glamour job of the 1970s, an air hostess, but the point was they wanted jobs. Three quarters of the girls I gave the paper to just wrote a single word: "famous".'

After school, and over the next few months that she was performing in *The Sound of Music*, I discussed the down side of fame with Dora whenever the subject came up. I talked with her about how, if you were really famous, you could never go anywhere without someone wanting to take a picture of you, even when you didn't want to have your picture taken. About how people you didn't know would know things about you that you didn't want them to know. I balanced this by telling her that it was all right for people to know that you were good at something, and to be respected for that. It was nice for some people to write, as they had on the internet, for instance, about how good she was at being Gretl and how well she could sing. But that was different from writing about her as a person and about her life.

We also talked about what she wanted to do when she grew up. Interviewers from both *The Jewish News* and *The Jewish Chronicle* had asked her whether she wanted to be an actress when she was older, and we'd discussed what her answer should be. Her first instinct was to say 'Yes,' or, 'But I'm one *now*.' But we talked about it and I pointed out that she was still only six years old, and she might find out about lots of other things she wanted to do when she was a bit older. I reminded her that only a year or so previously she had been certain that she wanted to be an astronaut (that was when she had been cross over how unfair it is that children aren't allowed into space).

She listened. Next time someone asked her if she was famous, she wrinkled up her freckled little nose and said 'no'. And the end of the *Jewish News* interview read, 'Asked if she wanted to be an actress, Dora insisted: "I don't know. I'm only six!"'

Maybe I shouldn't have directed her and should have let them print her first, unconsidered, six-year-old's response. Even though that would have been more natural, it felt wrong. I wanted to keep her feet on the ground. I don't know what the healthiest and most robust idea of self is for a six-year-old, but I'm pretty sure it can't be 'I'm an actress'. It's partly about the difference between doing and being. I was perfectly happy for her, even at her young age, to enjoy – and work hard at – her acting and singing and to do it at a professional level. That was an opportunity to stretch her wings and explore how high she could fly. I wasn't, on the other hand, happy thinking of her – and for her to think of herself – as an actress. That might sound completely contradictory, but it isn't. She might have been old enough to do a job, but as far as I was concerned, she wasn't anywhere near old enough to define herself by it. Definitions – even high-status ones – create limits. If you're an actress, you're not something else. If you are a person who does some acting, you can do other things as well.

I also wonder whether, unless they're specifically researching what children think about a particular topic, the national consumed-by-adults media should have direct access to small children. Grown-up performers in the public eye get advice and training in how to cope with the press. They have publicists helping them to manage their image and still, often, can't. And shouldn't one of the joys about childhood be – once you've ascertained that your school skirt is long enough to cover any holes in your regulation black tights and that Mummy's used enough hairspray, hairnets and hairpins to prevent your bun unravelling during your ballet exam – freedom from the awareness that there might be such a thing as an 'image' to manage? Isn't that part of what it means to be innocent?

Also, I didn't want Dora to identify what she was doing now with what she would spend her adult life doing. I come from a family where several people have performed as children and then chosen to go off and do something completely different. And even though, as

Tracy Lane – Emily's mum and David Ian's wife – is fond of saying about newspapers, 'they're just tomorrow's fish and chip wrappings', once you've put something down in print, it's somehow more binding than just saying it. I didn't want Dora to feel like she'd already made a decision about her adult life. If childhood should be about anything, it should be about possibilities as yet undreamt-of, about a sense that there are things out there to be discovered, a whole world to be explored. I want Dora to feel that the future is an open, uncharted place, not something that's already mapped out for her. That being in *The Sound of Music* was just one of a whole host of exciting experiences that her life might hold – that although there might be more exciting acting and singing experiences ahead, she might also get just as big a buzz from a whole range of other activities – and I didn't want her, at the age of six, to rule anything out. Although, believing that there's some virtue in maintaining a degree of realism, I did point out that she was unlikely ever to make an Olympic sprinter.

A few months later, one of Molly-May's older twin sisters, Emily, delivered a speech at school, as part of her GCSE coursework. Its title was 'To Be Or Not To Be?'. Born into a showbusiness family – both her grandmothers run stage schools and both her parents performed as children, though neither does now – at the age of three Emily and her twin Laura watched their cousin on a TV commercial and announced, 'We want to be in *there*'. Soon, they were. And on the stage at the Palladium in *Chitty Chitty Bang Bang*. Now, Emily isn't sure whether she wants to continue to act as an adult. 'If I was guaranteed good regular pay from theatre and television I would possibly be more inclined to try the profession,' she said. She's shocked by the statistic that 'on any given day almost 95% of actors or actresses are out of work'. But 'the buzz that I get when I am on stage is unlike any other feeling I have ever felt . . . the adrenaline rush that you feel is better than anything else I have ever experienced . . . I love knowing that you are making a difference to other people's lives. I believe without music and drama, the world would be a place with no soul.' There might be other jobs that she finds just as fulfilling, that come without 'the fickleness of the business, the empty promises, exploitation and false hope of the dramatic world', that pay the mortgage and fund holidays. On the other hand, 'I could earn the most money in the world and be the most miserable person. Perhaps sacrificing lifestyle and a good income is worth it to be emotionally, spiritually and totally fulfilled.'

Now in her mid-teens, Emily still has plenty of time to decide. Or to try one path and, if it doesn't suit, to change course and try another. What's important is that she understands the implications of making a particular choice. And that's what I'd like Dora to grow up with: an understanding that it's fine to choose a career that, in all likelihood, will pay diddly-squat and involve long periods of unemployment, as long as you're willing to deal with the consequences.

At the time of writing, Dora says that when she grows up she wants to be an actress and – once reassured that she would be unlikely to get blown up if an experiment went disastrously wrong – a scientist. Or a horse-rider. Even though I couldn't help pointing out that being a horse-rider was probably more dangerous than being a scientist, I'm happy with those three options. They seem like a balanced mix, especially as she seems keen on pursuing them concurrently, and are reasonable aspirations for a child of her age. Only one of the three is probably beyond the bounds of the possible. But there's some virtue in maintaining a degree of unrealism, too. Especially when you're under ten.

Meanwhile, the last word on celebrity went, unbeknownst to Dora, to her cousin Millie. One day, shortly after Dora's stint on the show had finished, we were going over to my sister Nikki's house for tea. Millie also had a school friend coming to play. In the car on the way home, Nikki overheard Millie telling her friend that Dora would also be there. 'You know,' she said, 'my cousin. She used to be famous.'

On Sunday, 19 November, Jo sent me an email to say that Dora was 'deviating from the blocking', and asking if anyone had come to watch her in the show and had been 'coaching' her afterwards. Remembering Jo's warning about a child she'd had to release from her contract because her mum had been telling her to upstage everyone else, I panicked and sent back a long email saying that no one had been contradicting the director's instructions, and even if anyone had been, Dora wouldn't listen to them. Especially if it was me doing the telling which, obviously, I would never have dared to do. I also explained that 'Dora isn't the sort of person to do something wrong in order to get a better audience reaction in ANY aspect of her life. She's very serious about everything she does and always prefers being in the right to being popular, and can feel mortified by her own mistakes.' Which is true. I asked her about where she'd been on stage and where she thought she ought to have been, and she definitely thought she'd been doing it right. In some cases she thought she'd been the only person getting it right and everyone else had been wrong. Gently I pointed out that as she was the youngest and that Sophie, who was playing Liesl, was a grown-up, maybe, just maybe, everyone else was getting it right and she was making a little, unimportant mistake or two. I also told her that it didn't matter if she got it a bit wrong sometimes, as she was the youngest, but that she should ask children's director Frank Thompson where she was going wrong and for help to get it right, because it was important to try.

Jo emailed me back the next day telling me that she thought I was over-reacting: they just wanted to check that there wasn't anyone else giving Dora contrary advice, no criticism was intended, and Frank would sort it out and everything would be fine. I replied ascribing my hysteria to PMT – which was, mostly, a lie; I suspect I would have (over-)reacted in exactly the same way at any other time of the month – and then called her for more reassurance. She gave me some, reminding me that Dora was six years old and that in the course of a two-and-a-half-hour professional show, it's not actually surprising if a six-year-old makes mistakes and that it can actually increase the 'aah factor'. I didn't tell Dora that bit. I didn't want to give her any ideas.

As the show, the kids and their parents bedded in, everything started to settle down into a regular rhythm. Within a few weeks, we mostly knew what would be happening when, which made having a life marginally more possible: although, as *The Sound of Music* was such fun, I didn't necessarily want one. I found myself watching the show about once every two weeks. Around the middle of November, I'd discovered www.theatremonkey.com, which not only provides reviews of West End shows, but also features some very useful information about which seats in each theatre are the best value for money, which offer sufficient legroom for people who need it more than I do, and which are restricted view. Here I found out that there are, at the Palladium, standing tickets. Unable to afford the top-price tickets that Jo had organised for us, I took to buying one of those for £20 each time I wanted to watch the show. You stand at the back of the stalls, where you can lean on a brass rail. The view isn't bad at all – because you're underneath the royal circle, you miss out on the enormous red banner with the German Imperial Eagle on it, but other than that, you can see just about everything. There's also seat XX1 that, for health and safety reasons, is never sold. If you get in quickly, you can sit in it once the show starts. But I found myself often choosing to stand, even when no one else had taken the seat. There were often one or two other parents or strangers there to chat with (the most exciting of whom was Sister Mary, the Real Life Nun from the US) and, as quite a fidgety person, I enjoyed the freedom of movement. Also – a bonus – if I needed the loo in the interval, I could beat the queue, even if I waited until the last glorious note of Lesley Garrett's 'Climb Ev'ry Mountain'.

While I was loving being in the audience, Dora was loving her time on stage and beginning – uh-oh – to enjoy signing autographs at the stage door afterwards. Even though I hadn't wanted her to get any ideas, over the next few weeks she started to get some anyway.

In Noel Streatfeild's classic *Ballet Shoes*, when Pauline Fossil, the actress of the family, lands her first job (she's twelve) in the theatre as Alice in *Alice in Wonderland*, she becomes 'very conceited'. The combination of the applause, the reviews and the fan letters, and the fact that the adult cast members are kind to her and obviously think she is good at her job, all go to her head. She starts expecting her adoptive sisters Petrova (the aspiring mechanic) and Posy (the dancer) to fetch and carry for her at home, and Winifred, her talented but plain understudy, to do the same for her in the dressing room. Eventually Pauline's behaviour spills over into the rest of the theatre, and the boss of the company makes her the understudy and Winifred Alice for one performance. This upsets her enough that a good cry (privately, in the bathroom at home, naturally), initially about how unfair the whole business is, segues, as she calms down, into a consideration of her own behaviour, which then mends itself. Shirley Temple Black wrote in her autobiography *Child Star* about her own 'sense of self-importance' as a child – which affected her behaviour towards others in a way she regrets (and she seems to be a woman with very few regrets): 'Only an idiot could have lived in the glare of such a central spotlight and been unaware of her prominence.'* It is nigh-on impossible for anyone to remain completely unaffected by public adulation, let alone a child.

When Dora was on stage, every time she opened her mouth, a large chunk of the 2,300-strong audience went 'aaah'. After the show, there would usually be a crowd of people hanging round the

*Shirley Temple Black, *Child Star*, p. 152.

stage door. A few would ask the children for their autographs, but most would clap and cheer when they came out and tell them how brilliant they were – and in the case of the little ones, how cute. Dora didn't remain unaffected by public adulation.

It started with her coming home from school and announcing, 'You can call me Gretl.'

'Er, no. We will call you Dora because that is your name.'

'But I want you to call me Gretl.'

'Well we're not going to.'

And 'It doesn't matter if I get things wrong, because I'm the youngest'. Yes, well, but that's not quite the attitude . . .

Her tantrums increased in both frequency and, although I hadn't thought it physically possible, volume. She was, evidently, receiving some excellent vocal training.

'I am cute,' she insisted on one occasion when she had been anything but. I explained that in my eyes, cute is as cute does.

'But I *am* cute. Everyone says so.'

She started expecting more things to be done for her: 'I have a dresser at the theatre. Why can't *you* help me put my school uniform on at home?'

At the theatre, Russ, the chaperone, did his bit to help the kids keep their feet firmly on the ground. 'I joke with the children. "Come on now, let's practise for your next job. Kentucky Fried Chicken." And the kids are laughing their heads off. They sit down: "Would you like a Kentucky, sir?" Just to keep them in reality.'

Back home, I tried to do mine.

'Yes, sometimes you are cute. At other times, when you're naughty, you're not. And part of the reason people say you're cute is that you're playing a cute part. It's your job.' In a quiet moment we discussed the difference between being cute and playing a cute part. The process was helped by the fact that Dora had already announced that she wanted to play a baddie so that she could wear a wig. I didn't quite understand the connection, but hey, whatever bit her biscuit . . .

'If you were playing the part of somebody nasty,' I pointed out, 'you wouldn't want the audience to think you were *really* a nasty person, would you?'

That made a small inroad. She shook her head. I could tell she was thinking about it. But what made all the difference was Julie Andrews Edwards's book. We were reading *The Great American Mousical* whilst waiting for the next batch of *Harry Potter*s to arrive from Amazon. Set amongst a troupe of theatrical mice on a Broadway substage, the book features a big-headed prima donna mouse called Adelaide, who throws regular tantrums. She is also unkind to the pretty ingénue mouse, Wendy, with whom Dora identified. One night while I was reading her an episode in which the leading lady is particularly nasty, Dora turned to me, her eyes open wide in a state of shock and declared 'I don't want to end up like *Adelaide*,' and instantly mended her ways.

There's not much you can rely on in life. But you can usually count on Julie Andrews. And I was very proud of Dora for having worked it all out for herself, and – once she'd figured out right from wrong – for sorting out her own behaviour.

Although Dora has a half-sister on her father's side, she doesn't live with us, so Dora is, effectively, an only child. This meant that we didn't have to cope with the effects of her being in the show on any siblings. It can be hard to be the brother or sister of a child who's doing something high profile. To start with, an awful lot of time and energy goes into organising the performer's schedule – and that's a lot of time and energy that isn't available to you. Then there's the kudos they're getting, the excitement generated by what they're doing, and the level at which they're doing it, which can make your everyday achievements at school and any extracurricular activities pale into insignificance. And that's before you even consider the money, which, as we're talking theatre, while it may not be much in real terms, is likely to be a lot more than any pocket money your parents are giving you. 'It's not fair,' complained the younger brother of one of the *Sound of Music* kids about his sister. 'She gets all the fame AND all the money.' 'I suppose,' sighed the older sister of another, a boy who has spent several years in the business, 'that there's absolutely no point asking if we're going on holiday this year. We won't be, because *he'll* be working.' Low-level grumbling, and the sense of injustice that your needs are treated as less important than your sibling's, can, sometimes, escalate. 'I could,' Paul Petersen told me, 'recite more than a score of suicides from the less famous siblings of prominent child stars.'

Obviously, if you work hard as a parent to even things up, and have a value system in which the performing child is viewed as 'just a little girl who's having a very nice time' – which is how one of the mums described her daughter to a radio producer who rang up to ask if she could interview her about what it was like being the mother of a star (she declined the invitation) – there's a better chance of dealing with sibling jealousy. But it's not a given. The fact is, if your brother or sister is doing something very exciting and getting paid for doing it, whilst simultaneously taking up more parental time and energy than usual because they have to be taken to and collected from somewhere inconvenient at difficult times of the day, it's tough. Who wouldn't feel just a little hard-done-by? Paul Petersen told me about his family's experiences.

'I got a wonderful job in a big movie called *Houseboat*, with Cary Grant and Sophia Loren. It meant moving to Washington DC and living in a hotel. What an upset for my family! My mother left behind my older sister Pam and her infant daughter Patty and her job at Lockheed and came with me for five months. There were ramifications to that choice.'

Three weeks before Paul spoke to me – 'and, mind you, this is forty-five years after the main fame part of my life – Pam met a gentleman

at a party. She had already been warned that this fellow knew she was
my sister – imagine living with that for your whole life. For the first
time in my fifty years of celebrity . . . when she met this man, in his
mid-sixties, he said to her, "Pam, how did Paul's fame make you feel?"
It was the first time someone asked *her* about the impact on *her* life.'

I asked Mark Lester how his sister coped with his success. 'I don't
know. Maybe she had issues with it. She always used to trail along in
my wake and was in a couple of films I did, in the background as an
extra. But she was a chubby little girl and really not very photogenic.'

'Er . . . are you good friends now?' I asked. 'How would she feel
about being described like that?'

'I don't know. But it's true, she was quite chubby as a child.'

Back in London, Laurie suddenly needed some of my attention.
One late November morning he woke up in agony, his left knee so
swollen it looked like one of his buttocks had slipped down his leg
and settled there. Several trips to our local Accident and Emergency
unit proved fruitless. A couple of doctors extracted fluid from the
joint – a procedure that simply added extra pain to the whole
situation as his knee just swelled up again. In desperation, he found
a private specialist and forked out for an emergency operation. This
was followed by a month on crutches and him not being able to work
during December, usually his busiest month of the year (juggling on
crutches is harder than juggling on stilts, something he often did in
his twenties). Worse than that, we also couldn't go away anywhere
because Dora was working and her contract didn't permit it. And
worst of all, his wife was completely obsessed with *The Sound of
Music* and the whole phenomenon of child performers and didn't
seem able to sustain a conversation about anything else. So although
I was there for him physically and made sure that almost everything
that needed to be done got done (bar the housework, obviously), I
wasn't there for him emotionally in the way that you would expect a
just-married wife to be there for her new husband – especially a
husband who was in excruciating pain.

It wasn't long before I bored him to Bournemouth, where he went to spend a few days recuperating in Lilli's flat, where he was properly looked after, didn't have to listen to a one-track monologue about *The Sound of Music*, and also didn't have to deal with stairs.

A CRAZY PLANET FULL OF
CRAZY PEOPLE

I did wonder, when Dora first started rehearsing for *The Sound of Music*, what impression she would get of Nazism. Would she pick up on any of the brutality that's hinted at in the show's story? Or would she just sail through, having fun like most other six-year-olds would, and not notice the political stuff? Would she end up thinking that a Nazi was a nice person who put on a costume and pretended to be nasty on stage?

Naturally, it's a particularly sensitive topic when you're Jewish. I – and many of my generation, born in the sixties, whose parents were born in the thirties – imbibed the horrors of Nazism and the Holocaust from our families along with, and as part of, our earliest religious education. It wasn't history for our parents and grand-parents: even for those of us whose families weren't murdered.

Nazism hadn't loomed large in Dora's early childhood in the way that it had in mine. In fact, *The Sound of Music* was her first encounter with it. Jeremy Sams's direction and Robert Jones's set design highlight the political aspects of the show. Captain von Trapp and Baroness Schraeder break off their relationship not (as in the film) because the captain is in love with Maria but because (as in the original stage version) they disagree on whether or not to resist the

Nazis should they invade Austria. When the scene changes for the von Trapps' tense performance at the Salzburg Festival concert, huge Nuremberg Rally-style red banners festooned with black swastikas drop down at the sides of the stage and an even bigger one with the Imperial German eagle stretches over the audience's heads, completely dominating the theatre. The audience always gasps in shock.

But all this terrifying imagery went completely over Dora's head – both literally and figuratively. During the scariest scene – the one that follows directly on from the concert, when the family is hiding from the Nazis in the graveyard at the back of the abbey – the actors were crouched under the rotating oval, blowing raspberries at each other and trying not to laugh. According to Dora, this was all started by her stage dad, Alex Hanson, and continued enthusiastically by all the children as well as Sophie and Connie.

Dora's entirely understandable failure to grasp the evil nature of Nazism became clear one Saturday morning shortly after her cousins had been to watch the show. We were at my sister Nikki's house. The grown-ups – me, Nikki and our dad – were relaxing on the sofas, gossiping, Dora, Millie and Freddie were snacking and chatting round the dining table. It wasn't long before we heard some loud giggles and repeated cries of 'Heil!' We went to look. The children were Nazi-saluting each other and laughing manically. It was funny, but we stopped them and told them not to do it anywhere else. Heiling wouldn't have gone down well in Millie and Freddie's (Jewish) school playground.

On the way home, I started trying to explain to Dora about Nazism, and why we'd stopped their game. I managed to avoid my usual tendency to pitch my explanations slightly above the appropriate level, feeling that a lecture on the origins of Fascism, the Weimar constitution and the history of anti-Semitism might go even further over Dora's head than the banners. So I told her a bit about Laurie's mother Lilli, who, at the age of ten, left home in what is now Wrocław, then Breslau, and travelled to France with her father. She was eleven when he sent her off to England, alone, in 1938, on a kindertransport boat from Boulogne. 'Can you imagine,' I asked Dora, 'what it must have felt like for her to leave her mummy and daddy and come to another country, not speaking the language and not knowing if she'd ever see them again?' Dora could and did imagine. She cried a lot and needed a very big cuddle before she stopped and asked why the Nazis were so horrible.

December. Dora bounced about on my lap chattering excitedly and clapping enthusiastically while we watched Kettles and Alicia on TV singing 'The Sound of Music' and 'Do-Re-Mi' on the *Royal Variety Performance*. The girls had emailed 'good luck' to each other for their respective television debuts (I'd tried to monitor Dora's spelling, but hadn't always been quick enough) and loved watching each other perform.

A couple of days later, I was surprised, after the recent concern that Dora was 'deviating from the blocking', when an email from Jo indicated that she was scheduled to do *Blue Peter* with Kettles. The next morning, Dora woke up and told me that she'd just dreamt that Adrianna was doing it instead of her. Later that day, Jo rang to tell me that Adrianna, not Dora, would be on *Blue Peter*. Dora was slightly upset that she wasn't going to be on TV again, but her disappointment was tempered by excitement. 'Mummy,' she exclaimed, gripping both my arms and jumping up and down, 'I saw into the future. I really did. Does that mean I might be magic? Like in *Harry Potter*?' Her innate sense of justice kicked in too: she and Alicia had already been on TV, Lauren was due to perform with Mittens on *New Year Live* on New Year's Eve. So it was only fair that Adrianna should get a go too. Shana, Adrianna's mum, rang later to check that Dora wasn't too upset, so I was able to reassure her that she wasn't. In the event, as well as the in-the-studio live performance featuring Kettles and Adrianna, they showed film of Kettles rehearsing with Alicia as well as electronic press kit footage of Kettles with Dora.

On the same day, Dora was presented with a special certificate by her headteacher. 'This is not,' Mrs Kendall said emphatically, as I squirmed in my chair at the back of the school hall, embarrassed at my child being singled out, whilst simultaneously grinning ear-to-ear with pride, 'for being in *The Sound of Music*. It's for everything else you're doing *while* being in *The Sound of Music*.' We put it on the mantelpiece where, before long, it was obscured by Christmas cards.

Dora and I watched *Blue Peter* together. 'There we go,' I said. 'You did get to be on after all.' Despite my best endeavours, however, she didn't get a Blue Peter badge. Embarrassing confession time. I emailed the programme to ask if, as they both appeared during the show, Dora and Alicia could have badges, not because Dora had expressed any interest in having one, but because I wanted her to. The reply was a polite but firm 'no', on the grounds that both children were in the background of the footage. I could, I thought, argue that they were both, in fact, featured, but in the end I decided that the battle wasn't worth fighting, mostly on the grounds that I'd be too embarrassed to admit to having fought it. Also, I was still cringing after the Julie Andrews Incident.

In fact, the cringing only stopped finally a year and a bit later, when I discovered that even Sylvia Young had had her own stage mother moment. 'When my daughter did her first audition for a commercial,' she told me, hands covering her face, 'and came out, I asked her how it went. She said, "It was very good. They asked me if I liked cornflakes, and I said 'No, not really.'"' I went back in,' Sylvia continued, 'and told them that she did like cornflakes. I was just very naïve and I thought I was being helpful and giving them info that they might need! Now I go red with embarrassment thinking about it.' Then she added, 'If you put that in the book, let me see it before you do, so I'm not embarrassed.'

I asked her why, in her opinion, stage mothers have such a terrible reputation, and whether we deserve it. She thought for a moment. 'There are certain stage mothers who will not recognise their own child's limitations and the talent of others. And that is where it gets very stupid. It's not just the mothers, fathers can be worse. And grandparents. My God! Face an angry grandparent . . . The problem is the minority who build their children up in their own mind and to their child, and they mislead their own child and expect too much. And that's very sad when that happens.

'But the majority of mums are not deserving of that stage mother title. They're quite sensible and take it in their stride and don't boast.'

I asked Redroofs' Sam Keston, too. She waxed eloquent. 'Why the reputation? Because they are a nuisance. They have aspirations beyond those of their children and are always looking for glory because they have produced a genetic marvel. They are often seen as living their own dreams through their children. Real stage mothers, although I'm pleased to report that we don't see very many, are quite repulsive, get in the way of the job in hand, and are honestly quite scary. They do more damage to their children than they will ever know and are guilty of ruining their children's childhoods. Of course stage mothers have their equivalents in academia – at least these kids aren't forced to take extra maths!'

She paused for breath. 'They can,' she added, 'be retrained. If the zoo is very firm.'

'Are a lot of us like that?' I asked, worried. 'Without realising it?'

'It's okay,' she replied. 'You're safe.'

Given the Julie Andrews and the Blue Peter Badge Incidents, perhaps not as safe as she might think.

Just before Christmas, the adult cast of *The Sound of Music* clubbed together, organised a party for the children and bought them all presents. If the spot-on appropriateness of Dora's present – a decorate-your-own cuddly unicorn – was anything to go by, a great deal of care and thought had gone into the whole arrangement. One of the Nazis dressed up as Father Christmas and distributed the gifts. There was a sing-song. Everyone had a lovely time. The children also did a 'secret Santa' for each other. Dora (or rather I) had to buy something for Greg, the Kettles' Friedrich. We were supposed to spend five pounds or less. Dora's secret Santa – who turned out to be the Kettles' Brigitta, Caroline – gave her a pair of blue Disney princess slipper socks with individual toes. She was thrilled. They were, she said, *exactly* what she wanted (apparently Molly-May had some). I didn't have a clue what to buy Greg, but having found out from his mum that he liked chocolate and practical jokes, I settled on a book of *Immature Pranks*, which wouldn't really be immature for a twelve-year-old, but he could always save some of them until he was older, and something called an Oops-a-Daisy: a plastic cow key-ring that pooped little brown sweets. At home, Dora, Laurie and I watched the BBC documentary about Connie, Dora providing extra commentary. At the Palladium, I'd stand at the back of the stalls about once a fortnight, sometimes alone, sometimes in the company of one or more of the other mums, loving the warm, soft feeling of almost belonging.

There's a moment in the show – the supreme Kleenex moment – when the children sing 'The Sound of Music' to Baroness Schraeder, and the captain realises, as Maria has just shouted at him, that he doesn't know his own children. All the girls – except Liesl – run to him for a cuddle. Then Kurt holds out his hand manfully for his father to shake, which he does, and pulls him in for a hug. I wasn't watching (Dora wasn't on) when, two days before Christmas, during the matinee performance, Kurt and the captain miscalculated and Kurt's head connected painfully with the captain's chin. Michael, who was playing Kurt, managed to keep it together for the rest of the scene, but as the show progressed, he developed a headache and started to feel sick. He was whisked off to hospital by Elizabeth, one of the chaperones who, handily, used to be a nurse.

For every other one of Michael's performances during his run, at least one of his parents had been around. But that day they'd dropped him off and headed up to the north of England, where they were performing a Christmas show with their ABBA tribute band, Y'Abba D'Abba. They'd arranged for one of the other von Trapp kids' parents to pick Michael up and return him home, where his almost-sixteen-year-old brother would be in charge until their parents returned – which they were due to do in the early hours of the morning.

His trip to hospital nixed that. Even though checks revealed him to be completely fine, the doctors couldn't release him unless he could be discharged into the care of an adult. When, earlier in the day, I'd heard about what happened, I'd rung his mum, Carol, to offer help if needed. I knew she'd do exactly the same for me and Dora, plus we live nearby and have a spare room. At half past ten, Elizabeth dropped Michael off at our house. I pulled out the sofa bed, fed him cheese on toast, lent him one of Laurie's vests to sleep in and left a note for Dora to say there was a surprise for her in the spare room, and it was called Michael. Next morning – Christmas Eve – Carol and Steve popped round to collect him with a huge tin of Celebrations and stayed for a while and it felt like an impromptu party. Laurie taught Michael a couple of Arabic drumming techniques and lent him a drum. The rest of us laughed and chatted and ate chocolates until it was time for me, Laurie and Dora to start packing to go to my father's house for Christmas.

I watched the show on Boxing Day, when Dora was on with Geese. Even after repeated viewings, the magic of *The Sound of Music* wasn't palling. Christmas Day had marked the mid-point of Dora's contract, and although there were more performances ahead of her than behind her, I was starting to feel conscious of time passing. As we headed into the New Year, everything seemed to be happening much quicker: the weeks, the shows, the gaps between them – everything, in fact, except the cold night-time waits by the wheelie bins – seemed to whizz by. A couple of weeks later, I was in again. This time she was on with Kettles, and most of the other parents were in the audience, several standing with me at the back of the stalls. 'Did you see?' one of the dads said. 'Andrew Lloyd Webber's in tonight. He's standing at the back of the sound desk.' I looked over. There was no one there. But the door into the bar behind was swinging.

Of the three teams' parents, whilst the Mittens mums probably spent the longest on the phone to each other, the Kettles mob were by far the loudest and most boisterous. When we met, we did a lot of jumping up and down and squealing, whilst clutching each other's arms. On this occasion, we were, if anything, slightly more over-excited than usual, and before Russ took them into the theatre, we wound our children up to fever pitch too. They ended up getting told off for talking and mucking about backstage. Dora came out that night feeling upset and sheepish – it was the only time she and Molly-May had been in trouble. I was surprised that we didn't get told off too, given how much noise we made, clutching each other's arms and squealing in the auditorium.

Although I never tired of watching the show, after a couple of months of schlepping Dora to the Palladium and picking her up after ten at night, I got progressively more fed up. The temperature had dropped and the dark wheelie-bin waits were becoming increasingly unpleasant. When I set off from home to collect her, I yearned for the evenings when I wouldn't have to leave my warm, paper-strewn sofa to stand and shiver, waiting for a small girl to come out, sign a few autographs, climb into her car seat, have a short tantrum (although in a mid-January epiphany I discovered that the application of a pain au chocolat and a carton of apple juice could prevent these) and then fall asleep. But every time I went in and watched the show, I felt completely different. My inner stage mother and I were in perfect agreement. We wanted it to go on for ever.

But of course, it couldn't.

★

On 12 January, Jo emailed all the parents:

> Hi guys.
> Today we had the final casting for the next teams and inevitably
> we are going to have some gaps. To assist us make decisions
> would you let me know whether you would stay on if you were
> asked. <u>This is not an offer</u> to anyone at this stage but it would
> help us if you could let us know. I realise it is a big decision but I
> would be really grateful if you would let me know as soon as
> possible! The new contract would finish in August and we will be
> unable to accommodate any holidays.

I consulted with Laurie and we agreed that, although both Dora and my inner stage mother would love to continue, as responsible adults we should overrule them both. Dora was tired and I felt that six months of her life was a lot – and certainly enough – to dedicate to a musical. The following term she'd be doing her SATs, and although she was keeping up well with her work and the school had been delighted for her to take part in the show, I thought Mrs Kendall would not take kindly to her absences continuing. She had also grown quite a lot in the nine months since she'd first auditioned, and was turning into a giant Gretl. She was, I suspected, probably too big to stay on in the role. Unlike her co-Gretls, all of whom were small for their age, Dora isn't, and, at nearly seven, looked like a nearly seven-year-old. Even if I'd been wavering, which despite Dora's pleading and my inner stage mother's desires I wasn't, I suspect I'd have decided it was better not to say 'yes' only to be told that they didn't want her to continue.

There were other reasons too. Whilst waiting outside the stage door in the cold dark of winter wasn't exactly my idea of fun, it was, I thought, preferable to Dora spending her long summer evenings in a theatre when she could be outside playing with her friends. In winter, when the alternatives were messy craft activities that never produced results equal to either the effort we put in or what we'd envisaged in the first place, or nagging her away from too much telly, it was the perfect way for her to spend her time. But summer is mostly for fresh air, running around and being noisy: it's not the ideal time of year to be spending two days a week trying – and usually managing – to control your natural ebullience while waiting quietly in the subterranean dark of backstage. Then there was the matter of my relationship with Laurie. Not many newly married husbands have to spend most of their first year of wedded bliss playing second fiddle to a bunch of nuns, Nazis and stage mothers. Despite occasional bursts of irritation at my obsessive interest in the show and everyone and everything to do with it, he'd been astonishingly supportive and tolerant. But if Dora had ended up carrying on, I think he would have divorced me.

A lot of the other parents said 'yes' to their children continuing. Six of them stayed on for the second run. We arranged to go on holiday to France at the very beginning of the Easter holidays – leaving the morning after the last night that Dora might possibly be performing. We were all looking forward to the break – especially Laurie, who hadn't been this long without a holiday in years, but was bearing up remarkably well, especially given that he was simultaneously being horribly neglected by his wife and recovering from an operation. Towards the end of the month, Song, the younger of our cats (named after the Korean footballer who scored the penultimate goal against Turkey in the 2002 World Cup playoff), died and we were all sad.

As January froze into February, the emails from Jo started to thin out. There were odd rehearsals and vocal clean-ups to tell us about, and the final version of the Gretl schedule, which had Dora finishing on Monday, 19 March, and then a big thank-you to all of us. But overall it felt like the end of a love affair – the kind that fizzles out when you gradually find you have nothing more to say to each other, rather than the sort that ends in an explosion of argument and recrimination. I found a couple of ways to fill the void. I was worried that our remaining moggie, Jarvis (who, being fat and stupid, was badly misnamed after Jarvis Cocker), was feeling bereaved and lonely, and whilst I didn't want to hurry him through the grieving process, I felt he needed a companion. We were all feeling a bit bereaved and lonely: Song had been an engaging animal who demanded lots of attention, and we missed her. I started looking for another cat. Or, more accurately, I threw myself into a full-on cat research programme, and although at first Laurie appreciated the fact that my conversation had broadened to include a second topic, the novelty wore off pretty quickly.

Russ and his colleagues were organising little parties for each team of children, which would take place between the matinee and evening performances of the last Saturday they were on. These would be lovely, but meant that neither the kids nor us parents would have the opportunity to celebrate together and say goodbye properly. So a few of us mums got chatting and decided to organise something ourselves. I emailed round asking everyone for ideas for venues and themes, and Tracy Lane wrote back immediately, generously and possibly foolhardily – did she know what we were like? – offering her and David Ian's beautiful house in Buckinghamshire and volunteering to help with catering. After a lot of information-sharing and a little bit of discussion, the parents all agreed that this would be fantastic, and we settled on Sunday, 18 March as the date most people could make.

Meanwhile, there were payslips to open and cheques to bank and spend. As the days grew longer, I took Dora to our local bike shop to make her first purchase: a shiny silver bike with gears – more gears, in fact, than she'll ever need. She also wanted a pair of Heelys: the trainers with built-in wheels in the heel. I also thought they looked like really good fun, but had some reservations – mostly about the relationship between how much they cost and the length of time for which they could be used. Like shoes, she'd need a new pair as soon as her feet grew. We'd discussed the relative merits of Heelys and roller blades, and because they are adjustable and would therefore last her through several shoe sizes, I steered her towards the latter. I also thought they were probably safer: she would be more likely to don the necessary protective clothing and less likely to accidentally zip into the road and under a car. She donated ten pounds to Children in Need and also, just before the very end of her run, bought herself a cheap, grown-up video camera. I did think this might be a bit indulgent for a seven-year-old. But it seemed like a better, more sensible purchase than the sort of pink plastic Barbie house she might otherwise have invested in. ('I didn't know I could've bought a Barbie house,' complained Dora, when we read this through. 'You didn't tell me.') We now have several very wobbly home videos featuring loud, tangential, voiceovers. Despite her repeated offers to buy sweeties for everyone, the rest of her money is still in her bank account.

With all this bubbling away in the background, Dora continued to perform, on average, two days a week, beaver away at her school work and, when she got the time, socialise. One Saturday when she was having a post-show sleepover at Molly-May's, the two girls burst out of the theatre and told Molly's dad and sisters that they'd met Tony Bear. In-depth questioning revealed that the then prime minister had, indeed, popped backstage, possibly in the interval, possibly with his wife and one young child (Leo?), and was 'nice'. Further research revealed that he had asked Russ if he was Captain von Trapp.

Back in November, Dora had had to miss a sleepover birthday party, and had only been able to put in a fleeting visit at another do, where she couldn't join in the makeover experience as, two hours later, she needed to be at the theatre, looking like a five-year-old. Her bottom lip quivered and tears welled. 'When this is all over,' I promised her, 'you'll be able to see more of your friends, and get your face painted and your nails varnished.' It was time to start preparing her for the aftermath of *The Sound of Music*. How would we fill the void? What if this was the best thing that ever happened to her and it happened when being mature meant acting her shoe size not her age?

I had been warned by Russ, and by other mothers, that performing children – like grown-up performers – get post-run blues when their contract's over. And also that the last night tends to be very traumatic. 'Oh my God, the sobbing,' said Pippa, Piers's mum, who has loads of experience of this sort of thing. 'This business is one long round of goodbyes. On one show, this poor girl did her last date with her team, and stood outside the theatre sobbing with them for about an hour. Then she got called back in another day, because someone was ill, and had to do the sobbing all over again with another group of children. It's awful when it finishes, and you just stand there watching your child being horribly upset. And the more children there are in a cast, the worse it is.' That was something to look forward to, then. I'd better make sure that Dora had plenty to go on to once her run in the show ended. There was the holiday in France with her cousins immediately afterwards, which should postpone the misery. And I knew she'd be happy to have time to hang out with her friends and go back to her dance lessons. What else did we need to plan to keep her buoyant? Or should I let her experience the crash? Was it an emotionally necessary part of the process?

I devoted a lot of time and attention to worrying about this. Part of me – the stage mother bit – was keen to take Russ and his wife Linda's advice, which was to get Dora out auditioning for something else as soon as she finished in *The Sound of Music*. But I wasn't sure. That would mean buying into a particular kind of lifestyle, not only for her, but for me and Laurie as well. Not all shows are quite as demanding time-wise as *The Sound of Music* had been. There are, inevitably, more rehearsals when your child's in the first run, simply because the directors are working everything out as they go along. When they join a show that's already up and running, the commitment is less. Also, there are very few shows where the children have as much to do as in *The Sound of Music*. The children who play young Cosette, Eponine and Gavroche in *Les Mis*, for instance, do their bit and quit the theatre in the interval – even on the days when they're doing both matinee and evening performances. That means that they can get home to bed at an almost reasonable hour and hardly miss any school. But was it healthy to take that step? Would I then have committed her to spending her childhood either working or auditioning? On the other hand, if I didn't let her carry on and do more performing, which she loved, had a talent for and appeared to have suffered few, if any, ill-effects from, would I be stifling something in her? Is it either all – a constant round of castings and auditions, the majority of which come to nothing more than the cost of a return trip into the West End and three hours out of our day – or nothing? A life that, after the excitement of *The Sound of Music*, would feel a bit dowdy and boring? Could there be a happy medium? Could Dora do some performing – might she be satisfied with local am-dram shows? – without all three of our lives having to centre entirely around her schedule? If so, how, when the whole world of performing children felt so all-consuming, so seductive? Had I inadvertently opened a small, but quite dramatic, version of Pandora's box? I started asking some of the other parents about their children's agents.

Although I was more than happy standing at the back of the stalls, on a couple of occasions towards the end of Dora's run I managed to book day seats in the front row – the ones you have to queue up to buy on the morning of the show and which cost the same as standing tickets. I loved sitting there. It was a completely different experience from being anywhere else in the theatre. You could watch every change in facial expression, hear the whirr of machinery moving the set, and make eye contact with your child and her friends (but only during the curtain call, or they'd get into trouble). You could chat with members of the orchestra. You could see everything, except the actors' feet and ankles. One day when I was watching from there, I leaned into the orchestra pit to natter with Ros Jones, the children's musical director, who also plays keyboards in the show and every now and then conducts the orchestra. I asked her if she could spare the time to meet up for coffee and chat about what would be the best tack for me to take with Dora once she'd finished in the show. I liked Ros a lot. She was friendly and fun and seemed down-to-earth, the kind of person who would probably have sensible ideas about what to do with a post-*Sound of Music* seven-year-old.

Unlike me, Dora hadn't thought too much about how she'd spend her time after she'd finished in the show so I tried to keep it positive, focusing on the things she'd be able to do that she couldn't while she was working. She'd have the chance to ride her shiny new bike, play with her friends, go on holiday, do her SATs and her Grade 1 ballet exam (very exciting! Dora thinks tests and exams are fun and was slightly miffed to discover, when she started Year 3, that she wouldn't get to do another round of SATs). But she was sad about finishing and cross that we hadn't said yes to her doing a second run, even though she very sensibly recognised that she was probably getting too big to still be Gretl.

Towards the end of February, a flurry of friends and relatives descended on the Palladium – which meant I had to source tickets (much easier now the show had been running for a few months and I was on first-name terms with several of the box office staff), arrange to meet people and remember when and where I'd arranged to meet them. This was also the start of the busy time of the year for me, meaning that I needed to refocus so I could devote an appropriate amount of time, energy and attention to my work. I had already lost my librarian training work largely because my head and heart were at the theatre instead of in the library, and I didn't want to jeopardise any of my other jobs. Then there were tickets for Dora's last night. None of us mums could work out why that particular show was sold out, when there were tickets available for most other nights. Alan, who manages the box office and had been very helpful, explained: it was because Connie was originally going to finish that night. We told him why we were so desperate for tickets and he promised that just this once, *just this once*, he would let us reserve day seats. So most of us would get to sit together, which meant we'd be able to exchange glances, share tissues and, as one of the more experienced stage mums said, throw flowers at the children when they took their final bows. 'Can we really do that?' I asked, wondering whether I should practise beforehand, and if so, how and where.

Early in March, Mrs Kendall, Mrs Arin (Dora's teacher) and eight of her classmates made the excited journey from Harlesden to watch a matinee. I had coffee with Ros the same day, which provided my first opportunity to discuss what I should do with Dora after she'd finished in the show with someone who was in the business and knew her. First, and most important, would be piano lessons. Then, I thought, I would probably let her have an agent – if they would take her, the agency run by Molly-May's grandmother and aunts at Redroofs, rather than going to Young 'Uns, the Sylvia Young agency, which represented most of the *Sound of Music* children. I'd made that decision for two reasons. Firstly, I hoped it would help maintain Dora's friendship with Molly-May. And secondly, the Redroofs agency is very selective about the auditions they send children to, so they don't do that many. It's an ethos that recognises acting work as part of the children's lives, rather than, at this stage, a career. The children with Young 'Uns do have a juvenile career. They are always auditioning, usually working. It is a life choice made by them and their parents, and having got to know so many happy, confident, intelligent, beautiful, kind and down-to-earth children living that life – and several young adults who have graduated from it – it seems like a fine one. That said, I wasn't about to commit Dora and, by extension, Laurie and me to it.

The following Tuesday I met Tracy Lane, her mum Janet and her housekeeper Tania – a calm, sensible woman studying to be a nutritionist – at Costco in Watford to shop for food and drink for the end-of-run party. I had to join to go in with them, which involved paying a small fee in exchange for a small plastic card featuring a grainy black and white pic of me looking like a cartoon character whose face had been run over and squished pancake-flat. We grabbed a couple of giant trolleys and steered them around the warehouse, the size and contents of which left me feeling tiny, intimidated and completely incapable of deciding which varieties of cheese to buy. Fortunately, the others were much more confident and capable, and having decided that the food should be Italian because 'it's easier to decide what to make if you have a theme' and Mexican might be too spicy for some of the children, they filled their trolleys quickly, competently and comprehensively. This inevitably left me feeling even more dithery and ineffectual, but, hey, the food shopping was done. And at least I'd been there, lending moral support and smiling.

Tracy paid for the shopping, promising to let me know how much everything cost so we could divide the cost of the food amongst all the families, but she and David bought wine and beer, and juices for the kids. Tania and Tracy unpacked the trolleys and then repacked them on the other side of the checkout, whilst I hovered uselessly and Janet made a few well-timed and intelligent interventions. Then they packed their cars and Tania headed back to the house. I treated Tracy and Janet to a couple of truly revolting jacket potatoes in the Costco canteen and Tracy told me about her stage career – 'in the end, I got bored of having to do the same thing eight times a week for twelve months [that's how long the contract is for adult performers in musicals]. There I was, towards the end of my run, tapping away in *42nd Street*, thinking about what I was going to cook for dinner and the ingredients I'd need . . .'

Dora wasn't ready to finish the next Monday with Mittens. 'I wish I could do my last show with Molly-May,' she sighed, on more than one occasion. Before the final schedule had arrived, I'd emailed Jo to ask if there was any chance this might be possible – especially as I knew Adrianna would love to do Mittens' final show with them. But Jo kept the end of the schedule in line with the preceding few weeks, and who could blame her? Adapt the timetable to please one stage mother, and the floodgates would open and the requests cascade in: 'You did it for X, why won't you do it for us?' making her job – which involves juggling a mind-boggling number of variables – completely impossible. 'Never mind,' I said, and we decided to buy tickets for the other teams' final nights so Dora could be there and cheer her friends when they finished.

She was satisfied with that. But during the week leading up to her final few shows, I heard a whisper that her wish might come true. There was a slight difficulty with the schedule. It had been drawn up on the assumption that none of the children would be continuing in their roles. Adrianna and Alicia – two of the Gretls – *were* carrying on, and it now looked like they might be scheduled to do too many performances over the couple of weeks when their old teams were finishing and their new ones starting. There was a possibility that Dora might be called back to cover a few of their shows. I didn't mention this to her, in case it didn't happen.

She was, in any case, busy looking forward to the parties: the backstage team one, which, she was driven to a fever pitch of excitement to report, would involve not only a chocolate fountain, but also strawberries! And *marshmallows*!!! Then there would be the big party at Emily Lane's house and, on her last night, a pre-show dinner with me and all her friends in Mittens at Piccolino's, which Jack's mum Sally had organised. Meanwhile, I was busy. As well as shopping with Tracy that week, I had several meetings to attend, my first ever video edit to supervise and twenty novels to read and write about over the next four weeks. In the middle of a manic week, during which I was running around Tescos sweeping food into my trolley whilst simultaneously reading a novel about middle-class women trying to make sense of their lives whilst out shopping, a thought struck me rigid. End of run. Cards. Presents. What would we be expected to give and to whom? I rang Helen, my font of wisdom on such matters, and a couple of the others. Yes. There would be cards. And pressies. Yikes. That afternoon, I sat Dora down. Together we compiled a list of everyone she wanted to give cards and pressies to. We decided that, given the state of my bank account, which, after six months of *The Sound of Music*, was ailing like a wan Victorian maid, and the fact that I didn't know most of the people concerned well enough to know what they'd really like, she would make the presents for the grown-ups, and we'd buy gifts for the children.

On Saturday, when I dropped Dora off at the Palladium, I felt sad. She wasn't ready for it all to stop yet, and nor was I. My inner stage mother, I knew, would never be ready, but I had hoped that the rest of me would have had enough by now. Laurie certainly had. One or two of the other mums whose kids were finishing on the Monday were watching the show that night as well, but I resisted the temptation, travelled home on the tube, reading one of my work books, and turned my attention to cards and presents. This was my one and only shopping opportunity. I bought chocolates for the boys and jewellery and pretty little handbags for the girls on the two teams – Mittens and Kettles – that Dora had done all but a few of her shows and rehearsals with, and also for the other Gretls. I bought packs of cards for her to write – trying to make those as well would be more than we could manage.

What with the party on Sunday, and a Monday packed with work commitments, there was no way we could have all the grown-ups' pressies ready for Dora's final evening. But as we were planning to come and watch the other teams' final nights, we could drop the gifts and cards off then, which took some of the pressure off. In the end, our creative activities session stretched over the following week, took up the whole of our front room and left both of us looking preternaturally pale due to excessive exposure to powdered plaster. I mixed water into the plaster and poured the resulting gloop into fridge-magnet and mirror-frame moulds, while Dora painted and glittered, got frustrated waiting for the plaster to dry and made an impressive amount of mess. In total we produced four hand-painted cups, to which we added chocolate Easter eggs; one hand-painted suncatcher; three hand-cast and hand-decorated mirrors and twelve bejewelled fridge magnets. It doesn't sound that much when it's all compressed into one sentence, but it felt like a cottage industry. I was exhausted and hoped the plaster dust wasn't too carcinogenic.

Dora loved the chocolate fountain party. The children had decided weeks before that it was going to be a masquerade. At least the girls had. The boys weren't quite so keen on the idea, but were outvoted four to two. One of Dora's friends had given her a beautiful mask for her birthday – all black and gold glitter, with an entire mating display's-worth of black, gold and brown feathers splayed on one side. She donned her fifties-style pink party frock and even pinker jacket, and clutched her mask so it hovered over her broad grin. I let her take my camera in to the theatre with her, and judging from the slightly out-of-focus photos, a great deal of chocolate was eaten. And smeared. I've no idea how the chaperones and dressers managed to get the six children clean enough to go back on stage for the evening performance. Anyway, Dora came out that night with an even bigger grin and a carrier bag of cards and small farewell gifts. Amongst these were a couple of little books for messages. Dora hadn't been terribly organised about asking people to write goodbyes in her book: collecting autographs would have meant moving away from the chocolate fountain, and why would she want to do that? But the few messages she'd garnered were lovely, full of affection and generosity.

'Was the party fun?' I asked her in the car.

'There was a chocolate fountain. And Jack was *sick* because he ate too much chocolate!'

'What, really sick?' I asked, finding it hard to imagine sensible, grown-up Jack making himself sick on chocolate.

'Really!' she said excitedly. 'And Grace got chocolate *all round her face!*'

'Did you eat lots of chocolate too?'

'Some. I'm hungry. Where's my chocolate croissant?'

'I've got you this instead.' I handed her a pain aux raisins. 'I thought you might have had enough chocolate.' This was a lie. The shop had sold out of pains au chocolat.

'How were the shows?' I asked.

'Okay,' she replied, concentrating on eating.

'Only one more to go.' As I hadn't heard anything about the two following weekends, I assumed they'd managed to rejig the schedule without calling her back in. 'Are you sad?'

'I'll be sad on Monday,' she said, concentrating on her cake. 'I don't want any more. You eat it,' and she thrust a paper bag full of crumbs and one small, curved crust through the gap in the seats. I ate it when we stopped at traffic lights. She closed her eyes. *I'll be sad on Monday*, I thought. *I'm going to miss the show. I'm going to miss the people. I'm going to miss telling people that my daughter's in the show. I'm going to have to deal with Dora missing being in the show.* I made myself think about the next day's party. Must remember to buy the flat-bread . . .

Sunday's weather was pretty typical for mid-March in London. I walked round to our local twenty-four-hour supermarket to pick up the bread in the sunshine, then home again in the rain. While I was getting ready and chivvying the others along, Tracy rang to ask if we'd come earlier than we were intending. Dora decided not to wear a party dress this time, but to go 'cool', and put on a summer dress over jeans, finishing the outfit off with a denim jacket. I settled for black dress over black trousers that didn't quite match, but knew that, happily, nobody would care enough about what I looked like to notice.

I shouted at everyone to get into the car. 'Come on! We'll be late! LAURIE! WHAT ARE YOU DOING!?' Dora was ready by the door. Laurie wasn't, and seemed, as usual, completely unconcerned that my stress levels were rising rapidly. There was no way, obviously, that we were going to be late. We were leaving very early. 'THAT'S SO WE CAN HELP TRACY GET EVERYTHING READY!' Why was that our job? 'BECAUSE I OFFERED!' Why did I offer? 'BECAUSE I'M NICE?' Why didn't my niceness extend to him? 'ARE YOU TRYING TO WIND ME UP?' What made me think he needed to try?

'Can I wait in the car?' asked Dora helpfully.

We both went to wait in the car. I studied the route. I turned the engine on and then switched it off. I checked my make-up in the little mirror and wished I hadn't: somehow, like my dress and trousers, the different parts of my face didn't seem to quite match either. I turned the key again, and turned the car round to face the right way. 'Are we going without Daddy?' Dora asked.

'Here he comes,' I said.

Laurie double-locked the front door, walked slowly over to the car, opened the back door, slowly and carefully put a spare pair of shoes in the footwell and a precisely folded spare jumper on the back seat. Then he took off his jacket, folded it carefully, put it down next to the jumper and got into the passenger seat. 'Hurry up,' I hissed, scowling at him. 'Do up your seatbelt.' Then I realised that I'd forgotten to bring the bread, jumped out of the car, ran back to the house, opened the door, found it, then realised I'd forgotten a jacket, ran to the coat cupboard in the kitchen, dithered over which one to bring, grabbed one at random, double locked the front door, sprinted to the car and hung the jacket on the back of my seat, from where it fell crumpled on to the floor. I left it there and strapped myself in. Laurie, to his credit, said nothing and barely even smirked.

It was a quick and easy journey, and we arrived at Tracy's house in plenty of time to help out. Tracy's mum Janet, Pippa and Piers were already there, Pippa and Janet hard at work chopping things. Tracy set me to work preparing salad. There were four lasagnes – two meat, two veggie – already cooking and the same number of pizzas ready to go in once the lasagnes were cooked. Then there were drinks to prepare: we mixed massive jugs of something Christine's mum, Wendy, suggested, called River Thames (Coke and orange juice), and a basic virgin colada – pineapple juice and coconut milk. Laurie got stuck in washing glasses and I started putting out crisps. 'Keep the sweet things for later,' said Tracy sensibly. The sweet things included twenty-four individual brown-paper-package-tied-up-with-string cakes, decorated with icing-sugar red roses, each with a delicately placed raindrop on it, that Connie had sent for the children.

The kids and their families started to arrive. Carol, Steve and Michael brought their karaoke machine. The younger children ran around shrieking, hugging each other and playing. The older kids helped themselves and each other to non-alcoholic cocktails, complete with paper umbrellas, hugged and chatted. The parents gossiped, drank, helped out in the kitchen and photographed and videoed the proceedings. All nineteen of the children, plus family members came – even those who'd originally thought they wouldn't be able to make it. The karaoke machine proved a great hit. At the time, David Ian was working on the reality TV shows for *Grease* in both the US and UK. The soundtrack went on to the CD machine and all the kids who knew the songs sang, clustered around the microphone. Dora got the bug, and it wasn't until Laurie and I took her to see *Hairspray* six months later and I downloaded the sound-track that we were allowed to eject her *Grease* CD from the car stereo. I got slightly fed up of listening to it, but reflected that her *Grease* obsession had, at least, spared us the hell that is *High School Musical* . . . There was dancing. And a quick speech – David was away, but had left a letter for Tracy to read to the kids, talking about how hard they'd all worked and how well they'd done.

And then, suddenly, it was five o'clock and time to go home. After some tidying up and a lot of hugging, we left and drove home, and got there quickly enough for Dora to have an early night before her last show.

SO LONG, FAREWELL

Before Dora went to bed on Sunday night, we checked that she'd written all the cards for her friends performing the following evening and that we'd wrapped the presents. She was a bit uncertain about what to write, so we'd discussed a few alternatives: *I've loved working with you, good luck for the future*; *I'll miss you*; *See you soon, I hope!* I had supervised closely. When she'd been doing the good luck cards, the spellings and sentiments had been completely straightforward. But goodbye messages felt more complex. And after the Mother's Day card she'd given me the previous year, across which, in her best joined-up handwriting, she'd carefully formed the words 'I Love you so much Mummy so I send you a speshil mesig. Your the beast,' I thought with these cards I'd best keep an eye. We didn't want to accidentally spoil any friendships or cause any unnecessary upset.

Laurie took her to school on Monday morning as I had to go to a meeting and interview some people on video. I dashed home later – via Marks and Spencer, where I bought a bunch of roses, bathed and changed and, having made sure that I had all the presents and cards for everyone performing that night, grabbed a suitably huge wodge of tissues, carefully dethorned the roses to ensure the flower-throwing experience didn't go horribly wrong, and collected Dora from school slightly early. This was partly because it was a special night and I wanted her to have the chance to squeeze every last gram of enjoyment out of it, and partly because I wanted the chance to squeeze every last gram of enjoyment out of it. There was also a video edit to approve en route, supper to eat with all the other children performing that night and their families, and tickets for me, Laurie and my dad to collect from the box office.

We rushed home so Dora could change into other clothes and went straight into town. I asked her how she was feeling and she shrugged. I suspected that it didn't feel like the end yet, that it wouldn't until later that evening, when she was experiencing rather than anticipating it.

The editing took slightly longer than I had hoped, then we ran to the restaurant where we were meeting everyone else. A few of the others had already arrived and so we found places to sit – me at one end with some grown-ups, and Dora at the other end with her friends. We ordered quickly, as the kids didn't have long before they had to be at the stage door. While we were waiting for the food, I decided to dash down and pick up the tickets. I could have waited until we took the children down to the stage door, but I was tense with worry. What if it was too late to pick them up and the box office thought I wasn't coming and sold them to someone else? Anyway, there should be enough time between ordering and the food arriving to fit it in, and as Dora didn't care whether I was there or not and there were plenty of responsible grown-ups around to keep an eye on her, off I went, dashing down Upper Regent Street, across Oxford Circus, into Argyll Street, into the box office, out of the box office, back across Oxford Circus, etc., back to my risotto, and a wave of embarrassment as it was Lynn's birthday and almost everyone else had bought her a birthday present and I hadn't (because I didn't know it was her birthday) and because Adrianna was there (which I didn't know she would be) and I hadn't brought her present with me either.

In a scrummage of wrapping paper, the children exchanged and opened their gifts, forgot where they'd put some of the things, found them, thanked each other and ate some of their dinner and all of their ice cream as quickly as they could. Lynn and I volunteered to herd them all down to the theatre. Adrianna and her dad came too. It was raining and we were a bit late, which, naturally, everyone apart from me was completely relaxed about.

When we reached the stage door, Russ took me aside to say that Jo Hawes would be emailing to confirm that they did want Dora to come back the next weekend and the one after. I called Dora over and let him tell her there and then, hoping that knowing she was coming back for more might mean she would cry less that night. She jumped up and down ecstatically. Her wish had come true and she'd be doing her last performance with Molly-May! I was delighted, partly because she was so happy, but also because it meant that her last show wouldn't be anyone else's last show. That would, I hoped, make it all less traumatic, as there would be no mass hysteria, just one child wailing quietly and inconsolably. There was another up side for Dora. In a surfeit of jamminess, she would get to be at all three teams' farewell parties. The joy of this was not lost on her. 'Mummy! I'll get three goes at the chocolate fountain! *Three goes!*'

Lynn, Darren, Adrianna and I waved the kids off and went back to Piccolino's to finish our dining experience and collect all our kids' presents. There were cuddly toys and painstakingly handmade pots and fridge magnets, jewellery – Jack and his family had bought the girls silver heart locket pendants with *Sound of Music 2007* engraved on them – and pens and chocolates. A lot of people had gone to a lot of trouble. We sipped liqueurs and dunked biscotti, then paid the bill and made our way to the theatre, laden with flowers for throwing, our children's gifts and enough tissues to mop up a melted polar ice cap.

I met up with Laurie, who was grabbing a quick snack in Café Libre. My father joined us there. I put Dora's bag of gifts in the car and hovered around the table where they were both sitting, clasping our tickets firmly, checking the time on my phone (I don't possess an actual watch) every fifteen seconds. There were still twenty minutes to go before the show started and it would take us precisely two minutes to reach the theatre and another two to get to our seats. Laurie was reaching the end of his snack in a sensible, relaxed, unhurried sort of way – perfectly reasonable given that no hurry was called for. I, obviously, didn't see it like that and hopped around nagging him to get going. He ignored me manfully, until we were in the theatre and I calmed down.

We were sitting to the far right of the stage, in row A. I leaned over into the orchestra pit to say hello to Ros, whose keyboard-playing position was just in front of us. Then the voice of Nick Bromley, company manager, invited us to switch off our mobile phones and welcome that night's conductor, and the lights went down. We mums waved tissues at each other and made sad-but-happy faces. The music swelled. My smile spread. This wasn't, as it turned out, the last time I would watch Dora in *The Sound of Music*, but it was the last time I would do so from the front row, with a whole bunch of friends, making eye contact as we recognised the particular idiosyncratic touches each child brought to their role. Grace's hand movements during the 'Do-Re-Mi' scene. John's facial expressions when all the children end up in Maria's bedroom during the thunderstorm. Dora's ferocious shoulder-shrug when Grace, during the concert scene, tried to steer her gently to where she should have been standing, and Dora, absolutely convinced she was in the right place, refused to go anywhere. At the tear-jerking point in the play where the children hug their father for the first time, several of the kids in the cast actually started crying, which set off the mums.

My contact lenses weren't quite as salted up as they were the first time I saw the show – but it was close. At the end, there was the usual standing ovation, and we all stood up and threw flowers. One of mine hit Jack on the head – thank goodness I'd dethorned. Most of the children – and all of the parents – were in tears during the bow.

By the time Russ led the kids out of the theatre, the tears had evolved into full-scale sobbing. Except for John, who was non-chalantly dry-eyed, the von Trapp children were bawling. Which was slightly ironic, as half of them weren't actually finishing that night – both Grace (Brigitta) and Yasmin (Marta) were continuing through a second run and Dora had another six shows to go. But it was about the team splitting up as much as the experience ending. All three teams of children had bonded closely together. It wasn't only the show they'd miss. It was the intense friendships that had, inevitably, developed in the working environment. Laurie, Dad and I let the sobbing Dora hug everyone theatrically, then led her off to the car, told her she'd done fantastically and handed over her pain au chocolat.

The following Saturday – Dora's final performance with Geese team – saw a slightly reduced sobfest. As Olivia (Brigitta) was, like her little sister Alicia, doing a second run and scheduled to do too many shows that week, Grace was brought in to cover for her on the Friday and Saturday shows. 'It was my last *ever* show with Grace,' Dora cried tragically en route to the car, instantly forgiving her older stage-sister for trying to steer her into position. She perked up, though, when I told her that I had, on her behalf, ordered the video camera she'd decided to buy, and that she could take it to the party the following weekend.

Although Dora was very tired and in need of a break, I was glad she'd got to do these few extra shows. It gave her a chance to say goodbye to all the other children properly: the Gretls who she was covering for came to the parties, so she got to see them too. It made a proper end to the experience. Closure. For me too. Also, it meant that she finished only a couple of days before we were due to go on holiday with her cousins, so we'd be on to something else fun and exciting straight away.

The intervening week was full of school, dance lessons and early nights with me reading from *Harry Potter* (we were now on . . . *and the Goblet of Fire*). Then, suddenly, it was the end of term and her final weekend on the show. She was very excited about taking her video camera in with her. She also had a bag of gifts and cards for the Kettles team and the grown-ups, and my little digital camera, which I surreptitiously asked Russ to please ask a grown-up to take some photos on.

Because we had so much to carry, I'd driven into town that day. We were, as usual, early, and as I couldn't find an extortionately expensive parking space nearby, I waited on the single yellow line by the stage door. Molly-May started handing out her cards and presents. She and her mum Helen had made an impressive card. It was an *OK!* magazine cover pastiche, entitled *Oi!*, featuring pictures of the children: one from the press launch, the one of Kettles and Dora singing 'The Lonely Goatherd' that was displayed on the front of the theatre, and two from the end-of-run party, with the children all bundled in colourfully together. There was also one of Molly-May, looking fetching costumed up as Marta, with Russ, also looking fetching costumed up as Marta. The 'headlines' read 'ORIGINAL CAST VON TRAPP CHILDREN SAD TO LEAVE THE SOUND OF MUSIC'; 'Such fun from the very beginning!' and 'On and off stage we're just like a real family'. The one under the picture of Molly and Russ read 'The fun we've had with chaperones', and had two exclamation marks. Molly-May had also hand-painted eggcups for her friends – Dora's was dotty and said 'Gretl' on it. I popped these, and the other gifts and cards that were distributed before Russ came out to collect the kids, into the car, which I had to keep checking in case there were any traffic wardens in the area. By some unfeasible stroke of luck, I'd managed to reach the end of the run without incurring a single parking ticket. I didn't want to ruin my unblemished record on the last day.

After the kids had gone in, I found somewhere to park and went to give a small 'thank you' box of choccies to the box office staff and to ask Alan if there was any chance of one standing ticket for that evening's performance. I didn't want a seat: I'd already done the big-last-night-throwing-flowers thing, but I did want to be there to watch Dora's last show. No problem. He printed one out for me. I walked round the corner, bought a final pain au chocolat and drove home.

That night Dora's voice was uncharacteristically quiet, croaky and wobbly, but she just about held it together through the performance. I stood alone, leaning on my usual railing – the parents of all the others in the team would be there on Monday for their final night – enjoying the show but tearing up as waves of sadness about this fairytale experience being properly over washed gently over me. Never mind how Dora felt, I would, I knew, miss this like anything. My inner stage mother wasn't even speaking to me. She was in a complete strop, because I'd let Dora's time in the spotlight – her time in the reflected glory – come to an end. How could I deprive the two of them of all this pleasure? What was the matter with me that I thought it was time for Dora to stop? Yes, okay, she was a bit tired and she was doing her SATs next term and she was only seven. But so what? She was a pro. It was her thing and I should just let her carry on and do this all the time. Education? Smeducation. She's clever enough, and if she decides later that she's missed out, she can always go back to learn some more. Let her live for the moment!

At the end of the show, I rushed to the front and cheered her and waved. When I collected Dora from the stage door, she handed me a carrier bag full of the shoes she wore on stage. She was sad, but after she'd said goodbye to all her friends, I gave her a big hug and the pain au chocolat and told her that if she liked, we could wait so she could say goodbye to all the adult cast. We hung around and waited. She said goodbye to everyone. There were lots more hugs. We left after eleven, when Connie Fisher and Lesley Garrett came out, and suggested she could come back and be Marta when she was a bit older.

'Can I?' she asked me excitedly.

'We'll see,' I said. 'Did you use your video camera?'

'Yes,' she said. 'Lots. I was crying before the show and in the interval.'

'I thought so,' I said. 'Your voice sounded a bit croaky.'

'Yes,' she said. 'But I didn't cry on stage.'

EPILOGUE:
WHAT DORA DID NEXT

Went on holiday.

Did well in her Key Stage 1 SATs and Grade 1 ballet exam.

Played with friends old and new.

Restarted piano lessons (we adopted my Auntie Ruth's underused piano and all three of us are learning).

Participated enthusiastically in a singing and dancing summer school at Redroofs, then in a local am-dram panto.

Felt different.

'COME BACK RIGHT NOW OR YOU WON'T BE GETTING AN AGENT!' probably wasn't the most appropriate thing to shout down a crowded street after a child who'd scooted too far ahead, but it worked, even though we both knew it was an empty threat. A few months after the end of her run, I took her to meet June Rose, Molly-May's grandma and the founder and head of Redroofs Theatre School. They signed her to their agency. Dora has an entry in *Spotlight*, featuring two smiley black and white photos of her (with foliage) taken by my dad. People have often asked me if she's going to do anything else.

My answer has always been, 'If something comes up that feels right, why not?'

The *Sound of Music* experience was fabulous. Dora loved the feeling of belonging, the challenge of meeting the high standards required and the sheer, unbeatable buzz of performing. It was, I'm certain, good for her emotional and intellectual development and had no adverse effects on her schoolwork – although it wasn't brilliant for her relationships with her classmates.

She still leaps at every opportunity to sing, dance and act, not caring whether the production is amateur or professional, whether the performance takes place in a West End theatre, the local town hall, or simply in a living room in front of a couple of mums. But she gets frustrated if other performers don't take the quality issue as seriously as she does.

It's a good job that Dora doesn't care where she performs, as there's been a big gap between jobs. She was offered the role in the police drama that I turned down, then nothing for six months. So she didn't go out to work again until a year after she finished her run on *The Sound of Music*. It felt like an eternity to her. But to have upped her chances of getting work, I would have had to take a deep breath, plunge us into the full-on world of working children, commit us to life-eating rounds of auditions, and not be too picky about which roles we said 'yes' to. And even then, that would have been no guarantee. You can be perfect for one part – like Gretl in *The Sound of Music* – at the age of six and then not what the casting directors have in mind for anything else for years and years. Or, indeed, ever.

Instead, slightly grudgingly, I have given up my lazy Saturday mornings and now drive her to Redroofs, where she dances, sings and acts her way through tap, script workshop and musical theatre classes. 'I fit in here,' she says, happily. Then, a week before this book went to press, she landed two parts – a little job as an extra on the BBC production of *Little Dorrit* and a lovely role in a bright and quirky mixed live-action and stop-motion animation film. Made by graduate students at the National Film and Television School,

Goodbye Mr. Pink features a young brother and sister, Alex and Rose – Dora plays Rose – dealing with the death (of old age, as the director specifies, rather sweetly, in the script) of their pet rabbit.

I still don't fully understand what drives people to get up on stage or in front of the camera. Or why the act of performing seems to come so naturally to some and not to others. Having observed Dora and her pals, I'm convinced that, in the main, it's not about attention-seeking. If anything, it's quite the opposite: about fitting in and being part of something, the desire to contribute, and so to belong, rather than the wish to stand out. I've found myself explaining this to a number of people who, when Dora experienced a period of fedupness at school, told me that she must be missing all the attention.

'The actors I know,' Boyd Tonkin told me, 'are, in most cases, the opposite of egomaniacs. They are people whose skills of cooperation and group working are incredibly highly developed.'

Aside from the economic imperative, which has, through the ages, always been a powerful factor propelling people into the entertainment business, why do people perform? I asked Catherine Hindson, who lectures in performance studies in the department of Drama: Theatre, Film, Television at Bristol University. She told me about the discipline, introduced and inspired by American academic and director Richard Schechner. 'Performance studies thinks about performance as a more general, extensive and complicated thing than what happens on a stage or a screen. Performance is something that human beings do, very naturally. It's something they share. So, any kind of ritual, any social occasion or event involves a human performance, and when we engage with other people, when we participate in those rituals that make up our everyday life, be they very small rituals, like going shopping, or bigger, more recognised rituals, like weddings or barmitzvahs, we are performing as human beings.'

So performing is a natural part of what it means to be human.

Everything we do is, in this sense, a performance. But that doesn't explain why some people are ecstatic on stage pretending to be someone else, while given the choice, others (like me) prefer hiding under a duvet. Or why, when you watch your child's first nursery class assembly, there are some three-year-olds standing there heads up, singing (or shouting) at the tops of their voices, and grinning excitedly into the audience, while others stare at their shoes, twiddle their plaits and mumble. Catherine, mother to a small daughter, doesn't know, either.

I asked Sam Keston (now Dora's agent), Sylvia Young and Maggie Melville-Bray if they think the children who perform are in some way different from their peers.

'Before they are given their first "break" or once they're established?' Sam asks, before answering both questions. 'Raw talent is indefinable but very easy for us to spot. A sparkle in the eye, an awareness, an inner confidence, wisdom beyond his or her years. These children are often very centred. Again, though, it depends whether we're talking stage or television. The screen loves vulnerability, and self-possessed children appear far from vulnerable! Once they are working,' she continues, 'these kids exude a sort of adult "way". Going to work in the theatre, or carrying a big TV or film role, is far from a hobby. It's a massive responsibility that is likely to put them into a different headspace from their schoolmates.'

Sylvia and Maggie aren't sure there is any difference. 'You do,' Maggie says, 'see a spark of something and then it's exciting to develop that. It's the same with swimming. Or showjumping. It's an enthusiasm too.'

'I think it's inborn,' says Sylvia. 'It's an instinct to get enjoyment from something that you hope is also giving enjoyment to others. A stage performance is totally different from anything else. The adrenalin. There's something unbeatable about theatre.'

'Performing,' says Maggie, 'is like winning.' But she also thinks that if there is something different about performing children, it's that they're not scared of failure. 'They're not frightened of falling flat on their faces and having to pick themselves up again.' It is, she says, a characteristic of successful people, who fail more than unsuccessful people. 'It's a personality type,' she says. 'They relish a challenge.'

Dora certainly does. She's the same upfront, enthusiastic person she was when I asked her if she wanted to audition, but also different, changing in the ways that all children change as they grow. She wants drama taught at her school (good idea) and to do more auditions and more performing – professional and amateur. Having witnessed a motorbike accident (thankfully one in which no one got hurt), she's changed her mind about motorbikes and now doesn't want one because they're too dangerous. But she would still like to go into space. 'Mummy,' she announced recently, 'it's really not fair that children aren't allowed to.'